MAIN
STREET
BOOKS

DOUBLEDAY New York London Toronto Sydney Auckland

THE OFFICIAL GUIDE TO THE XENAVERSE

R O B E R T   W E I S B R O T

XENA
WARRIOR PRINCESS
™

FOR ANDREA
—R.W.

A MAIN STREET BOOK
PUBLISHED BY DOUBLEDAY
a division of Bantam Doubleday Dell Publishing Group, Inc.
1540 Broadway, New York, New York 10036

MAIN STREET BOOKS, DOUBLEDAY, and the portrayal of a
building with a tree
are trademarks of Doubleday, a division of
Bantam Doubleday Dell Publishing Group, Inc.

The author gratefully acknowledges the *Orange County Register* for permission
to quote from Kinney Littlefield's feature on *Xena* in its February 26, 1996, issue; and *Ms.* magazine and Donna Minkowitz for permission to quote from Ms.
Minkowitz's article, "Xena: She's Big, Tall, Strong—and Popular," in *Ms.*,
July/August 1996.

Library of Congress Cataloging-in-Publication Data
Weisbrot, Robert.
Xena, warrior princess: the official guide to the Xenaverse / Robert
Weisbrot. — 1st ed.
p.   cm.
"A Main Street book"—T.p. verso.
1. Xena, warrior princess (Television program)   I. Title.
PN1992.77.X46W45   1998
791.45'72—dc21   97-34926
CIP

ISBN 0-385-49136-0

First Edition

1 3 5 7 9 10 8 6 4 2

ACKNOWLEDGMENTS

This book began with a letter. In December 1995, I wrote to Steven L. Sears to praise two of his scripts for *Xena: Warrior Princess*. To my amazement and delight, I soon received not only a long, gracious, and witty reply, but also copies of the scripts I so admired. This spurred me to learn more about the many levels of creativity, often hidden from viewers, that make *Xena* uniquely compelling.

In preparing this book, I was privileged to have the cooperation of producers, cast, and crew members, whom I found as remarkable for their kindness as for their artistic talent. I am especially indebted to executive producer Rob Tapert, who allowed me the fullest access to all aspects of production and the fullest freedom in writing about him and the series. His unfailing generosity has been deeply gratifying, both personally and professionally.

Lucy Lawless, as gracious a person as I could hope to meet, took time amid an extremely demanding schedule to give numerous interviews and valued encouragement. Renee O'Connor afforded me an illuminating interview and, between scenes, helped me orient during my first day on the set.

This book greatly benefited from interviews with Peter Bell, Robert Bielak, Tim Boggs, Bruce Campbell, Edward Campbell, Sam Clark, Danielle Cormack, Ngila Dickson, Donald Duncan, David Eick, Rob Field, Dan Filie, Liz Friedman, Robert Gillies, Patrick Giraudi, Galyn Gorg, Chris Graham, Eric Gruendemann, Tracy Hampton, Charlie Haskell, Michael Hurst, Beth Hymson-

Ayer, Gary Jones, Bernie Joyce, Lucy Lawless, Hudson Leick, Joseph Lo Duca, Chris Manheim, Robert Mellette, Ned Nalle, Renee O'Connor, Kevin O'Neill, Willa O'Neill, Allan Poppleton, Diana Rowan, Sam Raimi, Ted Raimi, Saskia Reijners, Jason Schmid, John Schulian, T. J. Scott, Steven L. Sears, Chloe Smith, Kevin Smith, Kevin Sorbo, R. J. Stewart, and Rob Tapert. I am indebted, too, to Joseph Anderson for typing accurate transcripts of several dozen interviews, without which I would still be preparing notes for the book.

Eric Gruendemann, already balancing the myriad tasks of production, warmly expedited my work in New Zealand. Jane Lindsay arranged with notable efficiency for housing and contacts with cast members, and Joanna Henaghan helped in many ways before and during my visit.

My editor, Denell Downum, encouraged and guided my work, offered a wealth of valuable ideas, and sharpened my writing. I am grateful, as well, for her initiative and energy in committing to a book on the Warrior Princess. Nancy Cushing-Jones, president of Universal Studios Publishing Rights, also merits acknowledgment for extending an opportunity to me despite my inexperience in this genre. Cindy Chang, senior director of Universal Studios Publishing Rights, expertly coordinated my efforts with those of Universal, Doubleday, and Renaissance Pictures, and helped speed my progress. I would also like to thank Sue Binder, Jeff Cruce, Maggie Hickerson, and others at Renaissance for their thoughtful assistance.

Finally, I wish to express a personal word of appreciation to R. J. Stewart, for his warm interest in my work; to Brad Carpenter, a deeply valued friend and mentor; to my parents, for their encouragement and help; and to my wife Andrea, for her keen critical eye, her creative suggestions, and her loving support, all of which made for a far better book and a far richer experience in writing it.

CONTENTS

Introduction   *1*

1. TALES OF A WARRIOR PRINCESS   5

2. MAKING MYTHS:
   A Behind-the-Scenes Look   33

3. CAST PROFILES   121

4. FROM SHEENA TO XENA:
   Heroines of the Small Screen   149

5. XENA'S ADVENTURES: Episode Guide   163

   The First Season   163
   The Second Season   193
   The American Way of English   225
   A Xenaverse Timeline   228
   Production Credits   230

INTRODUCTION

On September 4, 1995, *Xena: Warrior Princess* debuted on hundreds of stations throughout America. Television executives knew they were taking a huge risk by having a female warrior invade that most masculine of genres, the superhero odyssey. Could a heroine with a dark past, they wondered, possibly survive, let alone conquer the world of syndicated TV action?

The answer, of course, was an unqualified yes. In its first season, *Xena* became the most popular new syndicated series, with ratings that surpassed the mighty *Baywatch*. The second season brought even greater success, as *Xena* became the number one syndicated action show. Along the way to ratings glory, *Xena* received a flurry of attention, including tributes from shows like *Ellen* and *Roseanne, The Tonight Show* and *The Rosie O'Donnell Show;* conventions where eager fans could dress up like Xena and practice her "yi-yi-yi" yell; and cover stories in magazines ranging from *TV Guide* to *Ms.*

Clearly, *Xena: Warrior Princess* struck a chord with American audiences eager to move past television's traditional formulas. Fans quickly embraced its vision of Xena as a strong and brooding character who once terrorized villagers with a ferocity that even Genghis Khan would have envied. Viewers warmed to the show's sensitive side as well, responding enthusiastically to Xena's deepening friendship with her young companion, Gabrielle. And the action scenes brought something new to American television, as Xena ruled with her sword and chakram (a circular weapon dating to sixteenth-century Persia), and with martial arts to delight fans of Bruce Lee and Jackie Chan.

But cutting-edge though Xena's sensibility may be, she owes her existence to a hero firmly rooted in antiquity. *Xena: Warrior Princess* began as a spin-off of another syndicated hit show from Universal Television—*Hercules: The Legendary Journeys*. To bring *Hercules* to life, Dan Filie, the senior vice president for drama development at

Universal, and Ned Nalle, then Universal's executive vice president, had called on two innovative young filmmakers, Sam Raimi and Rob Tapert. Friends since their days at Michigan State University, where Tapert roomed with Raimi's older brother Ivan, the two had first collaborated as undergraduates on an hour-long Super 8 movie, *The Happy Valley Kid,* which became a campus sensation. By January

1979, Raimi, a sophomore, and Tapert, just several months from graduation, felt ready for bigger projects, and dropped out of college to write, direct, and produce a horror movie. They soon discovered that attempting this without money or prior feature-film credits could make for a real-life horror story.

Just after resolving to pour all their time and money into their new production company, Renaissance Pictures, Raimi and Tapert were evicted from their apartment when neighbors complained of the noise from their artistic endeavors. They persevered and were able to lure enough investors to finance four months of filming, but ran out of money midway through their movie. Brushing off these disasters as temporary nuisances, they completed their film in 1981, handling ever more tasks themselves as the crew dwindled during the last five weeks of production to the star, the soundman, and the cook. Finding a distributor added more than another year's frantic effort. But in 1983 *The Evil Dead* at last began to haunt audiences across the country, and brought Raimi and Tapert a cult following among horror fans, critics, and fellow moviemakers.

A tongue-in-cheek supernatural thriller, *The Evil Dead* winked at audiences even as it jolted them with outrageous violence. The acclaim for its mix of humor and horror generated two sequels, *Evil Dead II* (1987) and *Army of Darkness* (1993), which were even more violent and also more polished than the original. With Raimi directing, Tapert producing, and a third college friend, Bruce Campbell, playing a reluctant hero beset by spirits out for blood (and souls), the films dazzled viewers with offbeat camera angles, fast-paced editing, and gripping effects on a budget as bare-bones as the movies' deadly skeletons. Among the ardent admirers of Raimi and Tapert's offbeat cinematic style were Universal's Dan Filie and Ned Nalle.

By late 1993, when Filie proposed the *Hercules* project, Sam Raimi was preparing to direct an offbeat Western, *The Quick and the Dead,* with Sharon Stone doing a Clint Eastwood turn as a mysterious gunfighter out for revenge. But fortunately for Filie, "Rob Tapert started to get the itch to make *Hercules.* He'd taken the 'Nestea Plunge' into the myths, started to feel hooked on the idea of retelling them . . . and he was seeing the possibilities."

Beginning with five TV movies in 1994, *Hercules,* starring Kevin Sorbo, appealed to both men and women, young and old, with exciting action scenes, special-effects creatures, fresh treatment of ancient myths, and exotic New Zealand scenery. And as Hercules, Sorbo displayed a winning blend of intelligence, humor, and vulnerability to complement his muscular frame and all-American good looks. The runaway success of the five TV movies inspired Universal to launch *Hercules: The Legendary Journeys* as a weekly series, which debuted in January 1995 to high ratings and critical acclaim. After landmark adventures involving lethal Amazon warriors, Centaurs, Satyrs, the world of the dead, and the fabled kingdom of Troy, Hercules had accomplished his most difficult labor: he had become the mightiest action figure on television. His triumphs now cleared the way for a Warrior Princess to embark on her own epic adventures.

TALES OF A
WARRIOR PRINCESS

E xecutive producer Rob Tapert, who (with Raimi absorbed in other projects) chiefly gave *Hercules* its vision and vitality, had every reason to relish the show's success. But he kept returning to a goal that had so far eluded him: "to incorporate action in a way that wasn't readily available on American television." The fights on *Hercules* were inventively choreographed and played to the hilt by Kevin Sorbo and the rugged New Zealand "stuntees." But these scenes still echoed many earlier action shows, whether sagebrush fare like *Bonanza,* crime dramas like *Mike Hammer,* or even an intergalactic "Western" like *Star Trek,* in which twenty-third-century characters still found as much use for an old-fashioned roundhouse as the Cartwright family.

Tapert hoped to add a new dimension to TV action by merging Hollywood fisticuffs with Asian martial arts. "I am a huge fan of Hong Kong cinema," Tapert explained. "I've seen all the movies of [director] Tsui Hark, [martial arts star] Jackie Chan, and [director] John Woo. So I wanted to find a way to bring aspects of that action onto American television. But, son of a gun, we found out that while Hercules can do punches and kicks, he couldn't incorporate the great acrobatic style that I really loved in Hong Kong cinema. It just wasn't endemic to that kind of all-American guy. So *Hercules* didn't turn out in many respects to be a showcase for action; it was the showcase for the all-American new John Wayne."

Tapert especially admired the Hong Kong actress Brigitte Lin (Lin Ching Hsia), star of a classic action film, *The Bride with White Hair* (1993). Lin plays a warrior-witch—fierce, steely, mysterious—

who serves a clan by slaughtering rebels, but then refuses to kill an enemy leader with whom she has fallen in love. As punishment she must walk a gauntlet where soldiers pummel her with sticks as she struggles forward. Lin's character barely survives, but she has broken free of the clan's power—and her old ways. *The Bride with White Hair* became Tapert's inspiration for bridging Hercules, Hollywood, and Hong Kong action.

"I had always wanted to make a movie with her," Tapert said of Brigitte Lin, "but she doesn't speak English, she's in her forties now, so her chances of breaking into American cinema aren't good." Instead he proposed to John Schulian, the co-executive producer and head writer on *Hercules,* doing "a story about a female warrior," modeled on Lin's character in *The Bride with White Hair,* "that would let us do Hong Kong action." Schulian replied that he, too, wanted to focus an episode on a woman, but of a different sort—a beauty who comes between Hercules and his best friend, Iolaus. So Tapert said, "What if you made her a Warrior Princess and combined the two?"

They called the new character Xena, though memories fade over just why. Tapert said, "I have no idea how [Schulian] came up with the name Xena. But an old sales agent who helped us tremendously in the film business and was very much our mentor told us, 'Anytime there's an *X* in the title, it gets people's interest!' " While Tapert and Schulian were fashioning Xena as a warrior-temptress who could challenge Hercules, co-producer David Eick suggested extending her story over a three-episode "arc." Meanwhile Dan Filie at Universal was already looking ahead to the new season and held out even more ambitious hopes for this villainess.

Xena almost became *Jason,* as Dan Filie and Rob Tapert both loved the 1963 movie *Jason and the Argonauts,* but legal questions over ownership rights ruled out adapting it for TV.

Filie wanted to create a new series that could build on the popularity of *Hercules:* "I'd been bugging Rob, saying, 'Let's do a spin-off before somebody else rips you off. If someone's going to rip you off, let's be the ones, let's do it.' So we had been talking back and forth about a variety of things." Filie liked Tapert's ideas for *Xena,* a woman warrior, and offered his own version, called *Bekka.*

As Tapert, Schulian, Filie, Nalle, and Eick merged their different ideas for Xena, it became clear that casting the role would be a serious challenge. A single actress would have to project beauty and sensuality, to suit Schulian's image of Xena, and power, ferocity, and implacable will, to match Tapert's vision. She must be charismatic, to warrant devoting the final three episodes of *Hercules'* first season to her character. For good measure, she must have the ability—and availability—to carry a series should *Xena* win over viewers and studio executives. Remarkably, a New Zealand actress surfaced with all these qualities—and more. Equally remarkable, she nearly missed getting the part.

> "The producers would like to acknowledge and pay tribute to Stanley Kubrick, Kirk Douglas, and all those who were involved with the making of the film classic *Spartacus.*"
> —Disclaimer from "Athens City Academy of the Performing Bards."

Looking back, the casting of Lucy Lawless as Xena has an air of inevitability, so strongly has she come to be identified with this larger-than-life heroine. But as with other pairings that now seem so natural as to make other choices all but unthinkable—Clark Gable as Rhett Butler, Humphrey Bogart as Sam Spade, Sean Connery as the "original" James Bond—Lawless needed an extra measure of luck as well as talent, winning the role only after other performers, including Vanessa Angel and Roma Downey, had declined to play Xena. Once chosen, though, Lawless so thoroughly made the role her own that Kevin Sorbo said admiringly, "Lucy *is* Xena."

Lawless was an actress with modest screen credits but extraordinary presence when she first came to the attention of Rob Tapert and the Renaissance team in 1993. They were then casting the first of five Hercules telefeatures, *Hercules and the Amazon Women*. Diana Rowan, the casting director on location, immediately suggested two New Zealanders for key roles: the eminent stage actor and director Michael Hurst as Hercules' best friend, Iolaus (he became the first actor hired), and Lucy Lawless as Hippolyta, the Amazon queen.

Nearly five feet eleven inches, with intensely bright blue eyes and a lithe physique that could suit either an athlete or a model, Lawless looked every inch the warrior queen when she came in to read for the

part of Hippolyta. "I remember her audition for that part vividly," producer Eric Gruendemann related. "This was back when we had the time to see some people live—not just on tape, like now—and she just sort of lit up the room. . . . She had a power and a presence, even though only twenty-five years old, and a maturity."

Despite this impressive showing, Lawless could not overcome a reluctance to cast a foreign actress with limited credits. Rob Tapert recalled, "We said, 'You know, we really don't want to go with a Kiwi in the title role.' We didn't have any experience. And Roma [Downey] was still just right for that part." Lawless won a smaller role in the film as Lysia, an intimidating figure even among the Amazons, who leads their army, disciplines the ranks, and makes even Hercules show proper deference to the Amazon queen. A small role with few lines, it nonetheless allowed Lawless to command the screen as firmly as her character controlled the Amazons.

Lysia in the script is little more than a garden-variety henchman, who barks orders at her sister Amazons, terrified male villagers, and Hercules himself. But Lawless gives her unexpected magnetism and shading. She brings an ironic, lilting tone to her first harsh words to Hercules: "If you're looking for men, you won't find any, not in the city of Amazons. *You're* the only one . . . And *I* don't think you'll last very long." She also looks strong and fierce enough to give credibility to her bullying, as when she pulls Hercules by a rope up the palace steps and gives her bound prisoner a lesson in humility: "I'm sure you're used to having your way with women, I bet they just fall at your feet wherever you go. Well, not here. Here . . . *you* fall at *our* feet." She punctuates her observation by kicking Hercules in the groin and dropping him to his knees.

Even in quiet moments Lysia radiates an aura of danger. After chasing away several Amazons who appear too friendly with Hercules, she smiles at her prisoner, her eyes virtually glowing with anger, and whispers, "If it were up to me, you wouldn't be caged. You'd be *buried*." Later, when Zeus tells Hercules, "I like a woman with a little fire in her eyes—but this one is all fire," the viewer can understand why even the king of the gods appears nervous.

Lysia is properly subservient to Queen Hippolyta, yet the sight of them together projects a radically different image. Lawless towers over the diminutive Roma Downey, conveying an aura of implacable resolve that suggests: here is the *real* Amazon queen. Co-producer David Eick was so impressed by the magnetism and menace Lawless exerted in every scene that during the postproduction he told the sound mixers, "Whenever Lysia walks we should hear the sound of heavy boots—no matter what she's wearing!"

When *Hercules* became a series, the producers asked Lawless back to play Lyla, a Centaur's human lover, in the episode "As Darkness Falls." A sharply different character from Lysia, Lyla is free-spirited, playful, seductive, and manipulative rather than fierce. She is ruthless enough to drug Hercules into a state of blindness, but later repents her action and helps him. The role allowed Lawless a fuller range of emotions than *Amazon Women,* revealing dramatic talents that went far beyond her imposing physical presence.

David Eick, overwhelmed by Lawless' performance as Lysia, pressed to cast her as Xena. But although Rob Tapert and others were also struck by her presence, questions remained. Should a Kiwi rather than an American actress play Xena? And was Lawless a seasoned enough performer? "We all noticed her," Dan Filie recalled, "we absolutely said she is really something. Who is that? Wow! But we weren't smart enough to figure out that Lucy was our star character." One executive summed up the doubts about casting her as Xena, saying, "Ah, she's a lieutenant, she's not a star."

There was also the matter of name recognition. Universal wanted someone well known, the better to lure viewers to *Hercules.* And, as Eric Gruendemann recalled, "Sam and Rob were then pitching to the studio an idea for a possible spin-off: a ruthless female warrior [who] becomes good. [So] the studio was looking for someone who had a TV 'Q' [popularity quotient] in America."

There was no general casting call to play Xena, but simply a call

to Vanessa Angel, a beautiful young actress with a radiant smile, exuberant personality, and her own TV series. Angel, a favorite of Universal Studios, had nearly been cast as Queen Hippolyta in *Hercules and the Amazon Women,* and had been offered the ongoing role of Deianeira, Hercules' wife, but instead went on to star in the series *Weird Science.* She did not appear especially athletic or suited to action scenes, but, as with Roma Downey in *Amazon Women,* wigs and stuntpersons were plentiful. Also, Xena would first wreak havoc as a temptress who comes between Hercules and Iolaus, and Angel needed no stunt double to convince viewers that either hero might fall for her character.

Studio executives were so impressed by Angel that they discarded their idea for a series based on the character Xena rather than cast another actress who did not already have binding commitments. Filie recalled thinking, "The crossover is gonna be good for *Weird Science* [also produced by Universal], it's gonna be good for *Hercules.*" But "we couldn't get a series option on her, [so] we didn't think of it as a spin-off, we were just going to do three episodes and out." Xena would die fighting at the end of the three-episode arc, and would be buried beside any hopes for a spin-off series.

The studio put Angel through a month's training in martial arts and horseback riding. Then she went off to see her parents in England, where she caught the flu. Right after Christmas, Eric Gruendemann relates, "we got a call that Vanessa Angel was ill and couldn't travel. By December 28 or 29, we were getting *really* nervous. It didn't seem she'd be able to pull it together." There was no slack in the shooting schedule for *Hercules,* which was set to begin filming the three-episode arc on January 5, in part to accommodate Angel's commitments to *Weird Science.*

By then the producers were looking at Lucy Lawless in dailies of the episode "As Darkness Falls," and wistfully reconsidering their earlier doubts. "She could have been the Warrior Princess," Rob Tapert remarked to John Schulian. Schulian emphatically agreed. When Angel pulled out, Tapert said to Filie, "How about Lucy?" But Filie winced at the thought of having Lawless play wildly different characters in consecutive episodes of *Hercules:* "Jeez, we just used her." Tapert assured him, "Ah, I can make her look different." But even with a guardian angel affording a second chance, Lawless had so cut herself off from the outside world that the producers could not reach her. "We tried to call Lucy," Tapert recalled, "but she was gone, was off camping. So we called three or four other women here."

Trying to contact anyone in Hollywood between Christmas and New Year's was a sure path to frustration. Managers, agents, and actors went off to celebrate the holidays, knowing that no business would be transacted anyway. As the ball dropped in New York's Times Square to usher in 1995, Tapert's overriding New Year's resolution remained to cast the role of Xena. He was still determined to find Lucy Lawless, who, "blissfully unaware" of the producers desperately seeking Xena, headed with her husband and daughter further through the New Zealand bush. "Well, I decided that nothing *ever* went on in New Year's," Lawless said. "Everyone went away, nothing happened, certainly no work comes up. So we had gone off together on this jaunty holiday to give our daughter the camping experience, traveling the length and breadth of New Zealand in a tiny French Beetle type of car that you could wind down the roof on, and stopping at various relatives' on the way. The producers tracked us through the relatives. 'No, she went to so-and-so, she's not here but . . .' "

Diana Rowan, the casting director in New Zealand, joined the frantic hunt and, as Lawless recalled, "phoned up my parents desperately trying to get hold of me because my agent didn't know where

Among the actresses Tapert sounded out were Roma Downey, Mindy Clarke, and Kim Delaney. By early 1995 Downey had hopes of starring in her own series, *Touched by an Angel,* and bowed out as Xena. Clarke, best known as the most fetching zombie in cinematic history, in *Return of the Living Dead III,* also declined. Delaney had worked with Tapert on two direct-to-video *Darkman* movies and appeared set to play Xena. But she backed out at the last minute to make a movie.

I was, I'd just left." So had her parents. But according to Lawless, one link remained between her and the outside world:

> *My brother happened to be stopping by that day to pick up some mail. He was only there for five minutes and caught the phone call. He somehow found the number of my husband's folks, who found the number of where we* might *be next—and we just* happened *to stop by that day, we had changed our plans and gone to that particular location, and there I was contacted.*

The call to arms as Xena, a critical career move, caused Lawless more than a little anxiety. After the producers gave her the good news, she said, "I went to a bus that morning and just burst into tears. I thought, 'I'm not ready for this!' " But then she moved ahead— *quickly.* "Within two days," Gruendemann related, "we were dyeing her hair and totally revamping her costume, which had been tailor-made for [Vanessa Angel]." Her light brown hair had already been dyed auburn for her role as Lyla in the previous episode. This time, the producers went with jet black. "We wanted to give her a fierce look, a darker, more sinister look," Gruendemann explained.

"The world's greatest female warrior wants to kill Hercules" is how Rob Tapert summed up Xena's galvanizing presence in her three-episode arc. The first segment, "The Warrior Princess," incorporating John Schulian's approach, would present Xena as a femme fatale who seduces Iolaus in order to turn him against Hercules. Then "The Gauntlet," which Tapert envisioned as a tribute to *The Bride with White Hair,* would show Xena forsaking her ways as a plundering conqueror and helping Hercules defeat the barbarians she had once led. "Unchained Heart" would complete Xena's turn toward good, as she realizes, under the guidance of Hercules, her new friend and mentor, that she must atone for her savage past. According to the story outline, Xena would die fighting at the end of "Unchained Heart"; but Tapert stood ready to spare the Warrior Princess should Universal decide to draft her for new battles in her own series.

"The Warrior Princess" opens in a pastoral land where a tall young woman fetches water from a well. Just beyond her vision two unsavory figures ready their knives and whisper to each other, "There she is. Let's do it!" Their words portend a classic Hollywood moment: a woman in jeopardy is rescued by a dashing man. But instead this scene bears the stamp, not of Hollywood but of Hong Kong; for although this damsel is surrounded by danger, she proves to be scarcely in distress.

The woman's placid expression suddenly gives way to a frenzied yell, as she decks one man with her water bucket before he can strike, then knocks down his accomplice. Other armed men swarm around her, but she makes short work of each, grunting as she kicks, punches, and flips them in turn. Then, glaring in disgust at her dazed and prostrate assailants, she adds a tongue-lashing that reveals her to be the real conspirator. "*Pathetic!*" the Warrior Princess scolds them. "If you can't learn to fight better than that, then you're never going to defeat Hercules. And I want him *dead*!"

Xena can entice as well as intimidate. She manipulates the lovestruck Iolaus into fighting Hercules while telling her troops, "You demoralize and weaken before you destroy. When Hercules realizes that he's killed his best friend, he'll be ripe for slaughter." Xena thrills at the chance "to rid the world of the son of Zeus," for then no one would dare stand against her army.

Unable to avoid battle, Hercules quickly overpowers Iolaus but refuses to kill his longtime friend. Xena's spell over Iolaus slips away as he begins to see that Hercules is not his enemy. Her plans thwarted, Xena commands her troops, "Get them! I want them *both* dead!"

Hercules and Iolaus hold off her soldiers, but as she rides away un-harmed and unrelenting, the Warrior Princess calls out, "You haven't heard the last of *me,* Hercules!"

The episode proved a dramatic as well as ratings highlight of the first season. Though Sorbo and Hurst expressed doubts that Iolaus could be so easily turned against his closest friend, any questions about the story line faded before the intense fan reaction to the char-acter of Xena, and the studio's discovery that Lucy Lawless could make her at once wicked and watchable. "Just as we knew when we saw Kevin as Hercules that we had something special," Dan Filie said, "we saw the Xena dailies and said, 'Wow! This is great!' "

"I knew that I wanted to do a tremendously dark episode," Rob Tapert recalled of "The Gauntlet," the second segment of the three-episode arc. "We'd done some lighter things in the first four to five episodes of *Hercules,* when we started talking about the script for 'The Gauntlet.' And if I have any one complaint about what happened to *Hercules,* it has become too light almost. And I personally have a big dark streak," Tapert confided with a laugh. "So I wanted to make a dark one just to see how the heck it would work."

Xena continues her pillaging ways in "The Gauntlet," as the commander of an army cutting a swath through villages in Greece. But her character and manner have changed almost beyond recogni-tion. No longer a cunning temptress for whom deception is a weapon of choice, Xena is now honest, blunt, and, like a Japanese samurai, almost ascetic in her devotion to the way of the warrior.

"Neither Xena nor her remarkably coincidental identical twin, Diana, were harmed during the production of this motion picture."
—Disclaimer from "Warrior . . . Princess"

Although ruthless toward her enemies, Xena re-coils at seeing a massacre of helpless villagers by her lieutenant, Darphus. "You're a butcher!" she tells Darphus, then turns at the sound of a baby crying. Xena holds the infant and warns, "If you kill this baby, you die next!" Her intensity is enough to make Dar-phus back away. But Xena's good deed does not go unpunished. Her softhearted conduct gives Darphus his chance to stir her soldiers to mutiny, and force her to step down "the only way a soldier can"—by walk-ing a gauntlet.

Xena is stripped of her armor as soldiers line

up with clubs on either side of a narrow pathway. Then, to the sound of slow, heavy drumbeats, the Warrior Princess begins her walk through the gauntlet of death. Clubs crack on her arms and body as she writhes in agony and forces herself forward. At first simply staggering under the assault, Xena begins striking back with her elbows and forearms to knock attackers off balance. But the weight of the clubs is too great and she collapses, barely stretching an arm across the line that marks the end of the gauntlet.

> "The Gauntlet"
> Salmoneus: "An army such as yours, with such a beautiful leader like you—you need publicity. Public relations!"
> Xena (scowling): "I prefer my relations to be *private!*"

Darphus exults at the fate of his former commander, but then, to his astonishment and dismay, Xena slowly rises as if from the dead. Her face ashen, her body taxed to the limit of endurance, she has survived through sheer strength of will. Forced into exile, she remains intent on retaking her army from the loathsome Darphus. And while she has rescued an infant, she is ready, even eager, to kill an adult: on hearing that Hercules is on her trail, Xena sets out to slay him in battle and, with one great victory, convince her former soldiers to rejoin her command.

When Hercules and Xena find each other, the Warrior Princess appears gleeful rather than afraid. Spinning through the air, Xena lands poised for a kick that sends Hercules reeling backward. She brings her sword down flush at Hercules' head, but he holds it fast between his palms and kicks Xena away. Xena closes with Hercules, swinging her heavy sword, laughing at the sheer joy of battling this great hero to the death. The two trade blows until Hercules knocks Xena off balance, pulls her over his shoulder to the ground, and holds his sword across her neck.

"Finish it," she insists. "Prove you're the greatest warrior." Hercules instead pulls his sword away, saying, "Killing is not the only way to prove you're a warrior, Xena. I think you know that." She is chastened by Hercules' words as much as by his strength. He tells her that he, too, is going after Darphus and asks her to join him. But she spurns his offer and stalks away, her pride wounded by defeat, her mind trying to make sense of all that has befallen her.

At Parthis, a village under attack by Darphus' army, Hercules fights off a dozen soldiers and more. At last troops close in from every

side, pummeling Hercules, but their advantage is short-lived. A familiar figure hurtles toward the soldiers on a rope, knocking several down and dispatching others with powerful kicks. Xena plunges into battle on the side of Hercules. The villagers soon rout their attackers, and Xena herself slays Darphus, lunging past his defenses with her sword after he had battered her to the ground.

"I'm glad you came back," Hercules tells Xena, whom he regards with new respect, even affection. "They weren't true warriors," Xena explains. "They had to be stopped." "Is it over now? All of it?" he asks gently. "Yes, it is," she replies, realizing at last that her passage through the gauntlet has purged her bloodlust.

Xena appears strangely shy when Hercules asks her, "So, what now?" Then she asks hesitantly, "What do you say we go find out together?" Hercules pauses at this unforeseen turn in their relationship, then brightens at the prospect: "Yeah." The Warrior Princess, fearless in battle but almost abashed in talking with Hercules, slowly breaks into a broad smile.

"The Gauntlet" stands out as the most intense episode of the entire first season of *Hercules*. Its scenes of battle and plunder have a disturbingly realistic quality, with horses thundering across the plains, women and children screaming, bodies littering the ground, and flames shooting skyward. The brutal gauntlet scene, especially, bears little resemblance to the playful, amusing fights on other episodes of *Hercules,* where stuntmen often go flying but no character ever seems too badly bruised for the experience.

Liz Friedman, the talented young aide to Rob Tapert who helped supervise the assembly of the episode, emerged in near despair from viewing the "director's cut," a long, utterly bleak version, without music. She worried, too, in the wake of the killing of Nicole Simpson, that the savage beating of Xena in the gauntlet scene might send the wrong message to viewers. Friedman quipped to Tapert, "It's like watching *Schindler's List—without* the inspiration."

Tapert and Friedman took steps to infuse inspiration and defuse the unrelenting grimness. The gauntlet scene was cut drastically, by as much as 80 percent. A stirring musical score by Joseph Lo Duca, highlighted by pulsing Bulgarian melodies and choral singing for Xena's theme, was liberally added in the mixing of the episode. And Bob Trebor, who played Salmoneus, was prominently featured for his comic repartee. Trebor had asked to improvise additional humor (such as a theme song for Xena, employing a walnut drumbeat) as a way of lightening the episode, and he received encouragement from the producer on location, Eric Gruendemann. Trebor's scenes came out of the editing room virtually intact, the better to play against the harsh tone of the episode overall.

Robert Bielak, who wrote the episode, recalled being startled by the harsh tone of the final version:

> *It wasn't a total surprise, but we did not realize how the director was going to make it darker even than the script was. . . . There were those awful scenes of [Xena's] having to run the gauntlet, you know, seeing a female get beat up like that. It's not your [typical] eight o'clock* Hercules.
>
> *Sometimes you don't notice the effect of these things until you see them on the screen in front of you. And when we saw it, it was like, "Wow. This really* is *dark. This isn't* Hercules! *This is like a feature or something."*

Still, this episode was dark by design. It bore not only the director's stamp but Rob Tapert's, and he and Liz Friedman deflected the more panicky attempts to soften the tone for television. Friedman recalled there were even suggestions to alter the story line by having Xena adopt the baby as her own. "I *strongly* resisted this," she said, finding the idea out of character for Xena and too maudlin for an otherwise hard-edged episode. In the end, the baby had to settle for regaining its father, but Xena was not about to forsake her "career" for motherhood.

For all its harsh edges, "The Gauntlet," like other episodes of *Hercules,* is still, at heart, an uplifting adventure. Although the Warrior Princess is brought low by a life of violence, her one pure act, saving a child, gives her a second chance, and through suffer-

"No Jumbo-Sized Cocktail Rats were harmed during the production of this motion picture."
—Disclaimer from "Death in Chains"

ing she is reborn. It is a case of Greek myth meeting Christian myth, as Xena's passage through the gauntlet turns a tragic tale into a story of redemption.

Fan reaction to "The Gauntlet" was anything but dark, as viewers responded enthusiastically to the remarkable performance by Lucy Lawless. Much of the horror generated by Xena's gauntlet scene actually stems not from the beating but from Lawless' ability to convey extremes of emotion: fear, mixed with pride and resolve, as she begins her passage, then intense pain, and above all, the will to fight and survive. Her beauty and wild-eyed abandon in action scenes also gives the story a riveting visual center. When Lawless—not a stuntperson— rides at full gallop, one hand on the reins and the other brandishing a sword, viewers can well believe that an army of men would gladly follow a Warrior Princess into battle.

By early 1995 the only Universal Action Pack entry besides *Hercules* to become a weekly series, *Vanishing Son,* was fast vanishing in the Nielsen ratings. Rob Tapert recalled, "After seeing a rough cut of 'The Gauntlet,' the studio came to us about a replacement for *Vanishing Son.* So we said, 'What if we do one on the "Warrior Princess"?' So we saved her life, because we were going to kill her at the end of the third episode."

Dan Filie described Universal's hard choice between retaining *Vanishing Son,* a quality series despite its falling numbers, and launching a series of untested appeal in *Xena:*

We're talking to the Tribune guys, who represent twenty percent of [syndication stations in] the country, and at that point they had to pick up for the fall, and they wanted to pick up Hercules *and didn't want to pick up* Vanishing Son, *and we did not want to be in a situation where we were not building on* Hercules. *If we don't have two shows out there somebody else is going to put on a show behind* Hercules *and we're going to give somebody else a hit.*

We wrestled with it internally, Vanishing Son *or* Xena. *And the problem was that* Vanishing Son *was a totally different show than*

Hercules, *it's kind of like putting* Miami Vice *after* The A-Team *or something like that; you know, it just doesn't match. So it was, "O.K., we're not hanging on to our* Hercules *audience, the best way to do that would be to have a show that comes from* Hercules." *So in a conference call . . . with all the different Tribune guys, Rob and Sam [pitched] this Warrior Princess idea. It was a great character. They had seen one of the episodes. But how are you going to redeem her? Because they had all seen her as evil.*

Universal and the Tribune group both faced a large gamble. Yes, Xena had excited audiences, but as a *villain* to play off Kevin Sorbo's immensely likable, morally upright hero. The question remained, could a woman gain acceptance in her own right as a TV hero, especially one whose past was stained with innocent blood?

Filie, whose commitment proved crucial to extending Xena's life—and her weekly adventures—later explained that despite her flaws she had never been simply a wanton killer:

See, we never really saw her like that, we saw her as being a warrior. . . . So we said, all right, she's been fighting for the wrong reasons on the wrong side. And in the course of these episodes we made it clear that she didn't kill women and children, and she only killed those who opposed her.

Nalle added, "And Xena stood apart from any female character we had seen on TV." The possibilities for developing her further appeared boundless.

Xena's passage from guest villainess to series heroine was still far from assured. "*Xena was* a very tough sell to the syndicators," Rob Tapert recalled. "Everyone believed there was no market for a woman superhero." Tapert assured the Tribune executives that *Xena* "would be something different. It wouldn't be a female *Hercules*. I cut a six-minute demo tape of Hong Kong movie action sequences" to show them. "I said, 'We don't have the time to deliver these at this level, but this is going to be the kind of action that she does. And it's different than anything on TV right now.' And the guys at Tribune went along," much as they had done with *Hercules* a year earlier. "They took a big step forward with us."

The concluding segment of Xena's story arc, "Unchained Heart," shifts the burden of villainy from the Warrior Princess, now a friend of Hercules, to an old foe of both heroes. Darphus, killed by Xena in "The Gauntlet," makes a comeback worthy of Lazarus in "Unchained Heart" when Ares, the god of war, raises him back to life, makes him invulnerable to weapons, and bestows on him a fire-breathing beast called Graegus. Darphus celebrates his supernatural good fortune by vowing to slaughter Hercules and Xena, and to conquer the world in the name of the bloody god Ares.

As Hercules and Xena set out to stop Darphus, Xena finds the ghosts of her past more menacing than any human enemy. A chance encounter with Iolaus, who still burns with memories of Xena's treachery, shows how hard it will be for the Warrior Princess to start fresh. Hercules just keeps Iolaus from drawing his sword, but his assurances that they are all "on the same side" provide little comfort. "Are you crazy?" Iolaus shouts. "She tried to kill us!" He stalks away, and Hercules barely persuades his embittered friend to return.

Hercules, Iolaus, Xena, and Salmoneus hunt for Darphus together but their alliance is both strange and strained. Salmoneus wants only to make business deals with Hercules and Xena, to publicize their heroic exploits with "the world's first celebrity biography." Iolaus meanwhile walks well behind the others, so he can avoid looking at or speaking with Xena. Alone with Hercules, the Warrior Princess confides her doubts whether she can ever make good her past:

> Xena: I have done terrible things. I've killed so many men I'll never wash the blood from my hands!
> Hercules: You've already started. You saved that baby.
> Xena: But when you help people, you honor the wife and children that Hera stole from you. There is nothing in my whole life that moves me that way.
> Hercules: You're wrong. There's the goodness in your heart.

Xena's newfound friendship with Hercules soon blossoms into romance beside a campfire. To Salmoneus the wonder is that it took so long: "As warriors Hercules and Xena have always been a perfect match," he scribbles in his diary. He adds, with his special blend of optimism and opportunism, "I find myself wondering about them falling in love, getting married, having children—hiring me to handle their finances."

In the final clash with Darphus' legions Xena seems to be everywhere, cutting down soldiers, rescuing Salmoneus before Graegus can devour him, and once more fighting Darphus. Although Darphus has Ares on his side, Hercules and Xena triumph by steering Xena's former lieutenant into the path of Graegus, who swallows him whole. Then Graegus, in turn, bursts into flames and perishes. As Hercules explains to an astonished Xena and Iolaus, "Evil defeated itself."

Having slain Darphus, Xena prepares to set out on new adventures—alone. Hercules urges her to stay, bringing out a softness in the Warrior Princess few others ever glimpsed. She implores him, "Please don't. You're going to make me cry. I haven't done that since I was a child." They kiss passionately, but Xena remains intent to leave.

Xena: There's so much in my life I have to make amends for. I've got to get started.
Hercules: I wish you'd let me help.
Xena: You already have. You unchained my heart.

Xena waves with mingled sadness and hope, and rides on.

"Unchained Heart" completes Xena's inner journey from schemer to honorable if errant warrior, to genuine heroine. In kindling a romance with Hercules, Xena says she wants to let him know her feelings "in case I die fighting Darphus." That line, originally written to foreshadow her death in battle, instead signals another kind of passage: Xena will indeed pay for her sins with her life, but now by dedicating it to a fight for justice. The series *Xena: Warrior Princess* will show her ongoing struggles to overcome both villainous foes and the weight of her own past.

Although *Xena* aimed to win viewers with even wilder action than *Hercules* featured, the woman warrior's dark past was scarcely standard kids' fare. Somehow the new series had to blend lighthearted adventure and humor, as in *Hercules,* but for a heroine whose life had been grim, angry, and violent. To walk this tightrope as co-executive producer, Universal Studios hired an imaginative veteran of sophisticated television writing, R. J. Stewart. A native of Canarsie, in New York City, Stewart grew up around the world. His father was a World War II veteran who

went back into the Air Force and lived in a succession of military bases in Virginia, Washington State, and a host of foreign nations. As a young teenager during the early 1960s, Stewart spent three years in Greece, absorbing the history and mythology that would later inspire *Xena: Warrior Princess*. Stewart's friendships with Native Americans in Arizona, where his parents retired, further honed an ongoing fascination with cultures beyond the American mainstream. It also spurred him to cultivate a gift for writing, beginning with a play about Native Americans that won him acclaim while still a student at Arizona State University.

After college Stewart aimed for a career as an actor, then "drifted into writing." But the road to becoming a TV writer came into view only after a nine-year stretch on other roads, working as a truck driver in Los Angeles. In 1982 Stewart submitted a script called *Good Company*, a fictionalized autobiographical drama. The producer Glen Gordon Caron read it and hired him on the spot for a show he was developing for NBC, *Remington Steele*.

Stewart's writing helped *Remington Steele* (1982–87) become a surprise favorite of audiences and critics, who responded to the droll, clever byplay between the show's stars, Stephanie Zimbalist and Pierce Brosnan. The series rolled on for five years, but Stewart, having attained a TV writer's dream of both creative freedom and security, left after a single season.

Although Stewart's abrupt exit from a hit show defied conventional wisdom, he was intent on following his patron, Glen Gordon Caron, to another network. To the inexperienced Stewart, this seemed a promising career move: "I saw Glen Caron as the real star of *Remington Steele*, so it made total sense to me to go with him to ABC. But Glen didn't have another show on TV for another few years." Stewart remained with Caron through the lean times, but moved on just before Caron created an even bigger hit series about a couple whose forays into detective work combine action, romance, and offbeat comedy. "If I had stayed with Glen just a little longer," said Stewart, "I would have been on *Moonlighting*."

Stewart remembers his weekend career change with great satisfaction: "On a Friday I was driving a van for Gore Graphics Printers over to MTM studios; on a Monday I was working across the street as a staff writer. This wasn't a coincidence. I asked to deliver to MTM so that later I could tell the story, 'One day I was delivering to MTM and the next I was writing there.'"

Over the next dozen years Stewart "jumped back and forth between features and television," making ends meet though still seeking
a creative break to rival his sizzling TV debut. He wrote a half-hour
TV sitcom for James Garner as a political newcomer, *Man of the People* (1991), and a short-lived series for the new Fox network, *The
Great Defender* (1995), about a street-smart Boston lawyer who gains
unforeseen status and even greater culture shock on joining a snob-
bish Beacon Hill firm. In between came feature films, including *Major League II* and a rewrite on *Waterworld* that helped buoy Kevin
Costner's troubled big-budget adventure. In the spring of 1995
Stewart readied for his agent to offer him his next TV series about a
lawyer, politician, or detective, just as Universal Studios began casting
about for a head writer on *Xena: Warrior Princess*.

David Eick, Director of Television Development for Renaissance
Pictures, was about to leave *Hercules* to help Sam Raimi create a new
series on CBS, *American Gothic*. As a parting contribution to the crew
putting together *Xena: Warrior Princess*, he suggested R. J. Stewart
as a writer of uncommon talent. Dan Filie warmed immediately to the
choice. "R. J. Stewart's a guy I'd worked with on NBC, a witty, smart
writer out of the Glen Caron school," Filie noted.

When Stewart's agent phoned with the good news, he winced
in dismay at the prospect of writing for a show called *Xena:
Warrior Princess*. His first comment was "What??" Then, at
his agent's urging, he took a hard look past the title. "I was
aware of *Hercules* only from the publicity. First they sent me
simply a three-minute package designed to hook writers into it, then they sent one episode [featuring
Xena], the other two were not yet fully produced.
The immediately appealing thing was Lucy, although at that time I had no idea of the actress
she was going to evolve into. But I did see she
was a commanding presence."

Stewart also liked the show's "cool milieu—
the world of the Greek myths was very exciting.
And there's a freedom you get when you write in a
period like this. On shows like *The Great Defender*,
you're so limited by topical issues, it's like hanging
an anvil around your neck and throwing it into the

waters of time. What we think is important this week is going to be so dated, whereas if you're dealing with ancient times and with issues not limited by current events, they will last forever. So I felt so much freer."

Well into negotiations with Renaissance Pictures, Stewart remained ambivalent:

> *I didn't know whether I wanted to be known for* Xena: Warrior Princess. *Then I started thinking: What have you always wanted to do? You've always wanted to tell grand tales. You love adventure. You wanted your shot at being the head writer on a show,* this *is your shot. By the time I got around to saying yes, I think my agent was a little surprised.*

Conferring with Rob Tapert, Stewart created a background for the Warrior Princess that, while not excusing her violent acts, helped explain sympathetically her turn toward the dark side:

> *Xena grew up a village tomboy, and she had some martial arts training. When her village was invaded by a warlord, she retreated to the hills, rallied and counterattacked, and led the village and her family to a victory. It's the taste for revenge that she got out of this that drove her too far. If this warlord had simply attacked and she had fought him off, it might have been different, but he won [at first] and did terrible things to the village. Xena was obsessed with revenge, she kept chasing him, and at a certain point, she fell into the rhythms of this lifestyle, she let go of her innocence entirely, and fell into a cycle of violence and revenge.*

"Argo was not harmed during the production of this motion picture. However, she is undergoing intensive psychotherapy to help her work through her resentment and feelings of distrust toward Xena."
—Disclaimer from "Intimate Stranger"

Although Xena's earlier barbarism posed challenges in getting viewers to sympathize with her, Stewart never felt tempted to play down this aspect of his heroine's life: "Oh, no, the darkness was the attraction to the character. I have a lot of respect for the guys [writing] over at *Hercules* because I think it's a much harder character to write for."

How to make Xena likable despite her history of evil? Stewart described Xena in her three-episode arc on *Hercules* as making a "radical conversion" to good. "Whether or not *philosophically* one believes in free will, *dramatically* this character obviously had to be one that we believe could totally change, that she could re-create herself with her actions." The series, then, could relate Xena's heroic deeds as she strives to make up for her misspent youth.

Whereas *Hercules* often teamed its hero with a fellow warrior-adventurer in Iolaus, *Xena* featured a younger supporting character, Gabrielle, whose wide-eyed naiveté, idealism, and sweetness would play against the harsh past and hardened nature of the show's heroine. R. J. Stewart recalled the genesis of Gabrielle: "This was Rob Tapert's idea, that Xena should have a sidekick. . . . So I had to get a handle on her, because she hadn't been created yet." Stewart then had an inspiration:

"I have a friend who reminds me a little of Gabrielle in that she left home when she was young, she's an immigrant from Thailand who came to this country at a young age. To say I based the character of Gabrielle on her would be ridiculous. But it started me thinking: What about a character who's leaving home?" Gabrielle joins Xena in order to learn about the wider world. As with anyone who leaves a sheltered life, "it's a scary thing." Gabrielle's odyssey of discovery helps make her "someone you can relate to. There are young people who do this all the time."

Renee O'Connor quickly stood out among the actresses who auditioned for the part of Gabrielle. Her career path had led from Texas to Hollywood—with stops in Disneyland, Mississippi, and Australia—before bringing her even further, to New Zealand, in 1994. O'Connor impressed Rob Tapert with her performance as the naive but spirited young woman, Deianeira, in *Hercules and the Lost Kingdom,* the second of the five telefeatures.

According to R. J. Stewart, Tapert from the outset had recognized O'Connor's promise:

I had never seen Renee, so the part of Gabrielle was not written for her. But the day I turned the first script in, Rob said, "You know, I know the gal who can play this part." And we looked at other people, because you never know for sure. We always had a fallback position with Renee, but we said, "Let's see what's out there."

Beth Hymson-Ayer, the U.S. casting director for both *Hercules* and *Xena*, remembered the "meticulous" search for an actress to play Gabrielle: "I saw about four hundred ladies for the role. Each of them did 'pre-reads' [scenes from earlier, unrelated scripts] with me, and the producers probably spoke with fifty ladies. We then tested six or seven [for the role of Gabrielle]." Musing on this exhaustive and exhausting search, Hymson-Ayer smiled and said, "It's extraordinary any television program gets cast given the time frame."

Hymson-Ayer felt that O'Connor brought qualities that were perfect for Gabrielle:

She had a wild sense of humor, an intelligence, and with all that still a youthful quality. Remember, in mythological times, Gabrielle could not be twenty-five, twenty-six years old and still living at home and dreaming of going off on adventure. The life span at that time was not that great, so that youthful look was

important, and even though Renee may not be eighteen, she definitely still has a wide-eyed, innocent freshness to her.

Hymson-Ayer also viewed O'Connor's aura of intelligence as crucial to the character: "Gabrielle is definitely not an equal to Xena in a lot of respects, but at the same time she is as clever, in her own way."

In addition to O'Connor, several actresses auditioning to play Gabrielle memorably filled out the role in other ways, as Dan Filie recalled:

> *The question in casting the part of Gabrielle was "Should we be looking for a young swimsuit beauty, a* Baywatch-*type girl?" And a couple of the girls who came in were just dolls, really cute. But because Lucy hadn't had a lot of experience in front of the camera, we wanted to make sure we had an actress there we could throw "exposition" to. You see, Xena is not the type of character who's going to go into town and tell everybody her story. She needs somebody else to do that. Just as everybody knows Hercules, well, everybody's heard of Xena, in our world: "Ah! Xena the Warrior Princess." She doesn't have to explain who she is. She's the gunfighter. She walks into town, and "Ah! Billy the Kid!" Gabrielle would be the one to relate Xena's tale.*

For Filie, the luxury of having Lucy Lawless, "a beautiful woman," as Xena simplified the casting of Gabrielle:

> *It came down to this:* Xena *is our sexy character, if people don't think that Xena, Warrior Princess, has sex appeal, we're out of luck! So we decided, "Let's get the best actress as Gabrielle," just as we had with Kevin [Sorbo] as Hercules. And in reading the scenes, Renee was just the better actress. There's just a feeling, a good quality to her that comes across on-screen. And, it's funny, because we cast Renee for one reason, and now I think she's an incredibly attractive, very sexy character as well.*

"For Him the Bell Tolls"
Gabrielle: "So you're going to let an innocent man die?"
Aphrodite: "Oh, come on, *no one's* really innocent. Well, maybe *you.*"

Shortly before Xena: Warrior Princess aired nationwide, co-producer Liz Friedman stared nervously at a

giant billboard heralding the new series and said to
Rob Tapert, "You know, Rob, we pretty much made
the show we wanted—and if it doesn't work, there'll be
no one to blame but us." Friedman needn't have worried. In September 1995, a year after Hercules began
its legendary journeys to Nielsen glory, Xena launched
a dizzying triple somersault toward ratings success,
critical praise, and cult status beyond all expectations.

> "Iolaus was harmed
> during the
> production of this
> motion picture.
> However, the Green
> Egg Men went on to
> live long and
> prosperous lives."
> —Disclaimer from
> "Prometheus"

Fans of *Hercules* could connect with many familiar pleasures on *Xena:* the verdant New Zealand
scenery, the mix of action and humor, the casual use
of modern expressions instead of stilted "classical" dialogue, and above all, the presence of a towering hero whose adventures unfold in a golden age of myth. Beyond these Herculean virtues,
Xena offers delights found nowhere else.

There is, first, the Hong Kong-flavored action that goes far beyond
anything ever seen on TV. Even the 1970s hit series *Kung Fu,* which
displayed Asian fighting techniques, had featured only slow-motion
fights in order to conceal star David Carradine's limited martial arts
skill. There is nothing slow-motion about the stunt work on *Xena:*
whereas Hercules is champion of brawn, Xena is all slashing movement:
quick, powerful, full-extension kicks, tosses of her deadly chakram that
bank unerringly off two, three, many surfaces to find their targets, and
airborne acrobatics that would be the envy of Olympic gymnasts.

The boldest departure from *Hercules* is the character of Xena herself—flawed, brood-
ing, dangerous, com-
pared with *Hercules'*
morally pure, easy-
going, approachable
hero. According to
co-creator and execu-
tive producer Rob
Tapert, Xena was
deliberately given a
more mature per-
spective. While Her-
cules stands out for

his decency, he said, Xena is a character in transition, who has still to find herself:

I get a chance to play with a lot darker things in Xena. That makes it a much easier show to write for. The best episodes in Xena are those where we peel away and see a little bit of the inside of her character. They're inherently more dramatic situations because she's such a conflicted character.

Leading *Xena*'s charge to popular acclaim, Lucy Lawless in the title role radiates not only beauty but also an aura of danger that commands the screen. "She's got the devil on her shoulder," Lawless said of her character, "and that's why you watch her. You never know which way she's going to jump." Lawless takes much the same route as Sean Connery, the screen's first and most formidable James Bond, who said of his dark approach to the role, "I begin with the serious side," letting in the humor afterward. Lawless, like Connery a performer of wry wit and emotional range, holds these qualities just beneath the surface in playing Xena. The Warrior Princess has deep feelings, concerns, even humor, "but the trick is just to keep a lid on it, keep a lid on it, keep a lid on it, which lends it poignancy." Lawless observed, too, "It's important to play the character straight-faced, so the audience can enter fully into the fantasy."

R. J. Stewart said that he could risk delving into Xena's dark side because "Lucy Lawless sells this character, in a dramatic and poignant and sympathetic way. I could easily imagine this scenario: that we cast another actress who might be fine, but who, when she plays the dark side, is scary and mean to be around. So it's unpleasant for the viewers. 'Ooh,' you want to say [as a writer], 'she's so good when she's cheerful, let's make her cheerful.' But Lucy sells that dark quality."

Stewart laughed as he thought back to an earlier TV star, Robert Conrad, as proof that the right actor could "sell" a dark hero. A

Renee O'Connor counted a staunch supporter among Universal's extended family, in Dan Filie's six-year-old son, Steven.

"My son had seen *Lost Kingdom* about, oh, four hundred times. And he's a big fan of Herc, and he *loves* Renee O'Connor. So I'd say, 'Stevie! You know Xena's sidekick? You think it should be Renee O'Connor?' And he'd say, 'Dad! It *has* to be Renee O'Connor, it has to be young Deianeira!' "

Three grueling weeks and several hundred auditions later, Stevie's judgment prevailed.

rugged-looking former stuntman, Conrad played a government agent in post–Civil War America—a James Bond figure on horseback—on the series *The Wild Wild West* (1965–69). "Rob [Tapert] and I have talked about this a lot, that *Xena,* in its fantasy element, is like the heir to *The Wild Wild West* phenomenon. Now, Robert Conrad could sell this dark sort of jeopardy: look at him in the freeze frame at each act break, glaring over his shoulder. So even though he was never cheerful, never smiled, never emoted, you totally bought his character. Now, Lucy *starts off* with that ability to sell jeopardy and convincing action, and then adds to it emotions and nuances that Robert Conrad would never dream about."

MAKING MYTHS:

A BEHIND-THE-SCENES LOOK

The myths shown on *Xena* are the product of many unseen efforts. Writers, directors, costume and set designers, special-effects experts, musicians, and other artists all enhance the screen magic woven by the actors. Their stories, though unfolding off-camera, are the stuff that TV dreams are made of.

THE WRITERS

Even on action shows like *Xena,* the pen is mightier than the sword. TV is a writer's medium: most producers are writers, and many executive producers double as head writers for a series. Rob Tapert, though not himself a writer, works closely with the staff on *Xena* because, as he observed, "the heart of a great episode is a great story."

Head writer R. J. Stewart early recruited as his top staff member Steven L. Sears, whose scripts brilliantly mix humor and adventure ("Hooves & Harlots") and evoke Xena's conflicts between her new-found humanity and her bloodlust ("Dreamworker," "The Price"). Like Stewart a "military brat," Sears acted professionally from age twelve and began writing three-minute pieces to enliven his auditions. These micro-dramas garnered praise from casting directors and spurred him to try his hand at screenplays. In 1984 he landed a staff position on a crime show, *Riptide,* then moved nomadically across genres, writing for *Swamp Thing, The A-Team,* and *Father Dowling Mysteries* before becoming supervising producer on *Xena* in 1995.

Sears delights in the dramatic possibilities of a character like Xena. "She has more demons than most of us because of her clouded past,"

he said, "but also unlike most of us, she is willing to confront them."
Yet Sears jokingly laments the widespread preconceptions about
Xena:

> *We're cursed by a title. When I meet people and say* Xena: War-
> rior Princess, *automatically they either think it's a cartoon, or
> they think it's cartoon-*like, *one or the other. And after they have
> seen some of the episodes, their response is completely different.
> They say, "I didn't know you could do stories like that, in that
> genre." Well, that's the point. We do swordplay, that's part of our
> franchise, but there are human beings here, and we're dealing
> with them.*

Midway through the first season, the Emmy-nominated writer Chris
Manheim (*ABC Afterschool Special*) became the third member of the
staff. Manheim has written some of the most offbeat episodes of
Xena, including "The Prodigal" (absent Xena) and "Altared States"
(forsaking Greek myth for the biblical story of Abraham and Isaac).
She also wrote the superb tale "Remember Nothing" (from a story by
Sears), in which Xena gets to live her life over as a peaceful villager—
"as if the Warrior Princess never existed."

A familiar presence at staff meetings is co-producer Liz Friedman,
who came to *Xena* along a less-traveled road strewn with footnotes.
After graduating from Wesleyan University in 1991, Friedman had
considered becoming a professor but instead was hired as Sam Raimi's
assistant after sending him her prize-winning honors thesis on feminist themes of "slasher" films. In 1993 she became an associate producer on the *Hercules* movies, helping supervise the postproduction,
and her creative role on both *Hercules* and *Xena* has steadily grown.
"*Xena* appeals to both sides of me," Friedman said. "The one who
identifies as a feminist and also the one who ran out to see *Rumble in
the Bronx* [with Jackie Chan] on opening weekend." At story meetings Friedman is vigilant on "hero patrol," ensuring that Xena always
appears intelligent, capable, and—as much as any male superhero—
larger than life.

Story sessions overflow with high-energy banter, as if everyone
were writing for a vintage comedy rather than an intense action hour.
This manic mood is on display at a meeting to hone a second-season

script, "Warrior . . . Princess . . . Tramp," in which Lucy Lawless plays Xena and two look-alikes: the ditzy Princess Diana and a promiscuous, street-tough guttersnipe named Robyn (rechristened Meg in later versions of the script). The fantastically complex plot has Robyn impersonate Xena in an attempt to kidnap the princess, assume her identity, and steal her kingdom. Farce rather than intrigue accents this episode, which offers a chance to show off Lucy's acting range and flair for comedy. It also gives the writers free rein to vent their already keen impish impulses.

The genial host of this story meeting is R. J. Stewart, the head writer and co-executive producer, whose 44-page script is about to be enthusiastically vivisected. His hearty laugh and jovial manner set the session's free-spirited tone. Sears and Manheim drift in from neighboring offices and are joined by Friedman and Tapert, who speak the writers' bantering dialect fluently.

> "Neither Xena nor her remarkably coincidental identical twin, Diana, were harmed during production of this motion picture. Meg, however, suffered minor injuries while preparing Aardvark nuggets for King Lias." —Disclaimer from "Warrior . . . Princess . . . Tramp"

No suggestion is too daring or unconventional to win consideration, usually accompanied by a hail of teasing comments. Friedman (re)discovers this when she observes that a character's amorous advance toward Xena, whom he has mistaken for the trampy Robyn, would be funnier still if he reached for her breast instead of her rear. This would "underscore the humor" of Xena's shocked, livid response, "Are you suicidal?!" For daring to send this scene into uncharted censor's territory, Friedman endures much ribbing as the show's feminist gone bad. Then Sears helpfully muses aloud on which would be the funnier breast, right or left. Spirited debate ensues over the dramatic, comic, and anatomical possibilities.

Tapert seems to flourish in the *Xena* staff's uninhibited atmosphere. In contrast to his incisive but unadorned comments at story meetings for *Hercules*, he communicates with *Xena*'s writers in a shorthand that whimsically blends cultural references ("Can we get a haiku version of the song 'Going Home'?") and alludes to movies of every sort (new and old, American,

> Steven Sears's favorite episodes of *Xena* are "Prometheus" and "Dreamworker."

British, and Asian) to illustrate variations on scenes from "Warrior . . . Princess . . . Tramp." Tapert also holds his own in the group's frequent irreverent exchanges, as when Sears suggests ways to compensate for the disappointing performance of a child actor in an earlier episode:

> Sears: Could we use a hand puppet [for the child]?
> Tapert: A hand puppet would be preferable.
> Sears: Maybe we can animate a kid!?
> Tapert (poking fun at his own love of special-effects techniques): How about a [computer]-generated kid?
> Sears: We could use "forced perspective" [creating the illusion of height] on everyone except one person, and he can be the kid.

Amid the writers' wild repartee, plot points are dissected, dialogue is reworked or trimmed, characters are sharpened. Sears scales back several preachy lines in a climactic scene in which Princess Diana's elderly father, King Lias, gives Robyn a second chance. Tapert questions the rhythms of a conversation after Princess Diana's baby is kidnapped: "Why would [her husband] Philemon wait through several lines of dialogue before announcing, 'The baby's gone'? Now, if *I* were a father . . ." Tapert also observes that "the key plot device" of triple-mistaken identity "is too often lost sight of"; he wants it to register clearly throughout.

Refining the comic tone of "Warrior . . . Princess . . . Tramp" takes up much of the two-hour story meeting. The writers are most serious about the humor on *Xena*, which must reveal character and advance the plot as well as amuse. Friedman and Sears build on each other's suggestions for playing up Gabrielle's increasingly overwrought reactions to being jailed by the Xena look-alike, Robyn. Accustomed to enjoying Xena's complete trust, Gabrielle now stews in growing exasperation while Robyn spouts bizarre assurances that this is all part of a secret plan. The scene can make light of Gabrielle's predicament because viewers realize that the real Xena will at last set her straight; until then,

> "Warrior . . . Princess"
> Diana: "Tell me what to do to be a convincing Xena."
> Gabrielle: "Well, for starters, stop crying."

Gabrielle is left to scream at each new snub and indignity, "Let me guess! It's part of 'the plan'!"

How modern to make the dialogue is an abiding concern for the writers of this ancient period piece. Stewart agrees to strike the term "put a hurt on you," which simply does not fit anyone's notion of proper "Amphipolis-speak." Changes in language also occur for reasons of propriety: Tapert strikes an insult to Robyn, "despicable slut," as "too harsh." Robyn's status rises modestly, to a "slag."

The producers and writers band together to protect the hero's character, recognizing that "we can't transgress certain bounds." A line slandering Xena's love life is clever but does not survive scrutiny, because that is "beyond the pale." The arrival of Xena a day late

to meet Gabrielle similarly must be explained, lest it violate the writers' rule that "Xena is all action. She cannot appear ineffectual—ever."

During a lull, a visitor remarks, "Everyone is so scrupulous about the credibility of each story point. Is there any concern to explain how there are three Xenas roaming Greece?" Tapert exclaims with mock indignation, "Who let this guy in?" Sears invokes Friedman's theory that there must have been a limited gene pool in ancient Mycenae. He also hints at a "foundling" theory of Xena siblings left on doorsteps, but "that's for the third season."

Such frothy explanations of the ground rules for Xena's universe mask a good deal of hard reflection by the writers on just how far they can stretch myths, timelines, and plain common sense in pursuit of a good story. One question they have wrestled with is how Xena can convincingly play roles in stories that never originally mentioned her. For example, she has acted as a defender of Troy against invading Greek armies; a peacemaker between Centaurs and Ama-

"No Males, Centaurs, or Amazons were harmed during the production of this motion picture."
—Disclaimer from "Hooves & Harlots"

zons; even an ally to the young Israelite warrior David against the Philistine giant, Goliath. Steve Sears is unfazed by the challenge of "restoring" Xena to her place in ancient history and myth:

> *Here's the way we rationalize it. First, Xena was a dark charac-*
> *ter, and few people want to write about a dark character, so her*
> *participation in certain events would have been omitted [by the*
> *Ancients]. Second, the "authorities" on mythology disagree*
> *among themselves. [The Roman poet] Ovid disagrees with Plato,*
> *who disagrees with [compilers of Greek tales] Robert Graves and*
> *Edith Hamilton. Also, Xena was a woman. Most of the histories*
> *were written by men.*

While Sears weaves expertly through such historical and literary subtleties, he does not overly fret about them: "The final thing I say to people is, if those reasons don't work for you, remember: it's a TV show!"

The cavalier crossing of historical eras and regions on *Xena* has also absorbed Sears. Though he and his co-writers are well read in history, they have placed Xena variously in Greek settings from 300 to 1500 B.C., in Rome centuries later, in towns that recall medieval France and England, and in other areas and eras that span a thousand miles (or so) and an equal number of years. "Now, we do span a huge timeline," Sears acknowledged, "but we have a common saying here: "Anything B.C. is fine." He adds wryly that when a fan pointed out

that Troy was far away from Corinth and asked how Xena and Gabrielle could possibly move from one to the other in consecutive episodes, "I said, 'The world was much smaller back then.' "

The crossing of timelines comes more easily because, at heart, there is a single frame of reference for all writers: the present. Sears tells of an early book about the TV series *Star Trek:* "It said that this series was *not* [as often claimed] about life in the twenty-third century, but it was about us *as if* we were living in the twenty-third century. Otherwise, we'd have no way to identify with these characters."

Flexibility also marks the writers' approach to mythology. While versed in the ancient stories that form the world of *Hercules* and *Xena*, they freely adapt these tales to their own dramatic needs. R. J. Stewart, whose voracious reading of myths dates back to his youth, emphasized their value if viewed simply as a starting point, not as shackles that would condemn writers to repeat old tales verbatim:

Let me give you the philosophy of [our writing]—I really feel strongly about this. . . . In the history of Western culture and civilization the Greek myths have been a taking-off place to tell stories. Knowledge of what the Greek myths were is important, but there's never been a slavish obedience to the myths in any generation as far as what is said.

And that philosophy, Stewart insisted, perfectly suited the ancient Greeks themselves:

There is a guy named Euripides who was a playwright, much closer to the source of these myths than we are today. He wrote a play called Helen. *Now, in that play he does not have Helen go to Troy, he has her go to Egypt. Now, why did he do that? He had to have been aware that most of the popular myths he heard had her go to Troy. I guarantee you, there was someone standing around, saying, "Euripides, we've got this great pyramid set!" O.K.? So Euripides did a practical thing to make the drama work. It has been going on ever since.*

The myths have nourished the imagination of writers for thousands of years, said Stewart. "Both historical and mythical characters from the ancient world have been used freely by everybody from Shakespeare to Goethe. . . . And today we again want to use the mythology as a foundation, a stepping-off point, for telling our [own] stories."

CASTING

Casting offices in New Zealand and the United States work full-time to fill roles on *Xena,* from guest villains to huddled villagers. Diana Rowan, who casts most of the featured parts from her home near Auckland, approaches the relentless deadlines with a mixture of good humor and terror:

> *Well, every week I have to find forty actors for* Xena *and Hercules, forty American-speaking actors. . . . Every episode I think we're not going to make it, this is not going to happen this time. This is it. Our last episode is being made. And somehow we pull through, and then we face the next script, which usually comes about seven days before we start to shoot. . . . So every seven days I'm casting one* Hercules *and one* Xena.

Finding the right actor for a role, according to the U.S. casting director Beth Hymson-Ayer, is "totally subjective, a matter of intangibles, and that's why you can't go to any school for it." Hymson-Ayer discovered this firsthand on arriving in Los Angeles in 1980, intent on converting her business administration degree into a career in international marketing research. Instead a roommate who worked as a secretary in a casting office alerted her to a vacancy and urged, "Hey, if you're in L.A., you may as well do something you can't do anywhere else!" Hymson-Ayer won the job, and the job won her over. She learned to trust her intuition for spotting talent, then rose as head of her own casting agency.

Beginning in 1986 Hymson-Ayer cast such hit series as *Hunter, Doogie Howser, M.D.,* and *L.A. Law.* But it was a hip undercover-cops drama on the rising "fourth network," Fox, that gave her the most freedom to break new ground: "*21 Jump Street* relied on young guest leads, giving them the chance to be some-

> "Despite Gabrielle's incessant hurling, Ulysses' ship was not harmed during the production of this motion picture."
> —Disclaimer from "Ulysses"

thing other than simply a victim or the daughter or son of a lead character. These eighteen- to twenty-three-year-olds *carried* the show, and it was wonderful finding the new talent, and getting them that break."

Since 1995 that knack for finding fresh talent has helped Hymson-Ayer flesh out the epic tales of both *Hercules: The Legendary Journeys* and *Xena: Warrior Princess*. Her discoveries have included goddesses (Alexandra Tydings as Aphrodite), heroes (Scott Garrison as Gabrielle's handsome but ill-fated fiancé, Perdicas), and villains (Hudson Leick as Xena's archnemesis Callisto). Hymson-Ayer remains lighthearted about these and other casting coups, saying, "You know what? This is fun. We're not curing cancer, we're not trying to set social standards or reach any morals here. It's true escapism."

Hymson-Ayer first auditions performers in a "pre-read," in which "we work from an unrelated script so I can get a feel for their instincts, their ability, and their quality." She will play opposite an actor in scenes that are largely unrehearsed but far from casual: "If you're doing a drug addict, a rape scene, a very emotional scene, it can get intense. And I'll keep pictures of people that I like or think I might be able to use at some point."

Actors called back for a second audition read for guest roles on *Xena*, and Hymson-Ayer will winnow dozens of hopefuls down to seven or eight actors to take to the producers. The pressure then escalates to "a whole other stress level," as finalists perform for a high-level audience that may include Rob Tapert, R. J. Stewart, Liz Friedman, and the director for that episode. When Tapert goes on location, he will receive videos of the final auditions. "But if there are really clear-cut choices," Hymson-Ayer explained, "we'll call Rob and say, 'It's hands down, this is the person.' And he'll usually sign off and go, 'O.K., go ahead and book 'em.' "

Tapert, who has encouraged unconventional casting, suggested an African-American actor, Bobby Hosea, as Xena's first love interest, Marcus. Hosea was best known for playing O. J. Simpson in a TV docudrama, but Tapert remembered him from an earlier action flick called *M.A.N.T.I.S.*, which he and Sam Raimi had produced. When *M.A.N.T.I.S.* was picked up as a TV series, the network wanted to replace Hosea with a white actor but, Tapert related, "we drew a line in the sand on this." Tapert was equally committed to casting Hosea as Marcus.

In addition to acting talent, physical skills often figure in the selection of actors. "When we cast the role of Callisto," Hymson-Ayer said, "I was checking to find out whether the actresses had any martial arts experience or training. Or how fit or athletically inclined they were. For example, could they ride a horse? Because the script calls for Callisto to ride, and so we needed someone who could look comfortable on a horse! We couldn't take someone green." Much depends, she explained, on whether an actor can be "doubled" for action scenes:

You see, there are stunts that can be cheated well and stunts that can't. It's much easier to cheat a fight with a stunt double than it is to cheat a simple riding scene on a horse. In a lot of the fight sequences or charging sequences on a horse you can have a double because it goes so quickly across the screen, but when Callisto is riding into town you really need [the actress] on that horse. Once you take her off that horse and get her into a sword fight with Xena, you can do your cuts to her face and then cut away and see just her arm and you can have a stuntperson in there doing the sword. Those are things viewers aren't supposed to realize—you're supposed to believe it's her the whole time. That's the art of entertainment!

While casting choices often come down to intangible qualities, fabulous good looks can also propel an audition nicely. "Yes, there's a certain type of actor that we look to put on both *Hercules* and *Xena*," said Hymson-Ayer. "Beautiful people! Beautiful women, hunky men. The costumes of the era certainly accentuate those attributes. The audience loves it!" From across the ocean, Hymson-Ayer's New Zealand counterpart, Diana Rowan, laughingly concurs: "The blokes have to be hunks, and all the women have to be—the American expression is 'babe-alicious.' "

> Rowan's biggest casting coup was her discovery of the eleven-year-old Anna Paquin, who won an Oscar for her work on *The Piano*.

Rowan had gained renown as New Zealand's premier casting director well before joining forces with *Hercules* and *Xena*, having cast the acclaimed film *The Piano*. An English actress who relocated on marrying a New Zealander, Rowan landed an unexpected double role in 1982: soon after she won a lead part in a film, the director asked her to help pick the rest of the cast. "He wanted someone to find fresh talent," Rowan recalled, "and he said to me, 'I heard you have a good eye for people.' I told him, 'You've got *totally* the wrong person. I wouldn't have a clue how to cast.' But he persisted, saying, 'Well, you just use your instincts.' " Rowan's first instinct was to recast her own role: "I actually thought that I was wrong for my part and that somebody else would be better. Well, the show got rave reviews for the casting!"

One of the half dozen New Zealand "lifers" who have worked on every *Hercules* and *Xena* production, Rowan brought Lucy Lawless to read for the first TV movie, *Hercules and the Amazon Queen*:

I know all of the actresses here and I'd already cast Lucy in the film Rainbow Warrior. *I was auditioning "babe-ish" women who looked like they could also be warriors as opposed to anorexic princesses. When she came in for an audition, I remember being impressed that this girl had something special. So when we were looking at casting the part of the Amazon queen in New Zealand, I pushed for her. And then, after the producers had decided to go with an American actress [Roma Downey], I kept trying to get Lucy back for another part. Eric [Gruendemann] even joked with me, "You related to Lucy?!"*

Rowan later pressed to cast Lawless as Xena and tracked her by phone through the New Zealand bush to reach her in time.

Rowan's sure touch extends to the smallest cameos on *Xena,* as evident in a casting session with director T. J. Scott for an episode called "Return of Callisto." Scott, who directed an earlier episode introducing Callisto, is pleased to have the lead roles reprised by the original actors, including the riveting Hudson Leick as Xena's crazed nemesis. This still leaves several featured roles to fill, and Rowan and Scott brainstorm to make each one memorable.

The youthful-looking, thirty-two-year-old Scott clearly enjoys working with Rowan, with whom he shares both consummate professionalism and sly humor. Of his approach to casting, Scott remarks that insight into performers comes in many guises, including bare: "The first thing I read on an actor's 'casting form' is their answer to the question 'Will you do nude scenes?' It says something about them!"

Rowan screens for Scott the videotaped auditions of six to eight finalists that she has selected for each role. The actors are in character, though not in costume: they wear jeans and T-shirts, and some wave imaginary whips and swords as they speak their lines. First up are candidates to play a tough prison guard, each spouting a sneering insult at Callisto, "What do you say, *dog?*" The second and fifth guards win praise for their menacing look, the third impresses with his acting, the sixth stands out for his distinctive personality (the eyes are alive, the spirit humorous) but he never seems tough enough to play a warden.

> "Although Xena finally conquered her dark nemesis Callisto, it took her weeks to get the sand out of her leather unmentionables."
> —Disclaimer from "Return of Callisto"

Because the head guard needs a junior partner, Rowan also shows Scott a half dozen auditions by young actors, explaining, "[This is] if you want to go with someone who is still learning to be a thug." On spotting an exceptionally handsome actor, Scott exclaims, "Why, it's Kurt Russell!" No, Rowan corrects him, the fellow on-screen is "more gorgeous than Kurt Russell. We throw that in once in a while just to cheer things up." They size up the candidates: "He's got a slightly off-the-rails look but not as much as the others." "An all-American jock look." "I like this guy because he's got a different edge."

After viewing all the "guards," Rowan and Scott consider how best to pair a rough-looking actor with a boyish one. Guard No. 5 clinches the role of head guard with his imposing physique. Scott observes, "For those who didn't see [the earlier episode], it makes Callisto appear harder" if she beats up a menacing character. A blond actor with a winsome expression wins the role of second guard because "his partner will look even scarier" by comparison.

Rowan and Scott next view finalists to perform a wedding ceremony for Gabrielle and her childhood fiancé. The taped auditions are culled from readings for earlier episodes, but Scott is unfazed: so long as an actor projects the right spiritual aura, Scott will gladly ordain him for the role. Rowan promises of one video clip, "You'll love this actor's look, but you may need to dub him." The monitor flashes a sight that transfixes Scott: a visage enveloped by a sprawling grayish-white beard, with a wild gaze that might well pass for spiritual ecstasy. Scott has no doubt that Rowan's choice is perfect; the eyes have it. He even waives the idea of dubbing the actor: "I can understand what he's saying." Rowan suggests that the character should have an American accent rather than this actor's blend of Kiwi and British tones, but Scott smiles at such concerns: "He's a Greek priest! Why would he have an American accent?!"

Apart from casting most featured roles on both *Xena* and *Hercules,* Rowan helps set their tone by encouraging actors to play modern characters rather than stereotyped Ancients:

> *The first note I give to all actors is that they should be as natural as if they were on the streets of New York or California today. . . .*

And with the gods, although they should have a charisma on-screen that raises them a little bit above the average mortal, I still encourage the actors to talk as though they're just going down the path. That makes it more accessible to the audience.

For Rowan the line between gods and mortals is not so sharp as between heroes and villains: "The 'goodies' I make as real as possible and the 'baddies' I encourage to go up a notch or two because I think that makes it more exciting and, after all, we're not talking about reality here in any shape or form."

Because "a script can be cast in so many different ways," Rowan makes a point of learning the director's vision for each character. Still, she will often play with that vision in unexpected ways:

I don't necessarily go with the first thing that comes into my mind because I think life's not like that. So if a script says, "A huge thug comes over the bridge," I think, "Now, how else could you cast this? What if you got a little person in the part rather than a big nasty-looking person?" For the same reason, it's quite nice sometimes to have someone who is really evil smile all the time, and appear really charming. In fact, it's really much more threatening. And when we did the three Fates [in "Remember Nothing"], I proposed to the director that instead of a babe as the youngest Fate it might be quite nice to go really young, to cast a twelve-year-old child! I like to push the boundaries that way, it's one of my quirks!

The small number of actors in New Zealand compared with Hollywood adds to Rowan's readiness to cast against type. "Say I want a warlord," she explained. "Well, warlords are two-a-penny in the series, and I will consider the standard six-footish, gritty, muscular sorts but we have a limited [talent] pool here, so I think, 'How else can I make this work?' "

Recycling of actors helps Rowan further stretch the limited supply. "When we first started," she explained, "we were extremely opposed to using people twice. I think too often producers will underestimate their audiences, assuming they won't notice things. And I don't actually believe that eye patches and beards really fool everybody. Still, we do, of course, have a problem because casting two series and five feature films from a small country is difficult." Increasingly Rowan has made a virtue of necessity and relied on the versatility of actors, aided by deft costuming and "serious prosthetics."

Rowan shoulders, as well, a complication unknown to Hollywood casting directors: the need to find actors who can mute their Kiwi (or Aussie) accents for a U.S. series. Eric Gruendemann, who oversees the production in New Zealand, related the difficulties of blending the babel of accents into a single American sound:

> *There are so many different speech patterns even in America: a Texas drawl is different from a Louisiana drawl. We decided on Southern California as the basic speech pattern. We have a full-time dialect coach for New Zealand actors (and we have a few from Australia as well). With high turnover and the speed with which you shoot a television show, sometimes you get [the consistency] and sometimes you don't. What you're hearing is a valiant effort to try to homogenize the sounds into a single Southern California-speak, which some people are good at and some aren't.*

According to Rowan, the challenge of finding New Zealand performers to mesh with Americans goes beyond taming an accent:

> *Everybody can see the difference between, say, a Frenchman and an Englishman just in the body language, and that's true of other nationalities as well—everything from how far away you stand and when you look at people you're talking to, and how intense you get about certain things. There's a whole physical and facial gesturing that goes on that isn't immediately obvious. If I'm looking at an actor on tape, I know before they say a word who are the Americans. I couldn't tell you exactly what it is—just a look and the way they stand.*

Rob Tapert is philosophical about the pitfalls in getting Kiwis to sound like Yanks, noting that the New Zealand accent, a close cousin to British speech, has its own charms. "I have a feeling that most of America feels that anyone from ancient times speaks with an English accent, so I think, in its own way, it kind of works for the show."

No wonder that Rowan casts a broad net for talent: "I do make it my job to know anybody who acts in any capacity on stage, screen, TV, and commercials." Nor does she stop there: "I consider every possibility, from the plumber to the electrician. . . . A waiter comes up and I'll say, 'Have you thought of acting? You know, you really should take up acting!' "

IT TAKES A VILLAGE: EXTRAS CASTING

The great majority of actors on *Xena* do not audition, do not play named characters, and do not have lines. Yet they are indispensable to the action and the atmosphere of each episode. These unheralded performers are the extras, and they are hired, assembled, and prepped by a young former model named Tracy Hampton, who wryly explained the boundaries of her casting domain: "If they don't speak, they're mine."

Asked if she herself had once acted, Hampton shook her head and said, "No, I'm not as good in front of the camera as behind it!" Despite such modest disclaimers, Hampton had modeled in Europe, Australia, and her native New Zealand, where her tall, slender form, green eyes, and auburn hair adorned magazine covers until she was in her early twenties. Then one day she decided, "No, this is enough. It was either you put your all into it or you walk away. And I took my money and went backpacking through Europe on my own for a half year. And then I got back knowing I wanted to get into TV production because I knew the agents and crews."

When Hampton, at age twenty-three, joined the production team on the third *Hercules* telefeature, it was not glamour that lured her: "As an assistant director without the title, I started off having to take extras out to the set in four-wheel-drives through mud at four in the morning. And then I'd work on set till nine at night, bring them all back, then get up and do it again." The grueling hours led Hampton to ponder the fate of her predecessor: "The lady who did the first two telefeatures just burned out—she'd had enough!" Hampton kept her balance by shifting to full-time work on extras casting. "I still do twelve hours a day but not sixteen," she said, adding that the key was to create a vast filing pool from which to "mix and match" extras:

I walked into an empty office with a box of photos and someone said, "Here, this is your job." Nothing of this size had been done before, so it was a matter of putting a system in place, listing each extra's photo, background, and any special skills, and finding people with a unique look: everyone has to have long hair or be weird, ugly, interesting, beautiful. You know, they can't look like your next-door neighbor.

Hampton and her co-worker, Marisa Borich, make sure that villagers are not simply recruited by the dozen; they are, to a surprising extent, custom-designed. "We put a lot of pride into considering all the different categories of inhabitants," she explained. Ethnic looks also vary from week to week:

We might cast "Mexicans" or, at this moment, "Africans," and since there's not that many African people here, we look for Maori, too. For an Egyptian setting, we've gone dark-haired, olive-skinned. One extra has been Asian in some episodes and this week he's Egyptian. New Zealand is so multiracial that you can find faces that give the desired [ethnic] influence.

Seventy or more extras populate each episode. The upper limit is ninety because, Hampton notes, that is the maximum number of costumes the wardrobe crew can turn out in barely a week. Assembling the extras on the morning of a shoot, Hampton explains their roles and exhorts them to bring emotion as well as motion to their scenes:

They cross over the sets a lot, walk through the shops, and, when the script requires, they're all scared or they'll look on in dismay. I call them "background artists" in that you really encourage them to act, not simply mill about. We've started telling people more of the story, so when they get onstage they have more of a feel for it. And we make them realize that they're not "rent-a-crowd," that every person is handpicked.

Most directors provide Hampton with a general mandate ("Egyptian palace guards and slaves"), but some go further: "T. J. [Scott] will give us a breakdown of exactly the ratio of ages and the looks he

> Robert Gillies
> designed his first
> sets for the New
> Zealand rock band
> Split Enz, in which
> he also played both
> sax and trumpet.

wants. He'll look at the files and go, 'I want this one and I want that one.' He doesn't restrict you, he just gives you a more creative style."

Hampton's job description does not include crisis management but, as she soon learned, it helps:

We got a call late one evening from some musicians we had cast as "Africans" to play drums. . . . We had outfitted these island guys with special costumes, and they were due at six in the morning on set, but they said, "Oh, yeah, Trace, we're not going to make it, because some of us are in Wellington [well south of Auckland] and, yeah, sorry." And I could only go, "But, but, but . . ." So, first thing in the morning, we were hunting for guys who looked like them, who could fit into the costumes and then pretend to play the drums.

The show's composer, Joe Lo Duca, provided the actual musical accompaniment from his studio in Detroit.

Balancing such professional hazards are the joys of "seeing the fresh enthusiasm of people, many of whom come from tough lives. They get an opportunity to have a good time, they get fed well, and they get to run around in costume and meet [others on set], and they love it, they just thrive on what they see."

SETS AND PROPS

Characters on *Xena* may sound like Americans in the nineties but they inhabit a world unlike anything viewers have known. Production designer Robert Gillies has seen to that. A soft-spoken, gentle man given to dry wit, Gillies creates the castles, chariots, temples, hurtling boulders (Styrofoam), and shimmering (gelatin-based) ambrosia that help give *Xena* an aura of myth and mystery.

The pace of production is such, Gillies said, that "there is never time to consult a reference, so you must rely on your accumulated store of images." His inspirations have come in many guises:

Comic books offer visualizations of other realities, a rich source of images by other artists. And I've always been excited with those wonderful National Geographic *reconstructions of a Mayan city: you can look over the page for half an hour, there is so much detail. Natural landscapes could be the inspiration for a set. An animal skull might give ideas for shaping [sets and props]. As soon as we started working, we ordered a whole lot of skulls and skeletons from a place in the States called Skullduggery.*

Movies, too, can prompt ideas, including Italian spectacles with their ancient epic heroes:

Yes, I can remember Son of Spartacus *[with Steve Reeves], which I saw at the age of about ten. The obvious ones, you know, Ben-Hur, was classic stuff. And then also [the futuristic fantasy]* Barbarella. *I was about fourteen when I saw that and I just thought the big maze city was fantastic. I have taken that maze as an inspiration for [designing sets].*

Gillies draws, as well, on images from other TV shows, especially those exotic to Western culture: "When TV first came to New Zealand I used to love a Japanese show called *Chintara* about ninja warriors. These guys could jump backward up three stories. And it was all set in feudal Japan."

A week or two before an episode is shot, Gillies confers with the director on what sets and props his crew of several hundred will need to build. For "Return of Callisto," director T. J. Scott requests two chariots for a battle royal between Xena and Callisto. (Happily the prop department has on hand the chariots Gillies had designed for *Xena*'s second episode, "Chariots of War.") Scott also asks Gillies to create a "kind of temple" for Callisto's hideaway, "but no god." "A godless temple?" asks Gillies, amused. "Just a lot of candles," Scott replies. "I really like what you did for [the god] Bacchus' lair [on an earlier episode]. It was a cave but it had an architectural feel to it, with those columns, and a little bit of hominess. Can you give Callisto's base an architectural exterior, so it looks more like a ruin than a cave?" Gillies

> "By popular demand, The Executioner will bring back his comfortable lightweight cotton-flax blend robe in a variety of spring colors."
> —Disclaimer from "The Execution"

agrees matter-of-factly; building temples and ancient ruins on short notice is routine. Only when Scott asks to use a particular location among the eight studio sets does Gillies demur, because another superhero has not yet checked out: "*Hercules* is filming there now, so there is no time to prepare this for your episode."

Scott has better luck finding an exterior set for a showdown between Xena and Callisto that will echo the chariot race in *Ben-Hur*. He books a "two-day package" to shoot at the spectacularly scenic Bethells Beach, some twenty miles west of Auckland. Gillies nods benignly, then adds a sly reference to his latest props for an episode featuring Julius Caesar: "If Rob Tapert's crucifying five people hasn't freaked out the [Auckland City] Council."

COSTUMES

> The producers had originally envisioned Xena as a blonde, but Lucy Lawless suggested dyeing her hair black instead. She took as her inspiration the Argentine tennis star Gabriela Sabatini, who, Lawless noted, "looks like a Warrior Princess."

Outfitting the actors on *Hercules* and *Xena* demands an extra measure of creativity, for not only is each show a "period piece" but the period is constantly shifting. Dozens of craftspeople and coordinators share the labor, but the buckskin stops at the desk of head designer Ngila (pronounced "Nyla") Dickson. Slender, with long dark hair and striking red lipstick, Dickson cuts an elegant figure in an office piled with books (*Everyday Fashion of the Forties* and *A History of Men's Fashions,* among several dozen others) and exotic furnishings (a pink lampshade rests on an ebony female head bedecked with bells for earrings). Festooning the walls are mottoes attesting to Dickson's relentless pace ("Man who says . . . 'It cannot be done' should not interrupt woman who is doing it").

In designing fashions from peasant garb to royal robes, Dickson will often bend historical realism to a higher calling: to give clothes flair while indulging her wildest imaginings. "I have these discussions with Rob

Gillies," she related, "and we just de-cide—for example, a week ago we were into *Vikings*. . . . Within tiny bounds, I can do anything. You know, demons and monsters, giants, damsels in distress."

Dickson's imagination extends to heavy-duty ornaments that might belong to ancient times or simply an alternate universe. For a "mystic warrior, a really evil person," in an episode called "Dreamworker," she designed a headdress with curved horns, consisting of "a lot of glue, leather with shellac over the top of it, and a lot of fastening to make [the parts] stay [together], because they're quite heavy and they're quite often used in a lot of stunt action."

Dickson takes special pride in the costumes for "all the warrior women," beginning with Xena herself:

The undergarment is all leather, and the breastplates and all the decorative pieces that go on—the gauntlets, armbands, and shoulder pieces—are made from copper and lined with leather. Now, copper is a "living" material and it requires quite a lot of maintenance. But even though we make armor out of plastics for the stunt people, I really choose to stick with the copper for Xena because the texture and the color and look of it is just so good. . . .

Since Xena's first appearances, her outfit has changed on two levels. One was we didn't want it to be quite so dark and warriorlike as it had been on Hercules. *Lucy had a lot of trouble with it in the first episodes because it had so many pieces and layers. It was just very hard to wear. So we decided to strip it down, put in really good design elements, and make it more utilitarian. . . . It is a much better, simpler shape than we had originally for that character.*

These alterations were still "minute," Dickson said, compared with the fashion revolution that Gabrielle has experienced:

> *Her clothing has changed so much because the character herself has evolved: from a naive village girl to an Amazon princess to marriage to having a child [in a third-season episode]. . . . One change, of course, is that Gabrielle has been wearing less! Renee [O'Connor] has gotten so fit, her stomach is very flat, she looks extraordinary. So we want to get more of her on the screen!*

A meeting between Dickson and director T. J. Scott to prep the episode "Return of Callisto" reveals intricate planning to outfit everyone from the lead characters to the villagers who flit silently across the screen. More than most directors, Scott has precise ideas of how the color and cut of clothing can set the mood of a scene. He and Dickson converse in a knowing shorthand as they brainstorm and banter their way through a series of fashion possibilities that veer from the unconventional to the outrageous.

No role is too small to merit a dress code, including even the six prison guards who will appear in the "teaser" just long enough to be slaughtered by Callisto:

> Scott: I want to give a maximum-security feel. This is not a bumpkin prison, but more high-tech, something beyond a routine local jail. (He hands Dickson a diagram of his color scheme for the guards.) Here is my "T. J.-can't-draw sketch."
> Dickson: So, you want "high-tech B.C."?!
> Scott: Um-hmm. Guards with their jackets off, wearing gray-black T-shirts underneath.

The veteran villainess Callisto, Scott and Dickson agree, should retain her revealing and form-fitting outfit. Scott also specifies the look he has in mind for Callisto's warriors: it should be primitive, exotic, over the top. Their style, he observes, says "*Mad Max* with money."

Peasant villages on *Hercules* and *Xena* may lack amenities, but none is too poor to sport its own color scheme. Dickson, alert to Scott's preferences, smiles as she asks, "Blue village or brown village?" Scott goes for brown, observing that "earth tones recycle [actors] well because the extras don't stand out as much," so they can appear repeatedly in different guises.

A village girl who should stand out, because Xena will save her from Callisto, inspires Scott and Dickson to conjure a more stylish, *haut*-peasant look. "She should look like a young Xena or Callisto," Scott remarks. "Perhaps her stockings should come up like their boots." Dickson sketches Scott's ideas, but finds the image too "mod" for a Greek village. "It's the [sixties'] minidress look," she cautions. Scott jokingly suggests some ancient accessories: "O.K., should we give her a chakram?" For such a young girl, Dickson admonishes, "better make it a Frisbee."

For the young village women, Dickson suggests a surreal approach: "motorbike girls with darker colors, reds, purples—real biker chicks." Scott appears intrigued, and Dickson continues, with a mischievous gleam, "Why don't we do the sci-fi version, while no one's looking, see if we can slip it in, a look so modern it goes backward [to ancient times]?" Scott raises only one concern, that "the dresses should differ from Callisto's, so they won't compete with her." But Dickson, having earlier outfitted the flamboyant actress who plays Callisto, assures Scott, "Don't worry, we won't allow any competition with Callisto—not that anyone *could* compete with Hudson [Leick] when she gets that look in her eye."

The fashion highlight of "Return of Callisto" centers on Gabrielle's wedding to her childhood fiancé, Perdicas. Scott and Dickson agree that the actor who plays Perdicas, Scott Garrison, is so handsome that his outfit should play on his good looks. Perdicas was last seen fighting in the Trojan War, and Scott notes that even in a wedding costume "it should still feel like he's a warrior." "Softer leather, so he's more huggable?" Dickson inquires with a laugh.

Outfitting Gabrielle presents a dilemma. In perhaps the most distinctive dictum on TV fashion since *Miami Vice* barred "earth tones" in favor of pastels, Rob Tapert forbade the color white in filming *Xena,* a dark show with a dark heroine. But taboos are meant to be broken, albeit carefully. With Tapert's concurrence, Scott suggests lifting the ban on white for Gabrielle's wedding dress. Dickson adds a deft touch to highlight Gabrielle's purity: "Flowers in her hair?" Scott nods enthusiastically and builds on the image: "A wreath through her hair."

> "Cecrops' Joie de Vivre was not harmed during the production of this motion picture."
> —Disclaimer from "Lost Mariner"

The character of Xena poses the hardest costuming challenge, relating to the stringent time constraints that loom over the production of every episode. Scott would like to give Xena a warmer look, remarking that she "can't wear her armor to her best friend's wedding." Dickson demurs, having just spent nearly all of a two-week "vacation" working round-the-clock on outfits for a segment of *Xena* featuring Julius Caesar. Especially painstaking was Xena's uniquely stylish pirate's costume, with flowing violet robes covered by gold coins (*Captain Blood* by way of Givenchy), "which my prop department never wants to do again." "We've just hit an incredible wall in fitting Lucy," Dickson beseeches. "Unless another costume is absolutely needed . . ."

Scott is sympathetic but implores, "It's a *wedding*. Xena is the *bridesmaid*." It is a familiar predicament for Dickson, whose reputation for conjuring feature-film costumes on a tight TV schedule keeps expectations high. She pleads once more the impossibility of creating another outfit. Then, breaking a slight smile as Scott looks on in admiration, she begins expertly sketching the possibilities.

THE NEW ZEALAND CONNECTION

From the first telefeatures through the newest episodes of *Hercules* and *Xena*, producer Eric Gruendemann has been Rob Tapert's indispensable, inexhaustible liaison with the New Zealand production team. Gruendemann is not only the writers' and executive producers' representative but also the studio's representative, overseeing the many-faceted production and following it through into postproduction. Attempting to explain his role, Gruendemann found it easier to list what he did not do: "The writing of scripts and ultimately much of the postproduction, such as the final sound correction and special effects, is done back in the States. But basically everything that happens in New Zealand is my domain."

Gruendemann entered the world of pictures by way of numbers, as a wizard in accounting. "I'd always had a great head for figures, business was second nature to me," he related. He earned a degree in business and marketing, with a minor in film; and typical of many young

graduates in Southern California, Gruendemann's film minor became ever more major in his career plans. Even before leaving college he joined Paramount's internal audit department as one of the studio-based accountants, or "watchdogs," and scrutinized budgets for *Top Gun, Beverly Hills Cop,* and other features. "We were like IRS auditors

Eric Gruendemann discovered the possibilities opened by the information age while filming *The Blob* in Louisiana. He bought his first fax machine to facilitate communication with studio headquarters in Hollywood.

making sure the books matched, and if spending was out of control we'd recommend ways to make sure the crew didn't find at the end: 'Oh, man, we're seven million dollars over budget!' "

During the 1980s the cost of making movies exploded, and Gruendemann found his career riding that upward spiral. "Once, this position was the lowest of the low, you were a bean counter and a geek. But then the studios realized, 'Hey, money is really important!' They were getting burned, and so right around the time I got into it, this became an important profession." As an independent contractor, Gruendemann worked on A-films such as *Torch Song Trilogy,* but he preferred low-budget projects because, he said, "I find it more challenging when you have to bleed a rock, make ten dollars look like one thousand dollars, than when you're just paying bills."

Gruendemann's talent for stretching limited resources impressed Rob Tapert and Sam Raimi, for whom he had worked on *Darkman II* and *Army of Darkness.* By 1993, when Raimi and Tapert were preparing the *Hercules* telefeatures, they asked Gruendemann, then twenty-nine, to scout locations that would let them deliver quality on a limited budget. Among the places Tapert asked Gruendemann to explore was New Zealand; he returned with several hundred photos and boundless enthusiasm over the possibilities.

Gruendemann's recommendation to film in New Zealand, though now universally hailed, at first dismayed some studio executives who feared the country was too remote (twelve hours by plane) and its film industry too young to sustain a Hollywood production. But Gruendemann believed that modern electronics and Kiwi resourcefulness could make this work.

For as long as *Hercules* and *Xena* have been filming, Gruendemann has felt he had something to prove:

> When I went to a foreign land [to shoot Hercules], many people said, "This is crazy, these are uncharted waters. Will you be able to build big sets? What will happen when a camera breaks down,

*or when you need costumes? Will you be able to pull this off?"
Then, when Xena came along, people said, "There's no way you
can do two shows at once, the quality of the shows will suffer." I
figured I could probably do it, but it was anybody's guess whether
it would bury me. Normally, for a show like this, I would have
one coordinator and one assistant; on [these shows] I have six coordinators. I have the largest office and production staff ever seen
or heard of; part of this is the international freighting of people
and equipment all the time. But the unquantifiable benefits of
filming in this beautiful land far outweigh the costs. And New
Zealanders are a wonderful bunch of people, hardworking, with
a great sense of teamwork, camaraderie, and humor.*

Soon after Tapert and Raimi seconded the New Zealand option, Gruendemann turned to a rising Kiwi producer named Chloe Smith to
help Renaissance set up overseas. As a child in the sixties Smith had
dreamed of becoming an artist, but her parents feared for her future
and insisted she go to college. She dutifully earned a degree in micro-
biology but still longed for a career in the arts. Marking time as a
"postie," as New Zealand mail carriers are called, she helped organize
a succession of literary and artistic ventures. A staunch feminist, Smith
started a collective, a women's bookshop called Daybreak. Then came
jobs with stage, modern dance, and film companies, including a stint
in 1994 as production manager on *The Piano.* The movie garnered acclaim just as Gruendemann began searching for someone to forge a
production team in Auckland. Smith recalled her invitation to spear-
head this venture:

*I'm sitting at home one night when the phone rings, and a very
gregarious—and I have to say very loud because prior to that
time I just found all Americans very loud—fellow said, "Hi! My
name's Eric Gruendemann and I'm going to be in Auckland
next week, and I'm doing some telefeatures about Hercules,
would you be available and interested?"*

Gruendemann, Smith, and another veteran of *The Piano,* production
accountant Keith Mackenzie, set up Pacific Renaissance as a New
Zealand branch of Renaissance Pictures. While Gruendemann coordi-

nated between Los Angeles and Auckland, Smith assembled the local production team and negotiated salaries and terms for everyone from the assistant directors to the horse wranglers. With the advent of *Hercules* and then *Xena* as series, her role continued to grow. "I issue three hundred contracts for the two shows, so in terms of the generation of paper, it's a nightmare," Smith said. "Forests have been destroyed." Still, she is not one to run an army from the rear, instead spending much of her time on set with the production team. According to Eric Gruendemann, "Chloe could probably give the first and last names and birth dates of every crew member."

Smith described her ongoing role as "providing resources to expedite the creative process," and providing "reality checks" to the producers and directors on what can be filmed and at what cost. She explained, "As the scripts come through, from the beat sheet right through to the finished form, I respond back to Liz Friedman and the writers, and say, 'There's too much exterior [filming], not enough interior. Remember, it's winter here, we need to redress this balance,' or 'You've got a million cast people here, we need to condense that,' or 'You know, we can't blow up the entire city, because we won't have a set to come back to.' "

Smith also eases the inevitable cultural adjustments by Americans joining the production, especially first-time directors. Even apparently simple matters like how long a workday lasts—and who gets to decide—differ markedly between Auckland and Hollywood. Smith said:

We [Kiwis] will agree to work twelve-hour days, but we would not agree to work fifteen-hour days. But the insistent suggestion of American companies who come here is that overtime is something that's just done back in America, whereas here it's very much by consensus. You have to ask the crew, ideally at lunchtime, whether they would mind doing anything from fifteen minutes up to one hour, and they have the complete right to say no.

Sometimes you can read the culture shock in the faces of directors who come down for their first show. It has never led to a direct conflict with the crew, but [the tension] is definitely there. And also, when you come to New Zealand and walk around, you might go, "Oh, it doesn't look all that different from what I'm used to, no, it doesn't. Why, they even watch American television sitcoms here." But there are always certain things! For example, Eric and I will watch something, and he'll roar with laughter, and it will go—swish—right over my head. Or vice versa.

Smith marvels that overall the bridging of cultures at Renaissance has gone so smoothly and generated such warmth. "I've never felt anyone acting like 'You're the Kiwi and we're the Americans,' " she said. "Quite the contrary, I've felt welcomed as part of a team. And there is quite a sense of pride, because we've done a job well together."

Smith is a rarity in the largely male world of filmmaking, not only as a woman with authority but as an unapologetic feminist who has named women to key roles in handling day-to-day logistics and finances:

The production team runs with a hierarchy of women. Women just seem to end up in these jobs because we're good at organizing, and we work in a very cooperative way. The coordinators like Jane [Lindsay], Moira [Grant], and Natalie [Celie] all work autonomously, and their authority is respected.

Smith smiles at the suggestion that her politics color her approach to the shows:

I am very aware that when we do the script readthroughs, I may question something, and the reac-

"No Hollywood producers were harmed during the production of this motion picture."
—Disclaimer from "The Xena Scrolls"

tion is a bit "Oh, there she goes again, the radical-feminist-separatist!" But interestingly, it's not just me. Sometimes I'll point out something in a script that seems sexist, and I'll look down the table, and all the young women who are sitting there will be nodding!

Happily, Smith finds, the men on the production team are responsive to her suggestions. "The teasing is always done with humor, and when I speak up, those are always things which tend to be acknowledged and changed. You know, the ancient stories are wonderful, but at the same time modern life has changed a lot. Quite honestly, if these shows had turned out to be simply shots of female anatomy like on *Baywatch,* I wouldn't be here."

Smith especially savors the portrayal of Xena as a model of strong womanhood:

I'm not saying I prefer her over Hercules—but as a woman she's completely that conundrum of shades of gray. She's very much the way life is. The logical versus the emotional a lot of the time: but she's strong. And if she mucks up, she'll admit that she's mucked up. But basically she's comfortable within herself, and therefore she's a strong woman within herself. And I also like the fact that she has a very solid friendship with Gabrielle, who began as the young nuisance. . . . And it's as if Xena's come down, Gabrielle's come up, and they've balanced off. Which is really what a true relationship is all about.

Smith, like Gruendemann, spends much of her time guiding the work of varied artists and technicians. The New Zealand production team gathers at least a week before an episode is filmed, realizing that a gram of prevention is worth a kilo of cure. Staff members go over scripts, anticipate problems, and map strategies in meetings high on energy and low on formality, reflecting the tone set by Gruendemann and Smith at every level of Pacific Renaissance.

On Wednesday, June 19, 1996, Gruendemann, Smith, production designer Rob Gillies, costume designer Ngila Dickson, director Charlie Haskell, and a half dozen technical experts assemble in the unlikely headquarters of Pacific Renaissance: a fraying building near

Auckland's harbor that betrays its origins as a warehouse. Their "conference room" is a long, semi-enclosed hall bedecked with four-foot posters of Hercules, Xena, and films by Universal or Renaissance. The high, unfinished ceiling, insulated with aluminum sheeting, lit by occasional fluorescents, and supported by a forbidding tangle of girders, underscores that Hollywood is an ocean away.

Each participant receives a pink copy of the script for an upcoming second-season episode, "The Xena Scrolls." Set during World War II, the story casts Lucy Lawless and Renee O'Connor as descendants of Xena and Gabrielle who meet on an archaeological dig in Macedonia. There they uncover ancient records of a great warrior princess who had long been lost to both history and myth.

Gruendemann presides at the meeting, sporting a baseball cap and a casual green shirt with white "Hercules" letters. At this early stage, questions about Xena's feelings or Gabrielle's motivations scarcely arise, even from the director; nor are any actors present. Discussion instead centers on how to expedite filming within budget and to highlight key plot points.

Recognizing that viewers will more readily accept the fantasy elements in *Xena* if the everyday details look right, Eric questions script references to certain "period" props. "Did they have Zippo lighters in the forties?" he asks Ken Drury, a fiftyish, balding, rugged-looking adviser on "mechanical effects," who assures him, "Yes, during the war." For a scene in which Renee O'Connor fires an automatic

The car in which Lucy Lawless arrives in the opening scene of "The Xena Scrolls" is an authentic 1940s black Lincoln.

weapon at sundry villains, Drury keeps the filmmakers honest about the limits of different weapons. Like Q, the no-nonsense armorer in nearly twenty James Bond films, Drury holds out the heavy barrel of a Gatling gun and briefs the crew: "Before we get too much further, the Gatling does not rotate, though it can be made to rotate if tripod-mounted. The other option is the Thompson [rifle]." He pulls one out of its case and briefly aims it, then exhibits the Gatling once again. Gruendemann asks, "Can we have fake shells feed into it? "Yes," Drury obliges, "how many rounds do you need?" "Oh, a couple hundred." Then Gruendemann gets ambitious: "If we could feed shells while the thing is smoking, that would be more effective." Drury says, "I can make it smoke as much as you want, or keep it clear." Gruendemann finally opts for a no-smoking policy on the gunplay, reasoning, "We can sell it all [just] with sound."

Renee O'Connor's safety generates a round of concerns, for although she does much of her own stunt work, the crew on *Xena* understandably has scant experience staging gunfights. Someone asks whether O'Connor's gun will have kick, because the retort of an actual weapon with such heft and firepower might knock down a slender woman. "No," Drury promises, "it won't have any kick." Haskell also wants to take special precautions for O'Connor. The staff agrees to let a stuntperson film much of this scene with the second-unit crew, and to rig scores of tiny explosive charges to simulate bullet hits. Haskell sums up the G-rated destruction: "This is one of those scenes where thousands of bullets are flying around, but no one gets killed." Not all the weapons, moreover, will be as sophisticated as Drury's models. Gruendemann asks Drury's son and assistant, Jason, to pick up various guns "at a toy shop, and holsters, too, if you can."

While staff members clamor to protect O'Connor from accidents, it is left to Ngila Dickson alone to guard the costumes from being purposefully demolished. A scene in which a villain and his henchmen repeatedly but futilely shoot at Ares prompts ideas for destroying everything around the god of war, including his vest:

Gruendemann: So Ares is taking the hits and nothing's happening. Would you like to put bullet hits in the wall behind him?
Drury: Yes, and we can pop holes in Ares' costume, too.
Dickson (wincing): Why don't we save the leather?!
Gruendemann: I don't think we need to destroy the costume.
Drury: Can we add a piece to the front, and leave the original costume whole underneath?

To Dickson's evident relief, Gruendemann plucks the costume from the line of fire, saying, "Let's just go with holes in the wall behind Ares. As Smythe fires the last one, Ares catches it and smiles."

Both Dickson's wardrobe crew and the makeup artists will tailor each character's appearance based on guidelines set in the production meeting. Gruendemann prescribes the comical look of a fraudulent French officer, right down to his fake mustache ("it can be a thin line but not twisted"). And the imposter's outfit, he tells Dickson, "should be like a French military uniform in World War II, but just a little bit off." As for Ares, the god of war, who arises from a tomb after several millennia, Smith makes clear that divinity has its privileges, saying, "I think he should be immaculate. After all, he's a god." Gruendemann amplifies her point for an appreciative audience. "Maybe a little dust on his costume," he says, adding, "but beyond that he should look like a stud muffin."

Rock slides and flying boulders are among the thrills for this episode that must be planned artistically as well as logistically. Gruendemann asks production designer Rob Gillies to design an avalanche (Styrofoam is the preferred geological substance) that "almost looks as though [people are] being pushed through a car wash of rocks." Haskell comments that a boulder Ares uses to menace Renee O'Connor's character would look more menacing with spikes. Gruendemann adds, "And it would be better if Ares is manipulating the boulder himself, rather than [settling for] a *Batman* [TV show] routine where the spikes swing on a pendulum" ever closer to Renee's head. After ten minutes of verbal grappling with the

> "No Sleazy Warlords who deem it necessary to drink magic elixirs that turn them into scaly Centaurs were harmed during the production of this motion picture."
> —Disclaimer from "Orphan of War"

boulder, Gruendemann concludes, "We can rig a couple of different ones that come down at various points, swinging in and out of [the camera] frame at various times."

While scanning Act IV of the script, the staff runs up against a wall: a magical wall that Lawless' character opens to reveal a secret passage. The original layout calls for rare jewels (or colored glass, whichever happens to be handier) to adorn the wall; when these are pushed in sequence, a door will slide open. Rob Gillies suggests another possibility would be to turn certain jewels toward different points of the compass. Then he asks an innocent, common-sense question that no one can answer: "Why haven't grave robbers taken these jewels?" Smith adds a logistical cavil: "Do we *need* the jewels?" Gruendemann shrugs. "No," he allows, "it can be hieroglyphics." The staff leans toward using mysterious metal symbols in lieu of jewels. "I can live with that," Gruendemann says. "Just so that it looks complex."

Rob Gillies speaks softly and only on occasion, but he expertly translates everyone else's comments by means of a charcoal pencil and a large drawing pad. Gillies' uncanny sketches include a Gatling gun poised on its tripod, a sarcophagus for Ares, a panel with mysterious raised symbols, and other objects that have figured in the two-hour discussion. Then, in the final moments of the meeting, Gillies is called on to make an unprecedented contribution to the set design: his office.

The final scene of "The Xena Scrolls" features Rob Tapert playing himself in a send-up of how the series *Xena* is launched, ostensibly based on the "ancient records" of her exploits. Gruendemann hopes to use Gillies' office as a stand-in for Tapert's. Although Gillies works amid a clutter of pastel sketches, architectural designs, and scale models of sets, props, monsters, and other fantastic creatures, Gruendemann asks with a smile, "Can we manage to make your office look extremely swank?" Before Gillies can reply, the prospect of his finally meeting a challenge beyond even his ingenuity prompts a round of affectionate laughter.

READ-THROUGHS

A quip by the comedian Jack Benny once sent several actors into astonished, uncontrollable laughter on an episode of his TV variety show, but drew barely a chuckle from the audience. "I don't understand it," Benny mused aloud, then added a line that brought down the house: "That ad-lib went over *much* better at rehearsal." Benny's wry admission of planned "spontaneity" sums up the boundaries of innovation by TV actors: they may say unscripted lines, but almost always by prior arrangement with the director and other cast members. The main occasion for actors to experiment with scenes, question story lines and dialogue, and suggest changes is the read-through, the first and most free-spirited stage of rehearsals.

Stories that bend a show's conventions leave extra room for actors to innovate, as evident in the read-through for "The Xena Scrolls." In addition to Lucy Lawless and Renee O'Connor, the session features producers Eric Gruendemann and Chloe Smith, director Charlie Haskell, and guest actors Kevin Smith, Mark Ferguson, and Ted Raimi, Sam's younger brother. On a rainy Tuesday evening they trickle into the Corymander Room of Auckland's Carlton Hotel, scripts in hand, to share hot coffee and a cold reading of their scenes.

Gruendemann presides, keeping a firm hand on a loose rein. He sets a light mood that encourages ir-

Cast and crew are such enthusiastic followers of *Murder One* that Eric Gruendemann has been known to start a read-through by announcing, "*Murder One* is on this evening, so there will be no questions and no script changes!"

reverence and parody (Gruendemann himself is a frequent target, but then no one wholly escapes). In this relaxed atmosphere, fresh ideas flow vigorously amid the laughter.

O'Connor is among the first to arrive, and her fellow cast members marvel at the sight of this clean-cut actress chomping contentedly on a small cigar. She explains that the cigar actually belongs to Janice Covington, her character in this episode, who is written as a tough, take-charge archaeologist in the mold of Indiana Jones. Gruendemann likes the idea, but not the thin, reedy joint, which "may remind viewers of something else." He and O'Connor begin a verbal quest for the right cigar, Gruendemann favoring a bigger, fatter variety, "so useful when characters are being shot at, it's always the first thing hit."

Lawless reads first, and she must convince audiences of the first major surprise in the script: her character Melinda Dillon is no Xena, but a sheltered scholar of ancient texts whose bumblings contrast with O'Connor's indomitable heroics. Lawless relishes the role reversal, and springs some surprises of her own. After shifting from her elegant Kiwi-flavored English to Xena's standard California brand, she glides suddenly into a plantation drawl. Gruendemann appears startled but game. "You going Southern?" he asks. But he and others break into smiles as Lawless tightens her hold on her accent and the character. She repeats a few words that stray north of the Mason-Dixon line, and, like a musician tuning her instrument, achieves perfect pitch: "Your *father*? *Fah-thuh*? No, that's not right." Then, brightening, she exclaims, "Your *daddy!*" Everyone at the table beams approval. Soon Lawless' delivery is vintage Southern belle, to which she adds a few broad visual touches, fluttering her hands expansively, simpering, and gazing with wide-eyed naiveté. When a few scenes later Gruendemann coaches O'Connor, saying, "I think you're annoyed with Melinda at this point. You're steamed up," Lawless declares in a flirtatious Southern manner that Blanche Du Bois would have envied, "And ahm just cool as a cucumber!" Her Melinda Dillon is now two millennia and a universe removed from the hard-edged Xena.

Lawless' flamboyance, matching the script's playful depiction of the lead characters as mirror images of their usual selves, also suits the male guest actors. As the predatory fortune hunter Smythe, Mark Ferguson speaks with diabolical glee and a cultured British manner bordering on effete. Ferguson nonetheless appears almost subdued beside Ted Raimi's comical Parisian officer, whose exaggerated recital of French sounds ("eeeeee," "euuuuuuhhh," "annnnhhh") would befuddle Inspector Clouseau.

Kevin Smith reprises his role as Ares, who awakens from long repose in a sarcophagus, kills off Smythe (a disposable lesser villain), and triggers Xena's own revival in Melinda's body, giving Lucy and Kevin new territory to explore their characters' intimate rivalry. As scripted, their scenes crackle with Ares' pride and Xena's resolve, but lack any hint of their latent erotic bond. Gruendemann interjects after hearing a few lines, "We'll put it to you, Lucy and Kevin, should there be some sexual tension between the two of you?"

Ferguson, spotting the need for an infusion of masculine charm in this scene, quips, "Better bring back Smythe." Then, resigned to his character's demise, he suggests having Xena and Ares kiss, so she can catch him off guard. Lucy is taken with the idea, saying, "Let's have Xena give Ares some of what he's been wanting all these years," then kick him—"and just to show Xena's not a total man-hater, Ares can appear almost to enjoy it" as part of their ongoing cat-and-mouse game. Everyone warms to this, till Smith recalls that the two characters will kiss for the first time in a later episode. Lawless refines Xena's gambit: let them *nearly* kiss and Xena can still kick Ares. Smith obligingly contorts in pain and ecstasy, prompting general approval and assorted bawdy remarks.

Gruendemann proposes to raise the stakes in their fight by making clear that if Ares triumphs, he will be free to aid Adolf Hitler, his disciple in spreading war and destruction. Lucy adds, "I'll bet that Thrace"—once Xena's domain, later part of Macedonia—"is not all that far from Poland," the first victim of Hitler's onslaught in World War II. It's an insight rich with historical resonances but no one picks up on it, perhaps sensing that viewers will already be primed for the episode's final fight: Ares, god of war, against Xena, undefeated mortal challenger—surely a contest that needs no further embellishment.

Chloe Smith observes that viewers by this point desperately want to see Xena and Ares "beat the stuffings out of each other," and

Haskell has clearly given this matter close attention. He details, blow by blow, just how their battle will unfold. Ares, being immortal, gets the better of things until, at a key juncture, Covington/O'Connor cracks her whip around Ares' arm and yanks him back, giving Xena the opening she needs. Another supporting actress might well have basked in her character's rare center-stage heroics, but O'Connor merely shakes her head. "Ares is a *god*," she demurs. "How can Janice possibly overcome a god?" At O'Connor's urging, Haskell tones down Janice's actions to "human" proportions; the whip may still lash out, but it has been demoted from a savage weapon to a timely distraction.

This still leaves the director with a tough question: if Ares is a god, how *can* Xena win? Haskell narrates a sequence of sword thrusts and chakram tosses, and stirs everyone's favorite ideas into this recipe for defeating the god of war. In all, it takes seven mortals nearly ten minutes of brainstorming, but they ensure that by episode's end Ares will be entombed once more in the sarcophagus.

The last scene features Raimi as a descendant of his earlier character, pitching to a Hollywood executive an idea for a series based on the newly discovered historical treasure, "The Xena Scrolls." It is a short, sharp parody that will later show Rob Tapert himself looking over the translated scrolls and saying, "Not bad. Tell me more about this . . . Xena." The read-through concludes—officially, but the actors continue to build mischievously on Raimi's pitch for a show called *Xena*. One adds, "Yeah, we'll get to film on beautiful beaches!" An-

other remarks, "And ignore timelines!" A third offers, "And keep using the same actors over and over!" Gruendemann laughs and says, "Well, we don't want to give away our *whole* production scheme." Everyone gradually files out, in time to catch the end of *Murder One*.

THE VIEW FROM BEHIND THE CAMERA

The character Xena has no equal in speed and energy, except perhaps for the camera crews that track her. A key architect of their edgy, experimental style is Donny Duncan, the show's director of photography. Together with Rob Tapert, Duncan crafted the principles of dynamic camera movement, offbeat film speeds, and rapid-fire editing that have given *Xena* a look unique in American television.

Duncan, a native New Zealander, discovered both America and filmmaking in 1975 as a seventeen-year-old exchange student in a Los Angeles high school. Until then he had pursued academic interests but a class on "media studies" opened up horizons in advertising, radio, television, and film. When Duncan completed a ten-minute movie for a class assignment, his career came suddenly into focus: "Quite simply I just suddenly knew what I wanted to do with my life."

Beginning as a sound recordist for nine months on a news team covering New Zealand's parliament, Duncan received a week's trial run as a cameraman assigned to cover the Prime Minister's press conference. Duncan recalled feeling "a little nervous" but "it all worked out fine." His first niche in cinematography secure, he spent the next fifteen years working on TV shows, motion pictures, and commercials, interspersed with independent projects making documentary films.

In 1984 Duncan went to Sarajevo, Yugoslavia, to shoot a behind-the-scenes look at the Olympics. The host city was then a bustling cultural haven, and Duncan's crew spent hours befriending and filming people in cafés and parks. The athletic competitions themselves receded in importance and were often covered abstractly, as in a montage that intercut all the ice skating dances over many days. The resulting prize-

"Chariots of War"
Gabrielle: "I'm looking for my best friend. Maybe you've seen her? Six feet tall, dark hair, lots of leather, fights like the Harpies in a bad mood? Her name's Xena."

winning film, *Zimska Olympiada* (Croatian for "Winter Olympics"), later became a document of historic note, as Yugoslavia disintegrated into warring ethnic factions and the beauty of Sarajevo faded into poignant memory.

Less acclaimed but no less warmly recalled by Duncan was a low-budget horror flick, *Death Warmed Up* (1984), that he shot as a homage to an American film trio: Sam Raimi, Rob Tapert, and Bruce Campbell. "Their movie *The Evil Dead*," Duncan said, "was our benchmark. We were going, 'Wow, the stylistic things these guys have done are so cool!' " Duncan marveled, too, at the cinematic karma that later brought all these artists together: "Jim Bartle, who was the director of photography on *Death Warmed Up*, later shot the original *Hercules* telefeatures. And then, ten years after making that film, here I was in Rob Tapert's office talking about shooting *Xena*. So things go around."

In 1994 Duncan began filming a TV fantasy series, *Mysterious Island*, but the contract for this co-production required bringing a Canadian director of photography to New Zealand, so Duncan "got the golden handshake after thirteen episodes." Rob Tapert was then looking for a cinematographer with the daring to take *Xena* in fresh directions and heard of Duncan through John Mahaffie, the director of photography on *Hercules: The Legendary Journeys*. At a meeting in June 1995, Duncan recalled, Tapert shared his ideas for making *Xena* different from *Hercules* and everything else on TV:

> "Excessive belching can cause brain damage and social ostracism. Kids, please don't give in to peer pressure. Play it safe."
>
> —Disclaimer from "The Greater Good"

Rob wanted Xena *to be a faster show than* Hercules. *And in what became a bit of a mantra, Rob said, "Think of it this way, Donny: if* Hercules *does fifteen great shots a day, on* Xena *we want to do thirty good shots a day." So, there would be more material for* Xena *but more compromises. Rob would say, "If we can possibly help it, we don't want to ever return to the same angle if we can change it, or do something new."*

According to Duncan, Tapert's love of Hong Kong martial arts movies influenced their approach to shooting *Xena*:

Those films had pace and movement, with a lot of aerial work, gymnastics and flips and spins, that lends itself to lots of shots and coverage. And to make those gags work, it has to be pretty [well edited]. You can't show everything in one big [take]. So that was one of the elements that we went through: to have more of a "guerrilla attack," with lots of different shots cut together. I'd like to think of Xena as being a little grungier and dirtier [than Hercules] cinematically.

Duncan drafted a style memo incorporating Tapert's ideas and his own technical innovations. The memo emphasized that *Xena* should display "more kinetic energy than *Hercules*." Duncan's prime directive was to "always move the camera as much as possible, tracking, countertracking," and to "remind directors not to shoot like TV but in a mini-feature fashion."

Duncan recalled meeting a director during the first season, T. J. Scott, who took to new levels the idea of making the camera an equal partner in the action. "Donny, I've got this theory," Scott said. "The audience is a baby and the camera is a rattle. And we've got to keep the baby's interest, so let's get out there and *shake that rattle!*" Duncan often relayed Scott's image to other directors because it so well expressed his own philosophy that *Xena* should in every way keep on

the move: "So whenever we're lining up a shot and it's kind of bor-
ing and we think it needs a bit more visual interest, we say—it's kind
of a catchphrase—'Hey, let's shake that rattle! Get the baby's interest!' " Still, Duncan knows to reach for the rattle selectively, even sub-
tly. "Sometimes," he said, "it may be just a shot that slowly closes in
on the actor. If it's a real tense, dramatic moment it's most effective."

Xena's budget-related use of 16mm film during the first two seasons, though grainier than the 35mm film on Hercules, actually aided
Duncan's high-energy approach:

> People naturally assume that you would jump at the chance to
> shoot on 35mm and say, "Yeah, wow!" But by shooting on 16mm,
> you can use cameras a lot lighter and smaller and easier to move
> around. And that's helped give Xena its look, especially in the ac-
> tion sequences. Also, my camera operator does a lot of work with
> the Steadicam. That's the special handheld camera we use over
> rough terrain and up stairways and in other places where it
> would be too difficult to lay tracks down for a camera dolly. Well,
> because of the lightness of the cameras, he can use Steadicams. In
> fact, we shot an entire episode ["Is There a Doctor in the
> House?"] with the Steadicam.

Varying film speeds further distinguish Xena's visual style. Whereas
24 frames per second is the standard speed for TV cameras, Duncan's
style notes call for shooting action scenes "at 22 frames per second on
at least one camera." When played back at 24 frames per second, this
yields a speeded-up picture reminiscent of fights in Hong Kong martial arts movies. Duncan encourages experimenting with even slower
speeds (20 frames per second) on tight shots, or close-ups, though
not on wider shots that would risk looking slapstick, "too [much like]
Keystone Kops." An approach favored by Duncan is "speed ramping," or adjusting the film speed while the camera is shooting, so that
a scene beginning at 24 frames per second might shift down to 22
frames per second; the result is a gradually speeded-up fight scene.
The reverse technique, "ramping up," lets Duncan "swing into slow
motion for action sequences."

Duncan is a perfectionist in his use of lighting. His style notes call
for lighting that not only makes Xena and Gabrielle "look good all the

time" but also helps define their characters: "Xena should maintain darker skin tones versus Gabrielle, who should be lighter to emphasize innocence [and] purity." Duncan credits the show's visual success partly to his "refusal to compromise on making Lucy look fantastic." Fortunately, he said, Lucy provides most of the technical miracles simply by showing up on set:

> *Now, I'm incredibly lucky. Lucy's got amazing natural beauty, fantastic big blue eyes, and bright skin, so it's not particularly hard work at all. But you've just got to be religious in your pursuit of that look. . . . What I found works really well with Lucy is a strong, soft key light [the predominant light source] that's coming slightly from one side, so that one side of her face falls into shadow and has good, strong contrast.*

> "The reputation of the Amazon Nation was not harmed despite Velasca's overly radical adherence to an otherwise valid belief system."
> —Disclaimer from "A Necessary Evil"

Duncan prefers lighting indoor scenes "because you have control, you can put the lights where you want them." For the show's many outdoor shots, "you've got to work a lot harder." He describes as maddening but routine the problems posed by New Zealand's unpredictable weather:

> *In Auckland at certain times of year, around the equinox, unlike any other part of the world, the clouds move across the sun so fast, there are constant whistling winds. The weather is changing, changing, changing, so it is rare to get even thirty seconds of stable light for a shot. The thing that drives me nuts and that I'm least proud of is where we've shot half of a sequence in brilliant blue skies and full sun. The second-unit film crew comes in, sometimes a week or even up to two weeks later, and they might be shooting reverse angles of fights or inserts of this and that. Or occasionally they may have to do wide shots, using doubles. Now, if they are stuck with a completely flat, cloudy, rainy day and the location's turned to mud, those are the things that show the most.*

Unconventional lighting techniques help Duncan give *Xena* a dynamic look. "Where[ever] it can be justified," his style memo urges, "light sources can be interrupted, fanned, flickered, [and] swept across." The memo also tells the art department that, in addition to smoke effects for atmosphere, "we need chopped-up feather down to drift through shafts of light and give an added atmospheric dynamic" to both indoor and outdoor scenes.

Duncan tempers his penchant for innovation by keeping in mind the key to good cinematography: "It's got to work as a package. Otherwise people may say, 'Oh, wow, the cinematography was great,' and you're thinking, 'Well, what's wrong with the rest of it?' " The most satisfying episodes for Duncan involve unconventional camera work "but still manage to tell a good story," such as the first-season tale of the Trojan War, "Beware Greeks Bearing Gifts":

> *We broke lots of rules in that one: I remember doing long track-ing shots behind big columns where half the time you couldn't even see the actors who were saying important dialogue. We'd do a rehearsal and I'd say to [director] T. J. [Scott], "Hey, you're losing these guys. We can't even see them!" And he said, "Great, love it! We don't need to see them, we can hear what they're say-ing." And he was absolutely right. You see the show and because it moves, it's got the pace, the imaging, the flow. And you don't need to see their lips moving a hundred percent of the time, you know? People can disappear behind things and come back. It's like the movie* Citizen Kane: *I loved where major characters in dialogue scenes are shot in complete silhouette. But you know who's talking; you know their shapes.*

Duncan sees his role as that of a problem solver to serve the director's vision. In a first-season episode called "Callisto," T. J. Scott wanted to film Xena and Gabrielle through the flames of a camp-fire as Xena confesses that her army once burned a village, killing women and children. Scott wanted, as well, to shoot the scene in a single take rather than have an editor later stitch together many different shots of the two characters. Duncan arranged for the camera operator to shift focus throughout the scene, panning between Xena and Gabrielle as each begins to speak. But as fast as Duncan found ways to expedite the filming, problems leapt up along with the flames of the campfire:

> "No oversized Polynesian-style Bamboo Horses were harmed during the production of this motion picture. However, many wicker lawn chairs gave their lives."
> —Disclaimer from "Beware Greeks Bearing Gifts"

We laid a dolly track sideways so that the camera could move smoothly across on a fairly long lens sitting back a ways to [take in the two leads and] the background. And the camera operator memorized the lines and did a fabulous job just going slow and panning between Lucy and Renee at just the right times. But in order to keep the fire in our shot, we had to build a long, wide fire from gas jets and then bury the jets from camera view with fake logs. Now, the gas jets were making such a hiss that it was driving the sound people crazy. In those situations we often decide to ignore sound problems and simply get the actors to "post-sync" the scene in the studio later on. And that happens to a surprising extent. However, in this case, because it was such a tense, emotional scene, Lucy pleaded with us. She said, "Guys, please, please, don't make me post-sync this scene. . . . I really want this one to be real, to be live."

Duncan now had to fulfill two contradictory goals: Scott wanted a fire large enough to be always in frame, and Lucy Lawless and the sound crew wanted a fire small enough not to muffle the dialogue. At first Duncan tried turning down the jets, which pleased the soundmen but left Scott without the desired visuals. After further failed adjustments, Duncan hit upon an inspired artifice to make everything appear natural:

I thought, O.K., I'll tell you what: We'll lay a track for a small flat-top dolly and put the fire on the dolly. We'll give a grip [an equipment mover] a video monitor so he can track the fire, move it at the same rate as the camera, and always keep it lined up with the actors. Now we could use a much smaller fire because the dolly would always keep it in frame. And with just a tiny fire, our sound problem disappeared. So that's exactly what we did and it worked perfectly. And the audience—well, you will never know unless you're really looking for it.

Lucy Lawless confers with Michael Hurst, who directed "A Day in the Life"

Duncan's search for fresh approaches has benefited from having a crew that shares his eagerness to experiment. "When production was starting up," Duncan said, "[line producer] Chloe Smith encouraged me to pick a keen, young, energetic, fresh team, and to promote promising people to high positions. She's got a theory that they will give you two hundred percent more than someone who is tired and bored and hackneyed in the job."

Duncan followed Smith's advice in luring talents like Cameron McLean, who had earlier worked on films as a "focus puller," or first assistant cameraman. When Duncan offered McLean a dramatic promotion to camera operator, "he just about fell through the floor." Asked if he'd ever used a Steadicam, McLean said, "No, but I'm real keen to." Duncan told him, "Good, you've got six weeks to learn," and put him through intensive training. McLean operated the Steadicam under supervision for *Xena's* first two episodes. By episode three, Duncan said, McLean was "really into it boots and all, and doing a great job."

Duncan also broke gender barriers by recruiting talented women for key posts, with the strong encouragement of Chloe Smith. Duncan noted, for example, that women head the six-person lighting teams on both the main camera unit and the second unit, a rarity among film crews anywhere in the world. "We have, in general, an egalitarian crew," he said, "and we get on really well, like a big family. It's sort of like being part of a traveling circus, in a way."

Duncan described the filming of *Xena* as a collaborative effort featuring "fabulous sets and props and dressings, stunning costumes," and other elements that "make my job incredibly easy in many ways." The blending of artistic visions is evident on the set of a second-season episode called "Destiny," directed by the executive producer, Rob Tapert. Duncan is shooting a scene in which Gabrielle tends a wounded Xena at a healer's snowbound cabin. Brown, silver, blue, and black bottles and flasks, a mortar and pestle, and pelts hanging from the ceiling attest to the healer's vocation and rugged independence, while his austere blue robe enhances an aura of stoic dignity. Scores of candles break the darkness while adding to the mystery of the healer's abode. Just beyond camera range the sound recordist extends a boom mike over Renee O'Connor and Nathaniel Lees, who is about to reveal that Xena is dying.

In stark contrast to the lightning pace of the finished episode, the filming of Lees and O'Connor moves with infinite pains and patience. While the actors chat, undergo finishing touches on their makeup, or fine-tune rehearsals, crew members lay tracks for the camera dolly. This mobile platform on wheels supports the camera and its operator, Cameron McLean, and allows a "dolly pusher" to move it along the rails. McLean can then pan in for close-ups, pull back to reveal more of a scene, and track actors as they move across the set. The planning and labor that go into these setups, though unheralded and of course unobserved by audiences, actually consumes more time than the filming itself.

In setting up his shots, Duncan resists a common timesaving practice on many TV productions, using cameras from two different angles at once. "The ideal source of light for one camera angle may only compound your problems in trying to light a scene from the other angle," he said. It would also "drive the soundmen completely crazy" because the increased camera coverage makes it difficult to place microphones close to the actors without being seen. Instead Duncan often employs two cameras facing the same way, "one nestled tightly beside the other," to get both a close-up and a mid-range shot of the same subject. This allows him to maintain exacting standards for lighting a scene while providing the director with a wider choice of shots in editing.

While the five-person crew readies the main camera, Duncan considers new possibilities to lead into Gabrielle's exchange with the healer. Standing on the edge of a bed, Duncan frames an overhead shot of Lucy Lawless with a pair of binoculars, to underscore Xena's weakening condition. But he discards the idea when Tapert decides to move directly to Gabrielle's grieving reactions. "We know what's happening [to Xena]," Tapert says. "This is about Renee."

"Her pulse is fading," Lees says of Xena while the cameras roll, prompting O'Connor to scream, "No!" Tapert calls, "Cut!" and says, "That was good. Can we try one more, at twice that speed?" The actors shoot four more takes, each apparently flawless. But as O'Connor explained, even when a director likes the actors' performances, scenes must often be redone for technical reasons: "It might be a matter of adjusting the camera angle, or perhaps the timing of a camera's [movement in] tracking an actor is not quite right, or there is a sound problem." After the fifth take, Tapert nods, saying, "That was good for me."

A key ingredient in filming "Destiny," as with so many episodes of *Xena,* is the natural beauty of New Zealand. "The locations really sell the show," Duncan said. His second-unit crew visits South Island for shots of snowcapped mountains and other "scenics." But "we rarely travel twenty-five kilometers [some fifteen miles] outside of downtown Auckland. Everything we see we can find pretty close by here." For "Destiny," the cast and crew spend several days on Bethells Beach filming Xena's fateful encounter with Julius Caesar.

Bethells is a cinematographer's dream, with its turbulent waves, hazy azure sky, and green hills rising in the distance above the rocks. "Destiny" makes rich use of this backdrop, enhanced by a motorized barge built by the prop department, for scenes featuring Xena as a pirate raider who falls in love with Caesar. And it is on this windswept

shore that Xena will be betrayed and crucified on Caesar's orders.

The technical challenges of filming the
crucifixion are formidable. Prop men set up
five giant crosses on the sands while crew
members under Duncan's supervision lay
down tracks for a camera to move past each
cross. Duncan also employs a crane, a large
camera trolley with a long projected arm
that can lift the camera twenty feet off the
ground, to film Xena straight-on. Throughout these setups Duncan confers with Tapert on shot selection as the two inspect
twin monitors, one containing a close-up,
the other a wider picture.

The day's lengthening shadows make
accurate lighting crucial even in this out-
door setting. Lucy's tall, tanned stand-in, Saskia Reijners, nimbly
clambers up on a cross so that the crew can record light readings and
make adjustments. Then Lawless herself climbs up a ladder, deftly re-
verses position, and eases into her rigging on the cross. She proves as
stoic as Xena, suspended by a harness and wearing the thinnest of
"rags" during a chill and blustery afternoon. Between
takes Lawless ably negotiates several tricky dismounts
on the ladder, throws on a purple robe, and jumps to
keep warm.

During a camera setup, the New Zealand actor
Karl Urban, wearing silver-tinted metal-and-leather
armor, reflects on his good fortune to portray such a
complex, calculating villain as Julius Caesar. He has
been rehearsing a scene in which Caesar looks at his
former lover, Xena, on the cross, and coolly orders a
guard, "Break her legs." "I like that line," he remarks.

The handsome, witty actor who plays the guard,
Daniel Ryan, takes a few practice swings with a giant
mallet. On Caesar's command he will approach the
cross and "break" Xena's legs with a blow filmed
until just before "contact." The camera will then

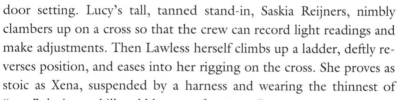

"Julius Caesar was
not harmed during
the production of
this motion picture.
However, the
producers deny any
responsibility for
any unfortunate acts
of betrayal causing
some discomfort."
—Disclaimer from
"Destiny"

Cast and crew take shelter from a storm during the filming of "Lost Mariner."

cut to Xena emitting a bloodcurdling yell. Ryan relishes this scene, though he assures a visitor this is unrelated to any past squabbles with his older sister, Lucy Lawless.

Filming extends till nine at night, with the aid of powerful lights, to complete scenes of Xena's rescue from the cross by the slave girl M'Lila. It caps a day of almost constant lighting adjustments by Donny Duncan, who began filming under brilliant blue skies and then coped for much of the afternoon with mercurial clouds and fast-ebbing sunlight. By the last hour a crew member who had dispensed sunblock-15 in the morning is handing out robes and hot-water bottles.

The need to stretch shooting schedules hours past sunset is routine for Duncan, who often uses his technical wizardry to convey the illusion of daylight. In the winter months especially, when his crew gets just nine hours of daylight to film what may be twelve hours of "sunny" outdoor scenes, Duncan will "turn night into day" by shooting close-ups with minimal background and by pulling out every floodlight:

> It's quite amazing what you can produce when you expose [the film] correctly, and suddenly what to the eye had looked like night, on film looks like the middle of the day. Viewers would be extremely surprised if they knew how many daylight scenes at this time of year were shot in pitch-darkness. And I've got a little trick sometimes—just so the producers and editors watching the dailies don't think we [crew members] have got it all cushy and sweet, I'll often get the camera operator to pan off the scene, right through the darkness, past the lights and the crew shivering and huddling in the cold, just so they know what we've had to do. It never makes the finished show, of course!

Also on film but unlikely to make the final cut is footage of Lucy Lawless helping cast and crew relax between takes. While shivering on the cross in the harsh wind, Lawless entertains the "Roman troops" below with a raucous rendition of the song "I've Got a Loverly Bunch of Cocoanuts." Later she whistles in clear, strong tones such crowd favorites as the theme from *The Andy Griffith Show*. Crew members unselfconsciously begin tapping, humming, or whistling in harmony. Then Rob Tapert readies for the next scene, and the outdoor concert hall instantly reverts to a hushed set. Lawless and the other actors move seamlessly back into character, the cameras roll once more, and Xena agonizes on the cross until "Destiny," in the form of the slave girl M'Lila, intervenes.

> Crew members use various codes to indicate when one of the producers plans to visit the set. Eric Gruendemann discovered that "The duck is on the pond" signaled his arrival.

STUNTS

With three major fights plus a number of smaller skirmishes to stage each week, stunt coordinator Peter Bell has been one of *Xena*'s indispensable off-camera heroes. As a farm boy in New Zealand, Bell rode horses, drove tractors and motorbikes, loved sports, and won two national boxing titles in his teens. Then, as a young man working in Melbourne, Australia, during the mid-seventies, he found that his childhood had provided the best possible career training.

When a friend answered a want ad for stuntmen, Bell went along, "just to see." He won a job doing live stunt shows, and later shifted to movie stunt work. His credits included A-list films such as *The Bounty* with Mel Gibson and *No Way Out* with Kevin Costner. But it was in Hong Kong action flicks that Bell performed his two most amazing feats.

Bell obliged a Hong Kong director by hanging out of an airplane 4,000 feet above the ground, climbing up and sliding down a rope until finally hoisting himself into the plane. The other, more dangerous stunt was for a movie called *Mad Mission IV*, in which Bell had to drive a car off one roof and onto another, six stories up and fifty feet across the street. Bell found that the building he would jump off of was two and a half feet lower than the one he was to land on. Nor did he have much room to stop: just sixty feet till he reached the far end of the second building at full speed. Bell fed this and other alarming data into a computer to learn the exact angle he would need to make the jump onto the second building and stop in time (eleven degrees). It looked ever more like a true mad mission, but Bell treated it like any other stunt that depended on careful planning:

> *We had to strip the car, put a 400 Chevy in it, put slicks on the wheels, and set up a launch ramp because 150 feet was [otherwise] not enough distance to get the speed I needed. And on the other side we put forty-four-gallon drums across the wall and then a sand barrier in front of it because there was no way that I'd pull up in time. I just crashed into it. And I had to be specific where I landed because the gag also called for the building to be demolished and collapse, and I would drive out at the bottom. . . . And I think I came down about six inches off the mark I had set. . . . It's really just basic physics that made it work.*

Bell later formed a company of stuntmen and stuntwomen, who appeared in all five *Hercules* movies and have since performed in every episode of the series *Hercules* and *Xena*. The team now counts around forty members, and Bell has used as many as thirty-four at a time. On average, about a dozen stunt players see action daily on at least one show.

Most of the stuntees, Bell said, "come with one special skill or other, whether it be martial arts, boxing background, gymnastics, mountain climbing, or perhaps they were good wheel men [or drivers]." Allan Poppleton, for example, was recruited from a martial arts school at age twenty-two for the TV movie *Hercules and the Amazon Women*. (He doubled for Amazons in fight scenes, his face concealed by a large animal mask.) Bell retooled his skills "so they would look good for the camera and what we want to do on the series." And once on Bell's team, Poppleton went to gymnastics class and also learned stunt riding and falls.

Most members of Bell's team are veterans of ten years or more, and Bell regards even those with five years of hard knocks as "recent arrivals." This, he ex-

"No Babies were harmed during the production of this motion picture."
—Disclaimer from "Cradle of Hope"

plains, is because "you can never, as we say, buy experience," which is crucial to making the shift from the gym to a film set. "We can show them what to do," Bell says, "but as far as the fight scenes go in both *Hercules* and *Xena,* a big part of doing the stunts is getting the timing

right: when you come in, how you 'sell' the hits to the camera, the flying through the air, and the impact on the ground that are all important things in a fight scene. And that takes *experience*. And so once you know, really know, how to fall properly, you can keep going in this business for quite some time."

Bell designs the fights on *Xena* as imaginatively and precisely as a choreographer would a dance, using a four-line system of his own devising. After sketching two stick figures face to face, each in a fighting stance, Bell draws a line between their shoulders, a second between their stomachs, a third between their knees, and a fourth, which he calls the "visual line," about three feet above their heads. Then he orchestrates fight moves that involve the viewer in all four zones:

Having planned and performed stunts for over two decades, Bell has found that fight scenes are the greatest challenge to sell to an audience:

You can crash a car, you can do a high fall, you can set yourself on fire, and they all look visual. And it doesn't matter what you basically do, that stunt is always going to look good. When it comes to a fight, however, you have to make *that look good. So I've always been a stickler with all my stunt people that whenever they do a fall, whenever they hit the ground, it must be with a good, solid hit.*

Landing on the ground is the icing on the cake for a fight. It makes the "punter" [viewer] feel the pain. You have the visual side of the fight, with the person who is throwing the blow, whether it be on Hercules *or* Xena, *doing a spectacular move, you have the hit, you then have the stuntee flying through the air or flipping through the air. This is all part of the visual. Then you have the landing, and we try to make that look as spectacular as we possibly can!*

When a guy takes a hit, he doesn't just fall over. Instead his feet will fly right up in the air and he'll come crashing down on his back. Or he'll flip right over and land on his stomach, or he'll flip out toward the side. So the landings are what I call the "feeling" part of a fight. When the stuntee hits the ground, the people watching him feel it and cringe. They say, "Oh!" and it makes them feel as if they're in the fight!

Another reason Bell values a good fall is that when a stuntee is knocked down in a fight, he seldom gets up again. "Sometimes we have two-dimensional fights where the two parties trade blows and move backwards and forwards. But ninety percent of the fights are one-dimensional. That is, the stuntees will come running in, take their hit, and go flying and crashing down."

Rob Tapert gave Bell broad freedom to stage fights on *Xena* that would convey the flair of Hong Kong martial arts movies. And while the stuntees cross over routinely between *Hercules* and *Xena*, Bell notes that their fights reflect the outstanding traits of each hero: the power of Hercules and the agility of Xena:

With Hercules' fights I still use those four lines, but when he hits somebody, I'll make sure that I've got some guys who, when they take a hit, exit the frame completely airborne. And we'll show them flying through the air, going long distances, and crashing down either through roofs or onto tables or whatever. . . .

Whereas with Xena, her style is more "martial arty" and acrobatic. And so I have her running up the walls, backflipping, running around pillars, running on guys' chests.

"The Greater Good"
Xena: "I wish the two of you would just get along." Gabrielle: "It's not like we're at constant war or anything. Argo doesn't like me." Xena (stroking Argo's mane): "Sometimes you have to have patience with things that annoy you." Gabrielle: "I never said she annoyed me." Xena: "I wasn't talking to *you*."

Asked which form he favors on Xena among the many different martial arts (karate, jujitsu, aikido, wing chung, and others), Bell said, "There's no real style whatsoever. I've bastardized a number of styles and I just have a vision in my head about the moves that I feel look good on-camera, and I put them into my fight scenes. But to me it works, so *that's* my style!"

Although viewers have remarked on the larger-than-life acrobatics of the stunts on *Xena*, about 80 percent of the flips, leaping kicks, spinning backkicks, and falls, according to Bell, are performed solely by the stuntees themselves. When mechanical aids like wires are used, it is most often to reinforce rather than replace the stunt work:

> *As far as running up walls, flipping over people, and all that, a big percentage of the stuntmen and stuntwomen can do that. But I have found that by putting them in a "flying harness" or in a rig, I can make the move look bigger and more spectacular. So if I have someone running up the wall, using a rig will help them get maybe another five or six feet higher than if they did it just on their own. And with everything in action scenes, the bigger you make it, the better it's going to look.*
>
> *When you see Xena leaping up, flipping through the air, running along kicking guys in the chest, she's in a flying harness and connected to a flying beam. At times the special-effects team will "remove" wires and cables from a scene in postproduction, but most of the time viewers simply would not notice them: The wires we use are blackened down and quite thin, because we're not jerking on them at all. Plus having a dark set helps!*

Because Xena stretches the boundaries of physical reality with her exaggerated leaps and flips, Bell's fight scenes glide dramatically up and down his four-line grid and reach the "visual line" above people's heads more quickly than the fights on *Hercules*. Xena's gravity-defying martial arts skills therefore actually make it easier for Bell to design her fights.

Lucy Lawless perfectly complements Bell's inventive staging of action scenes with her fierce aura, quick mastery of fight moves, and flair in riding, wielding a sword, and delivering full-extension sidekicks. Lawless laughingly recalled that her nickname in school was "Unco," for uncoordinated. But once cast as Xena, she plunged into

"Xena's memory was not damaged or . . . what was I saying."
—Disclaimer from "Remember Nothing"

a regimen of weight training, boxing, and kung fu classes, even traveling to Los Angeles to study with martial arts expert Douglas Wong, who choreographed fights in the movie *Dragon: The Bruce Lee Story*. Lawless absorbed his "white lotus" system of kung fu and learned moves with staffs and swords, impressing Wong with her agility and quickness in absorbing a range of techniques.

Apart from Xena's acrobatics, Lawless handles the brunt of fighting and has the bruises to prove it. She has endured black eyes, lacerations, a wrenched upper back causing neck pains, weakness, sinus problems, and blurred vision, plus a host of lesser injuries battling Bell's stuntmen and stuntwomen. Nor has she rested content with these risks. Rather Lawless has performed stunts that might give pause even to a stuntee, such as her fire-blowing scenes beginning in the fourth episode, "Cradle of Hope."

Although Lawless discounted the dangers in blowing fire, saying, "I don't do anything terrifically risky," she acknowledged thinking twice about the stunt after her trainer, a street performer, set his face ablaze during a practice session: "I saw that guy's face on fire and it gave me a terrible shock. . . . Oh, yeah, he's still alive, but his skin came off his face, it bubbled and peeled." Lawless added, "I've now gone through four coaches," presumably not all exiting in this grim manner. "When the circus leaves town, they vanish."

Midway through the first season, after merely exhorting Xena in the fight scenes, Gabrielle graduated from cheerleader to combatant. The writers gave her a staff, the least lethal of weapons, to preserve her innocence while still letting her defend herself. In Gabrielle's (and Bell's) resourceful hands the staff has taken on almost as many uses as a Swiss Army knife. She twirls it to keep attackers at bay, knocks them backward and forward, and pole-vaults over foes. She even uses it like a parallel bar: when a stuntee grabs her staff and pulls her around back to back, she flips over his back still holding the staff, then wrests it free and knocks him down.

Renee O'Connor's talent and gusto have helped make Gabrielle a major part of the action. Bell calls O'Connor "a great little athlete," adding, "I taught her how to twirl the staff and do moves with it, and she's gotten really good. And she has a ton of energy. When she steps through a fight, she gives it a hundred twenty percent. She really goes for it!"

Much of the fighting in each episode is filmed on the second unit, which completes or enhances scenes filmed with the principal actors on the main unit. This may involve shooting inserts of arms holding swords, legs kicking, and stuntees flying backward or falling. The second unit also works with Lawless' doubles for shots that are too difficult, dangerous, or simply time-consuming. Her main double is Geraldine ("Gerry") Jacobsen, a black belt in karate from Paeroa, New Zealand, who has long dark hair and high cheekbones like Lawless but insists, "We actually look nothing alike. I'm a lot shorter. She's got blue eyes, I've got brown." Gary Jones, who directed the second unit during *Xena*'s opening season, praised Jacobsen as outstanding and inexhaustible:

> *Whenever we doubled Lucy, nine times out of ten it would be Gerry. She was our fight double, and we also had a riding double, an acrobatic double, and two different body doubles. I'd have to say that Gerry was my favorite—a hundred percent enthusiastic, always up for just about anything. And she'd look up after a stunt and say, "Wasn't too good, huh? You need to do another one?" And she'd be right back into it.*

Xena's action scenes posed special challenges for Jones right from the opening episode, "Sins of the Past," which featured a fight on people's heads between Xena and the warlord Draco. Stunt doubles were rigged with wires that held up their weight as they jumped and somersaulted on the heads and shoulders of the extras. But Jones found it was no easy task to get his extras to look serious while actors were dancing about their heads:

Well, it was enough just to keep them from laughing. And we wanted to make their expressions genuine. Doug Lefler [the main-unit director] had shot the extras only at a distance. He had Draco and Xena on top of platforms, and the extras basically disguised the platforms from view so it looked like [the fight] was on their heads. But all the close-ups where stunt doubles really were on the extras' heads was all second-unit. . . . And it was kind of funny, because I said, "Doug, how do you want these extras to react?" and he goes, "Well, Gary, I left you the hard part. I was able to just do all the stuff from behind, *and I had them on the platform, so I didn't have to worry about it.*

Jones faced an added complication: a shortage of extras that forced him to cast his own crew members as villagers:

The main unit had forty extras for the fight scene. Our [second] unit started with twenty or so extras, but on the second day I was only allowed twelve to fifteen, and the third day I only had eight or nine, because of the way the budget works. So, by the time we got to shoot the close-ups on the third day, we had lost most of the extras. To pad it out, I grabbed all my second-unit crew and put them in front of the camera as villagers. When Xena pole-vaults on a villager's head, that's Karin, who did the makeup. . . . Xena does a handstand on top of Kirstie's head, who's our art director. And Rod, who does props, he's the guy whose hat gets spun around on his head when Xena's on top.

Nor was this all. "When Draco is standing on the head and shoulders of a villager, trying to balance himself before he gets knocked off, that's Rob Tapert, wearing a fake beard."

POSTPRODUCTION

The conclusion of filming in New Zealand is by no means the end of work on an episode. Many specialized tasks unfold for weeks after the last reels of film arrive in Los Angeles, including editing, adding music, visual effects, and sound effects, revoicing dialogue, and mixing the different audio tracks.

Since the first TV movies, Bernadette "Bernie" Joyce has coordinated all aspects of postproduction on both *Hercules* and *Xena*. Her credits include the pilot for the hit series *Kung Fu*, several *Bionic Woman* TV movies starring Sondra Bullock, and two *Darkman* sequels for Renaissance Pictures. "I became known as queen of the remakes for a while," she said.

Formerly a producer who "was first on the set, last to leave, and traveling to many different locations," Joyce shifted to studio-based work in order to spend more time at home with her children. Her workday still extends well into the evening but now includes home viewing of episodes in various stages of development. Fortunately her two teenaged children enjoy both *Hercules* and *Xena*, though they watch the shows with a trained eye that can be alarmingly adult. In this household, Joyce observed good-naturedly, the children may offer to help their mother with her homework:

> *My twelve-year-old can watch a show and say, "Oh, Mom, that's a bad loop," or "Mom, that's blue screen, I know it," or "Mom, that's a [stunt] double." So she's very savvy to all this now!*

Joyce said that after the crews in New Zealand finish shooting an episode, the team in postproduction has "about three weeks to edit and two weeks for sound. And within that time you do all the other things" like "color timing," a technique that helps give *Xena* its distinctive look:

> *When you watch the dailies, you realize each scene is shot at a different time of day. The sun moves around, and in New Zealand the weather changes drastically so that within one camera take the clouds can move. At the beginning of the take it can be cloudy and at the end of the take it can be sunny. Right? So we'll go through those dailies and match them so that it looks like it was all taking place at the same time. . . .*
>
> *Also, let's say we decide we want a scene to take place at sunrise or at sunset, we can warm it up and give it a little red. Or*

> "Joxer's nose was not harmed during the production of this motion picture. However, his crossbow was severely damaged."
> —Disclaimer from "Callisto"

sometimes we'll paint the hills and trees greener than they are. One of the attractions of our shows is the vivid colors and the beautiful countryside. . . . Yes, New Zealand is absolutely gorgeous, and we don't really need to do it very much. But once in a while when we have an opportunity we'll do a little painting.

Joyce said that all the technical features of postproduction have one basic goal: "to create [for the viewers] the illusion of reality." For a show dealing in myth and legend, that illusion must be especially compelling. And, Joyce added, by making each story as exciting as possible, "we hope to sweeten that reality."

EDITING

Entertaining friends at an elegant restaurant, Robert Field makes coins vanish and reappear, "bends" spoons with seeming psychic force, and instantly retrieves cards hidden in a deck. But it is his office job, as an editor on *Xena*, that provides the fullest outlet for his mastery of illusion. For in a recurring trick that leaves producers and fans riveted, Field, through sleight of hand (and computer), transforms many hours of unconnected, often repetitive fragments of film into a taut and gripping tale.

In 1970 Field enrolled at the University of California at Santa Cruz and ended up in a self-directed course of study in filmmaking. Intent to explore fresh ways to tell stories, he filmed a murder mystery that featured a series of flashbacks within flashbacks. This early effort sharpened his interest in entering the film industry. Six years later, Field recalled dryly, his eventual mentor, who made trailers, or coming attractions, for Universal Studios, looked at his film and pronounced, "You're no Steven Spielberg." But two months later, with Spielberg possibly otherwise occupied, the man hired Field as his assistant.

Although making trailers lacked the cachet of making feature films, the work honed Field's eye for striking visuals and rapid pacing. "Editing a show is about continuity and telling a story," he explains. "But the finest aspiration in editing a trailer is to position a product and successfully sell it." In 1985 Field branched out to work on a flick called *Cave Girl,* which posed his hardest editing dilemma:

It was a low-budget movie and the director kept pulling people off the crew to act in the film, so I actually appear in the film as a member of the mission-control team. And when I was editing that scene, I was thinking, hmm, the actor in me wants to cut to my close-up! But the editor says no, we've got to stay with the wide shot. So I would have these inner battles with myself.

Field's editing instincts won out, and he cut out his own close-up. "It wasn't right for the scene," he explained. "Not," he added, "that it was a great film to begin with!"

In 1994 Rob Tapert asked Field to cut a prologue for the *Hercules* TV movies, a condensed version of which is used for the current series main-title credits. When Xena began production the following summer, Tapert hired Field as an editor. A colleague, Jim Prior, was already at work on the first episode, "Sins of the Past." Field handled the next one, "Chariots of War," and the two have divided the load ever since.

For a typical episode, Field may receive as many as eight to twelve hours of film from the two camera crews (first and second unit) in New Zealand. Although editors are often thought of simply as technicians, Field's work involves ongoing creative decisions. He must decide on the best of several takes for every shot; whether to use close-ups or wide-angle coverage; when to use quick cuts (to give a scene more energy) and when to linger on an actor for more emotional power. And because the filmed material far exceeds what could ever fit into a 44-and-a-half-minute episode, Field, together with the producers, must choose which scenes or lines to keep and which to cut.

Field said that every director and episode has a unique style, and he tries to reflect this in his editing, as in the Halloween episode, "Girls Just Wanna Have Fun":

As the material for "Girls" started coming in, it seemed evident to me that this show was basically going to be like a roller-coaster ride through a haunted house! And that was the stylistic decision I brought to it. . . . The two dance sequences with

"No Bloodsucking Bacchae were harmed during the production of this motion picture. However, a few Dryads lost their heads." —Disclaimer from "Girls Just Wanna Have Fun"

*Gabrielle are heavily layered with dissolves on top of dissolves—
one face dissolving to another face. My aim . . . was to suggest visually the state of complete surrender that Gabrielle was experi-
encing with the Bacchae—she seemed under their spell. . . . When
T. J. [Scott, the director] called from New Zealand to ask me how
it was going I said, "Well, I don't know. It's pretty weird." He
replied, "Weird is good!"*

Typical of filmmaking generally, scenes that appear simple and natural
are often those that involve the most painstaking editing, Field said.
Action sequences, which have the fastest pace, because the cuts tend
to be very quick, are actually the most time-consuming to construct.
Perhaps the most daunting of all Field's editing tasks was the climax
of "Callisto," featuring a spectacular fight on ladders between Xena
and Callisto. Field looks back on it with a mixture of pride and battle
fatigue:

*The ladder sequence was comprised of 150 separate camera setups
shot over four days. It was an incredibly ambitious and compli-
cated scene, and a nightmare to organize. Imagine a vast jigsaw
puzzle, but with the difference that you not only have to figure out which pieces go together, you also have to cut and shape
each piece before you put it down on the table. Talk about mind-
blowers!*

Sometimes, Field said, the best editing requires simply letting a story
unfold without any special techniques, as when Gabrielle mourns the
supposed death of her friend Xena in "The Greater Good":

*Renee O'Connor is absolutely mesmerizing in that scene. So I
did what any editor worth a half a penny would do
. . . I just let the shot stay on her doing her work—
only cutting away from her when the progression of
the scene warranted it—and then back to her
again.*

> "The Black Wolf"
> Xena (speaking of
> Gabrielle): "She's my
> friend." Salmoneus:
> "She's your friend?
> You have a *friend??*"

Once Field has crafted all the individual scenes for an
episode, he assembles them into a full "editor's cut."
At that point the director comes in and specifies any

changes. The reworked version, known as the "director's cut," then goes to the producers, who send Field notes on what they may want to see changed, shortened, or at times added for continuity—perhaps a shot of an arm reaching for a sword or a horse galloping into the picture.

For the episode "Altared States," executive producer Rob Tapert phones with such requests as "Sell the fish better," for a scene in which Xena grabs the fish she and Gabrielle have caught and swings them against a band of ruffians. Field calls the second-unit crew in New Zealand and has them film a woman's hand reaching for the fish, and then inserts the shot just before Xena begins fighting. In a later scene, to amplify the tension where Xena is being chased and ends up leaping over a spiked hurdle, Tapert calls on Field to "heighten the jeopardy." Field "blows up" a distant shot of armed thugs chasing Xena and then inserts the magnified image just before Xena bounds to safety. Sometimes the producers' notes focus on setting a mood. For a scene in which Xena rides into a village, Tapert wants "a few nice little scenics" added, which Field extracts from digitally stored footage of New Zealand's meadows and mountains.

The producers' cut may require only a single pass or as many as four or five. The final stage often involves getting shows down to broadcast length. Most editor's cuts average between three to six minutes longer than the allotted time but some require more ruthless trimming. The editor's cut of "Callisto" ran fifteen minutes long and "The Greater Good" eighteen minutes long. In such extreme cases, Field said, he keeps to a hard rule: if a scene isn't essential to the story line, it must be cut no matter how entertaining:

After Gabrielle and Xena have discussed Xena's illness [in "The Greater Good"], Salmoneus tells Xena that she should have some of his chicken soup. "Soup is good food!" he proclaims. He then mentions that he would make some, but he has no knife to kill the chicken. Xena tells him he can use her breast dagger. So Salmoneus, in his exuberance to please, starts reaching for Xena's body. In the most steely of voices, Xena imperiously tells him, "The breast dagger is on the table!" "Sal" pulls back his hands, in his inimitable fumbling way, and says, "Maybe, uh, you should consider another name for that particular apparatus." We loved it!

But sadly, for a show much too long on first cut, it had to go—for the "greater good."

Once the producers sign off on a version, the show is considered "locked," and Field will go into an on-line editing room to add some final flourishes. On a typical day Field works on three shows at once. He summed up the three stages of his routine, plus a fourth that will not likely appear in an editor's manual:

1. Cutting raw "dailies" for the new show;
2. Working with the director or implementing the producer's notes;
3. Receiving the special-effects shots for a "finished" episode and cutting them into the show, and then into the edited master tape;
4. Pulling your hair out because nothing is going right, the effects shots are late, they don't look right, the deadline is fast approaching, the producer is asking for shots that don't exist, and lunch is two hours late.

With his reputation for quality work under pressure and his vain protests about impossible deadlines, Field recalls Scotty on *Star Trek*, forever insisting, "Captain, it canna be done in less than a week" while somehow coaxing his engines/editing bay to warp speed in days or

"Being that war is hell, lots of people were harmed during the production of this motion picture (but since television is a dramatic medium of make-believe, all casualties removed their prosthetic makeup and went home unscathed)." — Disclaimer from "Is There a Doctor in the House?"

even hours. The pattern was set early on, after another editor had worked on Xena's main title sequence for six weeks, trying for an artistic look in which images dissolved into white backgrounds. Tapert didn't care for it and asked Field to produce something more dynamic—within a few days.

Field was then working full-time on the fourth episode, "Cradle of Hope," and explained to coordinating producer Bernie Joyce that he would need a block of free days simply to gather material for the main-title sequence and several days more to actually edit it—which he simply did not have. Then, having established that it could not be done, Field delivered in two days a montage featuring Xena poised on horseback before a flaming village, riding at the head of her army, hailing the sea god Poseidon with her sword, and hurling her chakram. This cut became, shot for shot, the main-title sequence that is perhaps the show's best-known minute of footage and arguably the most stirring. For good measure, Field, drawing on his background in trailers, also wrote the copy for the prologue.

Again like Scotty—and so many on the Renaissance team, Field displays a warm pride in his craft, crew, and captain:

> [The quality of work in every department] attests to Rob Tapert's ability to gather people he has faith in and turn them loose on a show that is not only challenging to work on, but fun as well. Rob will give a little nudge here and there to keep you going the right way, but he lets you feel comfortable taking chances and exploring your own ideas.

Field called such freedom unique in his twenty-odd years as an editor, and added, "It is daunting, and it is also wonderfully liberating."

SPECIAL EFFECTS

The mythical creatures that menace Xena, from the winged Harpies to the sea god Poseidon, have all escaped from the computers of

Kevin O'Neill and his team of FX artists. As a child O'Neill was entranced by adventure movies featuring effects by Ray Harryhausen, a pioneer in the use of stop-motion puppetry. Harryhausen dazzled moviegoers with such creatures as the Cyclops and dragon in *The 7th Voyage of Sinbad* (1958); Poseidon, the seven-headed Hydra, and sword-wielding skeletons in *Jason and the Argonauts* (1963); and Medusa's serpent-laden head in *Clash of the Titans* (1981). "We all grew up watching films like this," O'Neill said of Harryhausen's work. "I think he inspired a whole generation of effects technicians that work in the business now."

O'Neill recalled making motion pictures from a young age, his audiences at first numbering in the single digits for Super 8 home movies "with stories based on visual effects." His role models included "Lucas and Spielberg, and the two guys I work for right now, Rob Tapert and Sam Raimi." Still, the leap from a passionate hobby to a consuming career did not come easily. "I actually started out as an accounting major or a business major," O'Neill said of his first year at Ithaca College, "because of my concern over the fact that my parents had invested their money in my education." But he suddenly realized that the business he wanted involved film, not finance, "and then I transferred into film school, taking classes in film production, editing, photography."

After working on a low-budget movie shot in New York City in 1983, O'Neill briefly fell back on the family business, distributing for Du Pont Plastics. "I was the Graduate, yeah," he quipped. But soon afterward an apprenticeship with a special-effects outfit paid off when a production company, Visual Concept Engineering (VCE), invited him to set up his own Visual Effects Division. O'Neill spent two years there doing title design work, opticals, and special effects for features. He went on to an eighteen-month stint at Apogee, a company founded by John Dykstra, who had headed the FX team for the *Star Wars* trilogy. There O'Neill worked on *Bram Stoker's Dracula, Cliffhanger, Last Action Hero,* and a film by Sam Raimi and Rob Tapert, *Darkman II.*

When Apogee disbanded in 1992, O'Neill worked on Universal's movie *Dragon,* about the martial arts legend Bruce Lee. The film's story line of a mythic hero battling both mortal and supernatural war-

riors provided ideal training for O'Neill's next assignment. In the summer of 1993 Tapert ran into O'Neill on the Universal lot and invited him to supervise the visual effects for the *Hercules* movies then in preproduction. O'Neill's flair in creating a bestiary of Centaurs, multi-headed Hydras, and other mythical wonders for the TV movies led to ongoing work on the series *Hercules: The Legendary Journeys* and then, in 1995, on *Xena: Warrior Princess.*

In order to handle the relentless pace of episodic television and still produce quality FX on a modest budget, O'Neill decided to forgo a central studio building and instead hire a "garage band" of artists who would work out of their homes while sharing images over the internet. O'Neill's "virtual studio," linking co-workers electronically, was perhaps his greatest FX illusion, permitting his team to do the work of a large studio at a fraction of the overhead.

O'Neill benefited from superb timing, for *Hercules* came along just when a "desktop revolution" was making powerful FX software programs widely affordable for the first time. Individuals could now create whole 3-D worlds on their home computers, and O'Neill intended to take full advantage:

> *The only way we could produce these effects in the time and budget allotted was to do it on desktop [computers]. The series* Babylon 5 *had actually been doing it for a year, creating entire environments in outer space in a computer. Now at* Hercules *we take original photography and add things to it, which is often harder to deal with. Because if you have an entire 3-D environment as on* Babylon 5 *you have complete control over the art direction and if something is failing technically you can adjust the look of something a lot quicker. But once you* photograph *something, as on our shows, everyone expects it to look a certain way: even if viewers have to imagine what a* creature *looks like, they*

know it's still the same grassy landscape, so that limits the adjustments you can make.

O'Neill recruited artists who had worked for top FX studios on A-list feature films. Kevin Kutchaver, whose credits included *Return of the Jedi* and *The Addams Family,* "was especially crucial for us," O'Neill said, "because of his special skill in combining live action photography with computerized 3-D creatures." O'Neill also hired Doug Beswick, a 3-D animator who had worked on *Gumby, Star Wars,* and *Aliens.* For the second season of *Hercules,* O'Neill, Kutchaver, and Beswick formed the company Flat Earth, and brought in as 3-D supervisor Everett Burrell, whose Optic Nerve studio had won an Emmy for makeup effects on *Babylon 5.*

The roster of talent in Flat Earth has shifted each year, but O'Neill continues to follow a basic rule in hiring that values art over electronics. "I found," he said, "it was better to hire people with creative backgrounds than to hire people with computer backgrounds to do creative tasks."

Some of Flat Earth's standard procedures would still be familiar to earlier generations of FX artists, such as blue screen photography and compositing. Filming against an iridescent blue screen remains the method of choice for extracting an actor's image so that it can later be placed into a scene. Compositing, the superimposing of images shot in different places and at different times into a single frame, is a process nearly as old as filmmaking itself. But O'Neill's team largely uses digital electronics to create and manipulate images, an approach on the cutting edge of FX technology.

While no two monsters on Xena spring to life in exactly the same way, certain approaches are common to many of Flat Earth's operations. Kevin O'Neill first confers with the director and the producers, Rob Tapert and often Liz Friedman, on what a creature should look like, how it will figure in the action, and what effects should be practical within the budget and time available. Once Tapert approves the basic concepts, the technical work of making a creature

"Sins of the Past" Xena (after defeating a Cyclops): "You know, you should find a different line of work." Cyclops: "Well, like what? I'm a *blind* Cyclops, for crying out loud!"

begins. A three-foot sculpture of the creature plus a detailed sculpture of the creature's head are built as models for the computer to replicate. Andy Clement, a 3-D animator, doubles as the artist who makes and paints most of the sculptures for Flat Earth. Beswick checks to see that the creature is being sculpted in a "flat" position, arms at its sides, feet slightly apart, to make it easier for the computer to process accurately. Otherwise, a dynamic pose might stretch the creature's limbs and create distortions when it is made into a computer model.

Bryan Blevins then takes the sculpture, called a maquette, draws a detailed grid on it, and, according to O'Neill, touches each point "with a sort of pen attached to a digitizing arm that translates all of this three-dimensional data into an object in the computer that looks just like it does when you hold it. Each point on the grid becomes a point in 3-D space in the computer, until you've got a 3-D object that replicates the sculpture you've been digitizing."

The digitized object goes to 3-D supervisor Burrell, who, O'Neill said, "has a makeup background and a sculptor's eye for how to paint and light our characters." Burrell inserts a "skeleton" in the computerized creature using a software program called "Bones," which gives the creature multiple joints and determines how it will move. In earlier decades Ray Harryhausen would insert a physical armature in his puppets; now the skeleton, like the rest of the creature, exists wholly in the realm of digital electronics.

Beswick now animates the creature according to the scripted action, after which it goes, along with film of the live action and any other background images, to Kutchaver. His task is to combine all images into a single scene, so that the computerized creature blends into the action so fully as to appear not merely alive but on the set with the other actors. The entire process from the first designs to the final compositing takes six to eight weeks.

The Centaur, a mythical being that is half man, half horse, was, according to O'Neill, "the effect that started it all in terms of whether or not we could do weird stuff like the compositing, or combining, of humans and animals." First appearing in a TV movie, *Hercules in the Underworld,* the Centaur since galloped into *Xena*'s legendary landscape during the tenth episode, "Hooves and Harlots." The sight of

Centaurs drawing chariots for Xena and her Amazon allies remains one of the series' most striking images.

Making a Centaur for *Xena* involves the precise merging by computer of a real person and a real horse in order to form a single fabulous creature. The process begins with the background or action plates. A trainer walks around the set with a horse on a lead. All the actors work around the horse with the understanding that an actor will later be added to these sequences.

The Centaur actors wear appliances that replicate the neck of a horse. They are used for close-up shots that don't require the horse half of the Centaur. However, for the wide-angle vistas that show the entire Centaur in motion, the shots are designed as digital composites—that is, a blending of different shots using digital technology.

Once the scenic backgrounds are photographed and reviewed, a blue screen is shot with the actors. From that point on it's just a selection process. All the possible takes are reviewed, not only from the perspective of trying to come up with the best take but also the best line-up of action between the horse and the actor. In all, the FX team works with three pieces of film: a scene of the horse on a lead with the trainer, generally shot in New Zealand. Then, a blank plate which is only the background without the horse—or humans—on which all the pieces of the scene will be superimposed or composited. Finally, the actor in his Centaur appliance, shot in front of a blue screen so he can be extracted and placed in the new background.

Once these pieces have been selected, the FX artists prepare the background. Typically, there are things in the background that must be eliminated from the final image: viewers clearly should not glimpse the trainer or the lead lines for the horses, or the horse's head. First, a kind of wire removal procedure gets rid of the lead, then the trainer and the horse's head are removed. Each element that is eliminated is replaced with a piece of clean background. The result is an image of a horse walking around the background with no head—a good start.

The actor who will play the Centaur (or at least, his upper half) stands or walks in front of a blue screen so that his image can be extracted from the background. The camera movement is corrected a frame at a time to match the moves and prompt the actor to follow the horse's action. Then the FX artists create more background work to blend the horse appliance into the real horse.

Marks drawn on the horse in chalk permit the FX artists to later track its movements a frame at a time, constantly lining up the horse's anatomy with the actor, and keeping them lined up so they're in constant sync. This is called a match move—the two must flawlessly go together. Then hours of fine-tuning ensure that the actor and the animal appear as one.

Since the birth of the first Centaur in Flat Earth's computers, O'Neill has fine-tuned the process. "We've changed the appliance worn by the actor so that it blends in more naturally. We've also changed the way the actors move, because a lot of times they weren't quite mimicking what a horse did as much as they were just hopping up and down." The most advanced digital technology is at work in compositing the Centaur, but the actor must help by "learning to move like a real horse."

Although *Xena* is less laden with special effects than *Hercules,* the Warrior Princess has been first to battle some of the most remarkable creatures, like the Harpies that guard Hades' palace in the episode "Mortal Beloved." Asked if wires were used for scenes in which the Harpies suddenly flap their wings and fly toward Xena into the sky, O'Neill replied, "No, there are no wires because there are no Harpies!" Instead the FX team used a computer mouse to manipulate the wings, filmed Lucy Lawless and a stunt double against a blue screen, and later composited the computerized Harpies, Xena, and a background plate of the palace into a single riveting image.

The god Poseidon who bursts from the sea each week during the credit sequence proved such a hit

> "No Winged Harpies were harmed or sent to a fiery grave during the production of this motion picture."
> —Disclaimer from "Mortal Beloved"

Xena advances warily in "The Death Mask"

Gabrielle shows off
her sculpted abs in
"Comedy of Eros"

Right: Callisto displays
her trademark glare
in "Callisto"

Below: Xena strikes a
classic pose in
"The Return of Callisto"

Xena charges into battle in "The Death Mask"

Below: An evil priest of Morpheus holds
Gabrielle at knifepoint in "Dreamworker"

Xena in
"A Necessary Evil"

Below: Xena and Hercules
take a defensive stance in
"Prometheus"

Xena is not impressed by Draco's belligerence in "Sins of Past"

Right: Salmoneus takes a turn as master of ceremonies in "Miss Amphipolis"

Left: Xena temporarily gets the better of her nemesis in "Callisto"

Callisto takes possession of Xena's body in "Intimate Stranger"

Below right: Xena clings to a decidedly seasick Gabrielle in "The Lost Mariner"

Above: Xena, Gabrielle, and Joxer on the lookout for bloodsucking Bacchae in "Girls Just Wanna Have Fun"

Gabrielle and Joxer in "Ten Little Warlords"

Below: Xena and Cecrops in "The Lost Mariner"

Above: Xena reveals her leather undergarments in "Altared States"

Left: Callisto gets ready to make trouble in "Callisto"

with fans that he was introduced as a recurring character during the second season. O'Neill described the birth of the god:

> *Poseidon was another sculpture that we designed. And then we had to come up with a "plug-in," which is a computer term for a software application that replicates water. Everett Burrell and Bryan Blevins were the two people at Flat Earth who handled that. Basically they shaped the water into the form of the sculpture that we had created and digitized. This was similar to an effect we did on* Hercules *for "the Enforcer" [a creature formed of water who rises from the sea].*

Flat Earth has experimented in other ways with water effects, as in the whirlpool Charybdis that menaces ships in the second-season episode "Lost Mariner." According to O'Neill, Charybdis represented a breakthrough on several levels:

> *We started doing more environmental 3-D effects. And for Charybdis we actually replicated [overhead photography from] helicopters moving over the ocean. The close-ups of the boats heading toward the whirlpool were done on location. But on the wide shots, the boats were also [computer-generated] 3-D.*

The most famous and frequent effect on *Xena* is neither a creature nor a force of nature but her trusty chakram, which may careen off many surfaces before unerringly finding its target. Xena's chakram exists both as a prop used on set and as a computer-generated image. During the early episodes, the emphasis was on doing as much as possible with a prop, to save money and time in postproduction. But as the

chakram's movements became ever more complex, Flat Earth began handling more of these effects. O'Neill explained how the crew on location and his FX team combine to keep Xena's chakram on target:

> *Several seasons ago [when Xena was introduced on* Hercules*], we actually made a 3-D chakram, digitized it into the computer, and have been using that ever since. I plot out with the second-unit team the actual physical gags that are going to occur on the set. And then we animate to when those objects [Xena is aiming at] are cued up and hit. So we'll receive film of explosions and things breaking apart as "practical effects" shot in New Zealand. And we animate the 3-D object in there later.*

Some of the most crucial effects on *Xena* are the ones we never see. Flat Earth handles the unheralded "cleanup" detail when the production uses wires or cables for stunts. Wire removal is a painstaking process that occurs entirely in the computer. "We have to come up with things to put in place of the wires," O'Neill explained. "You have to grab pixels [the smallest points on the computer screen] from around each wire and pinch them in and paint them over."

When Xena leaps from a tree to the mast of a distant ship in "Lost Mariner" or from one cliff to another in "A Fistful of Dinars," she is moving beyond the practical range of wires and cables. For such long-distance flights, O'Neill's team digitizes a 3-D image of Lucy Lawless or a stunt double tumbling in front of a blue screen. They then composite the image onto an action plate, and move Xena from tree to boat (or cliff to cliff) in the computer.

For O'Neill and his fellow FX artists who give *Xena* much of its mythic aura, the show has provided an exhilarating opportunity to take the achievements of their idol, Ray Harryhausen, to new levels. "I think that's probably the most exciting aspect of it," O'Neill said. "It's something that I wished all my life to emulate, and . . . now, finally, I produce this, in conjunction with a team of really talented, motivated people." Nor is he resting on his laurels. "There are always new challenges, new things we want to try," he said, confident that the ancient myths offer his FX team a world of endless possibilities.

"No cherries were harmed during the production of this motion picture."
—Disclaimer from "A Comedy of Eros"

MUSIC

Joseph Lo Duca, the composer for both *Hercules* and *Xena*, spent decades honing a mastery of many styles before embracing the challenge of setting myth to music. At age thirteen Lo Duca appeared in Detroit clubs as the warm-up act for rock stars Bob Seger and Ted Nugent. He went on to study jazz and classical music at the University of Michigan and then in New York City, where for three years he also imbibed Greek and other ethnic music. Much the way he improvised guitar riffs at events like the Montreux Jazz Festival, Lo Duca shunned rigid career plans in order to explore the possibilities of the moment. That openness brought an unexpected collaboration with two other young artists seeking a career breakthrough: Sam Raimi and Rob Tapert.

> **"Hooves & Harlots"**
>
> Terreis: "The Amazon world is based on truth. On a woman's individual *strength!*" Gabrielle: "I'm all for that. I've always considered myself as a single-minded person. Of course, if I got married, I'd have to ask my husband if that would be O.K." (Terreis glares at her.) Gabrielle: "That was a joke!"

Lo Duca in his early twenties had been winning arts council grants to compose jazz, which he found "wonderful honors but not exactly ways to make a living." He supported himself mainly by performing, until a producer for whom he had recorded studio background tracks said, "Joe, you're pretty good at this, what would you like to do when you grow up?" Lo Duca replied, "Playing jazz, touring, teaching, and, oh, maybe writing for films." That casual nod to cinema, Lo Duca recalled, led the producer to introduce him to Raimi and Tapert, then completing their first horror film and "looking for someone who could make frightening music." Lo Duca's score for *The Evil Dead* was scary enough to forge an ongoing creative bond with the two producers, who a dozen years later asked him to score the *Hercules* telefeatures.

Originally Rob Tapert had envisioned an exotic musical score for *Hercules,* possibly with Arabic roots. "Rob was very taken by a lot of ethnic and Third World music he had heard," Lo Duca recalled. "Also Peter Gabriel [the British pop musician who drew on Yemenite melodies and instruments in scoring a film about Jesus, *The Last Temptation of Christ*]." But, Lo Duca explained, he and Tapert changed direction as it became clear that Kevin Sorbo's Hercules was no exotic figure but a down-home American, transplanted to an un-specified age of adventure.

Still, *Xena*'s music has roots in some of Lo Duca's themes for the exotic supporting characters on *Hercules*. Lo Duca recalled that for the first telefeature, *Hercules and the Amazon Women,* he roamed far from the Hollywood norm in searching for music to represent the Amazons: "My first solution was to write something more Eastern European in meter, and I hired a group of female gospel singers to sing this chant, knowing that their version would be throatier and zestier and more warlike, but still feminine. And that happened to be a wordless chant. In Brazil they tend to sing 'lay ah la, lay ah lay ah,' and they work with those syllables. And being a big fan of Brazilian music, I found this was something that, without inventing a language, I could teach to a group of singers—and it worked. It was just based on those samba and other melodies that they sing, using those syllables, and I thought I can use that. I can make this work." Lo Duca grafted this Brazilian chanting style "onto an Eastern European rhythmic and harmonic base . . . not unlike what [the theme for] *Xena* has become."

Lo Duca's readiness to explore non-Western traditions found a perfect outlet in *Xena: Warrior Princess,* whose heroine is as mysterious as any of the guest characters passing through *Hercules*. Melodies are often written in minor keys, creating a poignant, at times mournful tone suited to Xena's dark past, stoic manner, and harsh world. And foreign influences weave through the music, centered on Eastern European dance and drum rhythms augmented by a female choir.

The episodes that introduced Xena on *Hercules: The Legendary Journeys* pioneered in blending far-flung musical traditions. According to Lo Duca: "We used instruments from all over the world to create a piece for Darphus, Xena's lieutenant in the "Warrior Princess" trilogy. We played conches, shofars, Chinese cymbals and digeeridoos; when combined with an orchestra the result is scary and unique."

Xena owes a special musical debt to Bulgaria, a nation with cultural roots in Russia, Turkey, the Balkans, and even ancient Thrace, just a chakram's throw from Xena's village of Amphipolis. The reedy instrument that leads off the main title sequence is a Bulgarian bagpipe called a gaida, which is made from the stomach of a young sheep or goat. Rob Tapert had wanted "an exotic sound right at the beginning," and Lo Duca decided to experiment with the gaida: "I asked the man to give me a glissando," a sliding together of notes "that's caused when you're first blowing the gaida up with air. It's kind of like [guitarist] Jimi Hendrix with his wild revving. I said, 'Play some funny sounds.' Sometimes I just let the musicians go wild, and I'd weave their performances in and out of the score."

> "No messenger doves were harmed during the production of this motion picture. However, several are reportedly missing in action and search-and-rescue efforts are underway."
> —Disclaimer from "Death Mask"

Lo Duca liked the gaida's "warlike sound combined with drumming and water castanets." Then, he recalled, "when I pressed deeper into the musical culture of Bulgaria, I found a shepherd's flute called a kaval that I use in love scenes. Overblown, the kaval produces a very chilling effect for Xena's chakram toss and her paralysis trick."

Both Xena's signature theme and the main title music feature a female choir chanting Bulgarian lyrics. The idea was Rob Tapert's, and it was a long time brewing. During the late eighties Tapert had seen the Bulgarian Women's Choir in concert, and, as he related, it made a lasting impression: "I kept thinking, 'How the hell can we ever use those [voices]?' And so when we were doing the three-episode arc on *Hercules,* I called Joe [Lo Duca] and said, 'Joe, what if we do it all with Bulgarian backup singers?' He went, 'Ahh! That's great!' So Joe got his big ethnic music group together out here."

Lo Duca had earlier used female choirs and Eastern European rhythms in heralding the Amazons, and he found this approach ideal for Xena, an Amazon in spirit: "This show was originally temped with *Conan* music," featuring heavy, ominous chords and deep-voiced male choirs. "I thought that that was just too masculine. Hong Kong action fighting scored with over-the-top [female] singing was very appealing to us."

But just what would the choir sing? Tapert had admired the Bulgarian Women's Choir simply for its impassioned, exotic style: "When I saw them and then when I bought a bunch of their CDs I didn't know what the hell they were singing." So Lo Duca jotted down in English "an ode to the Warrior Princess," then had the verses translated into Bulgarian—after some memorable false starts. "I actually tried to use a professor of musicology, but I quickly found that this wasn't going to work, because I had some real Bulgarians [in the choir], and they were looking at this, going, 'This makes no sense at all!' They were *not* buying it."

Lo Duca adapted quickly, asking the native Bulgarians in his choir to translate his lyrics: "And I would go over it [with them], and see what I could do to stretch things phonetically and syllabically, so they would actually be singing what I was writing. It certainly helped [their chanting] because it was an authentic inflection, and it helped me because I was getting an authentic rhythm of the speech."

The result was American TV's first (and still only) epic Bulgarian chant:

Jenata iazdi samotna	The Warrior Princess rides alone.
Neinoto minalo srazi ia	Her past drives her from shame.
Sreshtu voiskite ot tumen sviat	Against the forces of a dark world
Vouva za dobro tia	She fights for good, not for fame.
Rogovi zvunove idvat	Horns sound her coming, blare her name.
"Napraite put na voina!"	"Make way the Warrior! Cheer!"
Tupani biat vuv ritum	Drums beat a rhythm
Princhesata e pak tuka!	Let villains beware
	The Warrior Princess is here!

Still, one needn't know the fine points of Bulgarian to appreciate *Xena*'s distinctive melodies, powerful drumbeats, and soaring female voices. One ardent teenage fan, Lo Duca recalled with a laugh, "thought that we were singing 'Go, Xena, go! . . . Power Rangers!' " No matter, for the chanting conveys a mood that goes beyond language. "Warlike, chilling sounds help to create an atmosphere of ancient culture, even though the dialogue is contemporary," Lo Duca said. ". . . And while TV economics, as they exist today, demand that quite a bit of the music is synthesized, we always go out of our

way for the human cry. It adds mystery and intrigue to Xena's world."

Music drawn from Greek and related cultures amplifies the mythic roots of both *Hercules* and *Xena*. When Lo Duca needed a theme for Gabrielle, who hailed from a small Greek village, Poteidaia, he drew on a "source piece," a traditional Greek dance form. Yet he avoided using the bazouki, a Greek instrument resembling the mandolin, because "if we used it in a superficial way, it's going to sound like you're in a Greek diner. I know, because I played bazouki in Greek bands for belly dancers, when I first started!"

Lo Duca arranged Gabrielle's theme for an Arabic instrument called an oud, a smaller cousin of the bazouki that imparts "a much more rustic quality. And the bazouki samples that we used briefly in the score were just to get the impression that she's Greek. The more subdued sound of the oud also plays off the fact that Gabrielle, if you will, is 'Apollonian' [radiant and artistic, like the Greek god of sunlight, music, and poetry] and Xena's 'Dionysian' [wild and unpredictable, like the Greek god of wine]. So we found in Gabrielle's theme a nice little hook into her character."

Source music on the two shows can stray far from ancient Athens so long as it conveys deep feeling and a distinctive sound. The "Greek" funeral dirge in an episode of *Xena*, "The Path Not Taken," actually has roots among religious Jews known as Hasidim. Lucy Lawless recorded a rough, unaccompanied version while in a Los Angeles studio to "loop" additional dialogue for this episode. No one knew the meaning of the lyrics or even the language (as it happened, neither did Lawless herself: "I just trotted out funny words"). But Lo

Duca was enthralled: "Lucy's very reticent about her vocal talents, but I said, 'Oh, we have to use this song!' And Rob [Tapert] found a place for it." Even so, the song was nearly discarded because of time constraints in production, but the resourceful Lo Duca would not let a sleeping dirge lie.

Originally Lawless was to sing a polished version of her song in the studio or on location, but the tight film schedule did not allow this. "The best performance we had was on a third-generation, poor-quality cassette," Lo Duca recalled. "Yet there was something very moving about Lucy's performance. So we took that cheesy audiocassette and beefed it up as much as we could, and I basically played the background for it." It became Xena's bittersweet elegy for her slain lover, Marcus.

Lo Duca's remarkable openness to music from all areas and eras meshes with his own cosmopolitan ancestry. His forebears are Sicilian with an admixture of Spanish and, on his paternal grandmother's side, French. Lo Duca notes the Moorish influence, both North African and Arabic, on Sicily, plus the imprint of Greek, Byzantine, and later cultures spanning ancient through modern times. Each week Lo Duca seeks fresh ways to infuse the music of *Hercules* and *Xena* with elements of that rich heritage.

Lo Duca's work routine in composing for *Hercules* and *Xena* begins when he receives rough cuts of episodes at his home near Detroit, and exchanges notes with the producers about where music is needed and what kind. He described these shows as requiring "a lot of music, perhaps thirty-five minutes of a forty-four-minute episode. They're not sitcoms, or dramas like *Law and Order,* they're action-adventure fare. If a few minutes go by and there is no music, people get nervous. The producers are conscious of [how viewers go] channel surfing, they want [music] to keep the show moving." Lo Duca laughed. "Maybe there's too much music sometimes!"

Adjusting to widely varying resources makes for an added creative challenge. "The music is sometimes written for orchestras, sometimes for synthesizers, and sometimes for ethnic musicians," Lo Duca explained. The largest budgets are keyed less to the needs of particular episodes than to times of intense ratings compe-

"Beware Greeks Bearing Gifts" Gabrielle (staring at the huge Trojan Horse): "Do you want to go back for the Horse? It's bound to be a collector's item." Xena: "Only if you're gonna pull it."

tition: the "sweeps periods" in November, February, and May. According to Lo Duca: "Those are the shows that have the most punch, like the 'Warrior Princess' debut [on *Hercules*] during May [1995] sweeps."

For all the pressures and constraints involved in composing for television, Lo Duca freely acknowledges that compared with most other musicians, he has entered the Elysian fields in terms of support for his creative impulses. "I am given the resources of an entire symphony orchestra," he said. "That's uncommon for a composer in any field."

Lo Duca also employs cutting-edge technology at each stage of his work on *Hercules* and *Xena*. He composes and synchronizes to picture using his personal computer, sends files electronically to his copyists, and prints out music using notation software. Computers dispatch the performances cross-country to studios in Los Angeles over digital phone lines and cue melodies to points in each episode with split-second precision. "While the setting of the shows is B.C.," Lo Duca observed, "the music is made in ways that look to the millennium."

> "Senticles was not harmed during the production of this motion picture. However, several chimneys are in dire need of repair."
> —Disclaimer from "A Solstice Carol"

SOUND

At a "spotting" session for the episode "Callisto," producers Bernie Joyce and Liz Friedman, postproduction supervisor Todd Powers, and Tim Boggs and Jason Schmid of Digital Sound and Picture explore where to add or alter sounds. Only the actors' lines are preserved from the original production in New Zealand, and these, too, must often be redone. And if the footsteps, horses' hooves, rustling leaves, clashing swords, and crashing boulders on *Xena* sound "natural," this is a sign of painstaking effort, well after filming ends, to mimic or outdo these sounds.

The pre-credit scene, or teaser, on "Callisto" receives special attention, for it will introduce Callisto and cue her menacing, psychotic character. Friedman says, "We should start with a really hot fire, let it crackle," which can lead into an attack by Callisto's soldiers on a defenseless village. Boggs suggests adding a villager's scream to highlight the horror.

Friedman wants a "signature" sound for Callisto and says, "We should lay in a snake rattle during one of her crazy moments." Joyce adds that Callisto should sound "gleeful" on killing a man already lying on the ground, explaining, "Killing is like sex for her." On hearing this, Friedman observes with a smile, "We've corrupted you."

Everyone at the meeting recoils at a scene showing crucified victims of Callisto, though their horror is purely technical: a "dead" extra inconveniently stirs. Boggs salvages the scene by suggesting they add "a dying moan."

For a temple procession in which Xena rescues a priestess from the murderous Callisto, Joyce asks, "Do we want any chanting?" Friedman builds on this idea, saying, "Can Joe [Lo Duca, the composer] get some female chanting?" Boggs suggests that the chanting sound "hushed, awed." For such a special style of singing, Joyce says, "maybe we can find some chants in the music library," a computerized reference file of sounds, "just to get ideas."

Joyce and Friedman call for additional background dialogue to clarify or embellish the story line. When Xena enters a village after Callisto has sacked nearby towns claiming to be the Warrior Princess, crowd voices exclaim, "Is that Xena?" "I hear she turned bad." Boggs, as attuned to plot points and characters' emotions as he is to decibel levels and sound effects, asks, "Are these villagers expressing just fear or anger, too?" "It's all fear," replies Friedman.

"Here She Comes . . . Miss Amphipolis" Salmoneus (speaking of the disguised Xena): "A country girl at heart, Miss Amphipolis enjoys the simple things in life: weaving tapestries, making candles, and doing volunteer work with her local Hestian Virgins."

Several scenes are "spotted" for additional noises and dialogue in order to sharpen the humor. When an arrogant but inept "warrior" named Joxer menaces Gabrielle, only to be clobbered by her staff, he grabs his nose, spins around dazed, and stumbles away. Friedman calls for "the sound of a nose cracking" and adds, "We should rewrite some funny Joxer stuff" that [the actor] "Ted [Raimi] can deliver in a nasal tone."

War whoops count as highly as words in spotting action scenes. Friedman prescribes a battle cry for Xena's charge on horseback at Callisto. In the climactic fight between Xena and Callisto, Joyce and Friedman decide, actresses Lucy Lawless and Hudson Leick should add battle cries, shouts, grunts, roars, and whatever else: "Let them make it as wild as possible, as much as they want—they can really mix it up!" This is a long fight, and Joyce wants to vary the audio track with "many different sounds in different places." She encourages her eager crew to hold "a music and sound-effects party."

The most feared saboteurs of the sound crews are not modern vehicles but the swarms of cicadas that turn out for the location shooting. When these insects breed during New Zealand's late summer months of February and March, their incessant chirping may devour half the dialogue or more of outdoor scenes.

Much of the dialogue on "Callisto," as on most episodes, will later be revoiced in a process known as "looping" or automated dialogue replacement (ADR). According to Joyce, this is a time-consuming and tedious process, but necessary:

ADR is difficult for actors because you've got two things to deal with. One is sync—the voices have to sync up perfectly with the images. Two is performance. It's very difficult to get that spontaneity and that emotion that you have in production in a four-wall recording studio with a microphone. So it is one of the more tedious processes of postproduction. But it's necessary.

We probably have more looping than on other programs because of the complexities of our shows. For the fights and battles, we'll revoice all the reactions. We have wild lines in the background like "Get them!" and "Kill them!" We have a lot of accents in New Zealand that we will revoice so that the American audience doesn't get turned off to a foreign accent or simply for clarity. And we have to loop when airplanes pass overhead even if you can hear the lines, simply because there were no airplanes in this time period. Or you'll hear a truck or a motorcycle drive by.

Looping dialogue on occasion occurs before a scene is even shot, as in an episode called "Ulysses," which features the god Poseidon. Lacking a live Greek god to film scenes with other actors and then loop selected dialogue, the crew has the FX team animate a 3-D creature and hires an actor, Chuck Riley, to speak Poseidon's lines. This deep-voiced veteran of commercial voice-overs brings a different inflection to each new recital:

Ulysses is approaching. *You* know *what you're to do.*
Ulysses *is approaching. You know what you're to* do?
Ulysses is approaching. *You know what you're to* do.

Riley explained between takes: "I like to do triples [three recitals of each line], to experiment with different readings." After he delivers all of Poseidon's dialogue to everyone's admiration, Joyce considers ways to add to Poseidon's aura of menace. "There is one more thing I'd like to get," she says. "Can you just give a couple more wild laughs?" Riley asks, "Evil laughs?" "Yeah!" Joyce replies. Riley obliges with a torrent of long and short cackles, thunderous peals, maniacal bursts of glee. Then he steps sedately away from the mike and chats amiably with the sound crew.

In addition to dialogue replacement, many other sounds are added during postproduction. Joseph Lo Duca digitally transmits his musical score from his home in Detroit, and a music editor may supplement this from a library of Lo Duca's past compositions. A team of four or five "Foley artists" re-create sounds of body movements. To simulate the flapping of wings, a Foley artist blows rhythmically into a microphone. And the most distinctive sound on *Xena,* the famous "whoosh" at the raising of a sword—or an eyebrow—is created by a Foley artist shaking a bamboo stick.

Why whoosh? The sound literally echoes the style of Hong Kong martial arts films, where hands are not only lethal weapons but accoustical instruments of great power. According to Joyce, the frequent use of whooshes serves many ends:

Because Xena doesn't have the superpower strength that Herc has, we'll give her whooshes to speed her up. Or if somebody's about to get killed and she turns her head to save them, we'll give her a whoosh. We don't whoosh for just anything, but we do it at peak moments or when we need to make her look faster or stronger.

At first *Xena* featured extensive whooshing, to accentuate her dynamism and to add to the show's unique style. But in the second season, Rob Tapert called for using the effect with greater restraint. Clark agreed that "less is more," preferring to save the show's trademark sound for the most dramatic junctures or for over-the-top comedies like "Miss Amphipolis." But Patrick Giraudi, the show's chief recording mixer, noted objections by fans on the Internet that *Xena* was "beginning to sound more like other series." The sound technicians still engage in long, spirited debates on the question "to whoosh or not to whoosh."

The sound of Xena's chakram as it whizzes through the air, ricocheting off walls, helmets, and boulders, may be the most complex effect on *Xena*. It blends fifty to sixty different noises manipulated for speed and tone, among them the screaming of firecrackers known as jumping jacks and the screech of small primates called lemurs. Asked whether anyone thought simply to throw a chakram, Schmid smiled and explained gently, "It wouldn't make much of a sound."

The mixing of dialogue, music, and other sounds takes three days, including one reserved for fine-tuning, or "tweaking." This may be a matter of getting the composer, Joe Lo Duca, to send additional music over digital phone lines, or to adjust background sound levels. In the tweaking stage for "Miss Amphipolis," Joyce directs, "Bring up [the sound level on] the 'wallas,' " referring to a standard nonsense word, "walla," repeated by extras to convey crowd murmurings. ("Rhubarb" is another crowd favorite.) And when Salmoneus, the master of ceremonies for the Miss Known World pageant, realizes that the winner is actually a man in disguise, the technicians hunt for a cartoonish "boing," to underscore his astonishment.

> The sounds on *Xena* often have unusual sources. For a fast-flying bird in "Prometheus," technicians put in the sound of an F-16.

The final stage of mixing combines the many sound tracks onto a stereo tape for broadcast. A typical episode blends around sixteen tracks for Foley and backgrounds, eight for dialogue, eight for music, and up to fifty or more for hard sound effects. "Obviously the more action in an episode, the more tracks you're going to have," Joyce said. For shows heavy on creatures and sword fights, there may be a hundred or more tracks to mix.

The credo of the technicians involved in mixing is that the right sounds can enhance any scene, and that these sounds are out there, awaiting discovery through inspiration or sheer hard work. Giraudi recalled an episode, "Warrior . . . Princess . . . Tramp," in which they added a comical sound when the bumbling Joxer reaches for Xena's rear in a ghastly case of mistaken identity:

> We had an "ooga" horn in there, to make it more playful. Well, the director hated it. He said, "You can't make a gag funnier with a funny sound." Well, as soon as he left the room, we all passionately disagreed! We find that the fans love that sort of thing.

The episodes on *Xena* are not simply polished in postproduction. They are transformed. Editor Rob Field, himself a vital part of this process, marveled at the cumulative impact of the changes from the end of filming to the broadcasts that audiences see and hear:

I saw parts of the almost finished cut of "Callisto," and even though it was only six weeks previous that I had turned the show over to sound and optical effects, it felt as though it had been six years! It almost looked like something I had never seen before, or only dimly remembered. Only then did I realize how much work had actually gone into it and what it took to get it done.

Gabrielle becomes one of the Bacchae
in "Girls Just Wanna Have Fun"

Below: Xena displays some unexpected
skills in "Chariots of War"

Ares is dangerously appealing in "The Reckoning"

Xena and Gabrielle flee from the Horde in "The Price"

Below: The formidable Velaska briefly rules
the Amazons in "The Quest"

Above: Xena and Hercules share a passionate moment in "Prometheus"

Right: Joxer flashes a disarming grin in "For Him the Bell Tolls"

Below: Xena flies a kite in "A Day in the Life"

Gabrielle acquires a new wardrobe as an Amazon Princess in "Hooves and Harlots"

Left: Xena uses her fire-breathing trick in "The Reckoning"

Below: Xena and Gabrielle enjoy a rare quiet moment in "A Day in the Life"

Xena in
"A Necessary Evil"

Right: Xena finds
herself trapped inside
Callisto's body in
"Intimate Stranger"

Xena in her duel
with the warlord Draco
in "Sins of the Past"

Xena and
Gabrielle hit
the hot tub
in "A Day
in the Life"

Xena and Argo in
"The Black Wolf"

Xena battles a mysterious attacker in "The Reckoning"

CAST PROFILES

• LUCY LAWLESS—XENA •

Lucy Lawless became an adventurer long before she starred as one. Born on March 29, 1968, the fifth of seven children and the oldest girl, she grew up in Mount Albert, which she recalled as "a family suburb" of Auckland, "the first ring of suburbs outside the inner city. Nothing real exciting ever happens there, but it was a good safe place to grow up. As kids we used to ride our bicycles around the streets, and get into all sorts of trouble—minor trouble, but we thought we were real scalawags." Her father, Frank Ryan, became mayor of Mount Albert the year Lucy was born. He served twenty-two years, and remained in local politics as the financial chairman of Auckland City. Until the age of eight, Lawless was very much a tomboy who, like her four older brothers (and most other New Zealanders), thrived on rugby and other sports. But acting soon proved a more enticing pastime.

"[Lucy] used to get up on the coffee table with a seashell for a microphone and sing away," her mother, Julie, recalled. Lawless also found ways to broaden her audience: "My best friend, Michelle, and I would make a show for the old ladies in Mount Albert. We'd put on these plays, invent silly costumes." As a ten-year-old student in a Catholic convent she had her "first real part," playing a saleswoman in a musical about the Prodigal Son. As befitted someone who

Renee O'Connor on working with Lawless: "I'd say it's a respect two people have for each other. I really like Lucy as a person. We've bonded together. We listen to each other. It's a good friendship."

Lucy Lawless'
favorite episodes of
Xena are "Is There a
Doctor in the
House?" and
"Warrior . . .
Princess . . . Tramp."

then loved singing even more than acting, she later lost all memory of the role, but "I remember some of the songs. I was a much better singer in those days than I am now."

Lawless' singing was good enough to lead her away from early thoughts of becoming either a marine biologist or a pathologist, and she spent three years training for the opera. In 1986 she enrolled in Auckland University to study languages and opera, but left school after a year. "I found out," she said, "that I didn't have anywhere near the passion for a life with music that would keep me coming back for the knocks, but I seemed to have that resilience for acting."

Leaving the university came more easily than forsaking a career in opera, despite what had been a "wonderful" experience in Catholic school. "I really loved school, yeah, I'm one of those one in five thousand off the production line for whom the system really works." But "I never had any intention of going, at seventeen years old, [for] three or four years. That just seemed like an eternity. In fact, that year was kind of a bonus. I would have been gone at seventeen if I had the money. . . . I knew what I wanted to do, it wasn't to get a useless degree. . . . It never *occurred* to me to ask my parents for help in this way. I just wanted to travel, I *loved* my languages, I had been overseas with my mother when I was fifteen. We did an opera tour. I just wanted to go and eat the world, you know. And it's the best thing I could have done."

New Zealanders in their late teens typically pursue an "OE," or overseas experience, and Lawless pushed hers to the limit. At eighteen she picked grapes on the Rhine in Germany, then moved to Switzerland and, with her boyfriend from New Zealand, Garth, traveled through Greece. When the money ran out, the couple left for Australia, where Lawless worked as a gold miner in the Outback, a hard, arid region, often bitter cold, removed from coastal cities like Perth by more than five hundred miles of dusty roads. Nearly all of the miners were men, and she matched them in surveying, digging, driving trucks, and handling heavy industrial equipment.

Lawless kept at this grueling work for eleven months, later calling it "a way to make good money, for people who weren't otherwise qualified—a way to get back to Europe." Then, thinking of the grueling, dirty labor, the harsh terrain, and the isolation, she added with a laugh, "I don't know, just a bit of madness." Her plans took another unpredicted turn when, in 1987, she discovered she was pregnant. She and Garth married and returned to New Zealand, living in a tiny apartment, surrounded, she told Karen Schneider of *People*, "by mad old ladies with cats that drove me insane." The following year her daughter Daisy was born, and Lawless returned to work. She wrote and acted in plays, and her husband produced them and made videos as audition tapes.

At first Lawless starred mainly in TV commercials. Her roles ranged from a wife and mother who depends on the Auckland National Savings Bank to a harried professional woman whose electrical appliances come to life, tidying her home and fetching her slippers. Lawless welcomed the security—up to a point, turning down an ad for tampons that seemed a doubtful career move, though it would have brought her, in American money, some $30,000.

At twenty Lawless joined a comedy troupe on a New Zealand TV show called *Funny Business*. The audition went smoothly: she and another woman showed up just after two key actresses had walked off the set; both were hired at once. Lawless worked at the show two and a half seasons, enjoying the chance to "stretch my boundaries of the absurd." She followed this with guest roles in episodic TV, including an outing on the science fiction cult hit *The Ray Bradbury Theater*, in which she tries desperately to keep peace between her conniving husband and her paranoid but crafty grandmother, played by Jean Stapleton.

In 1990 Lawless appeared in the New Zealand short film *Peach*, as a lesbian who tries to rescue a heterosexual woman from an abusive relationship. "Looking back," Lawless said ruefully, "I can see I didn't know anything about [the role]. It's a demeanor, an attitude to life, which I didn't quite understand. Also, I was a bit intimidated by the part."

"No one was harmed during the production of this motion picture. However, Xena's ability to recover her body was severely impeded by Lucy Lawless' unexpected mishap."
—Disclaimer from "Ten Little Warlords"

Lucy Lawless on what she is proudest of: "My kid. And my relationship with Rob [Tapert]. I'm proudest of Daisy and I put her and Rob above all else."

Despite limited acting opportunities and uncertain prospects, Lawless moved to Vancouver, Canada, in 1991 to spend eight months at the William Davis Center for Actors Study. Her commitment reflected a belief that success would come with time—and unrelenting work: "Not [just] the hope, but the expectation. Absolutely. If you just work [so] hard that nobody works any harder. . . . My dad never said you can't. My mother always encouraged me, we went to see theater plays and things. . . . So [when rejections came] I just sucked it up. 'You didn't get the job, you didn't get the job, you don't look right, blah, blah, blah,' you'd be devastated for two seconds, and then you'd come back stronger than ever."

Returning to New Zealand early in 1992, Lawless appeared in a fact-based ABC movie with Jon Voight, *Rainbow Warrior,* about a French terrorist attack on a Greenpeace ship protesting France's nuclear policy. Her character, Jane Redmond, had few lines but ample "feistiness" that, according to Lawless, bore a close resemblance to Xena. Among varied later roles, kissing teen idol Rick Springfield on an episode of his series *High Tide* made for a personal, if not a professional, highlight that, said Lawless, made her "feel like a schoolgirl."

Also in 1992 Lawless became a co-host, or "presenter," for *Air New Zealand Holiday,* a travel magazine show broadcast in New Zealand and throughout Asia, which took her around the world. She entered a second season as presenter just as Renaissance Pictures set up in Auckland and began casting *Hercules and the Amazon Women.* Lawless won the key role of Lysia, the Amazon second-in-command, and was invited back to play Lyla, a Centaur's wife, in the episode "As Darkness Falls," when *Hercules* became a series.

Lawless interspersed her roles as Lysia and Lyla with ongoing work as a presenter for *Air New Zealand Holiday.* When a third season of this travel show beckoned to her with the promise of security, "I was very torn," Lawless recalled. "What made the decision a lot easier for me" was learning through the grapevine that "the deal they offered me was well below that of the male presenter. And in the end

I gave it up, and then the part of the Warrior Princess came up totally unawares."

Since the breakup of Lawless' marriage in 1995, she has been dating Rob Tapert, whom she called a "wonderful man" and a wonderful match:

We seem to be on the same wavelength, generally. We seem to like the same things and have the same twists in our psyches. And, yes, we enjoy the ironies and the badness and the heart in life.

On October 8, 1996, Lawless was in Los Angeles taping a comedy skit for *The Tonight Show* with Jay Leno when she fell from a horse. She was hospitalized for pelvic fractures, raising doubts about her future and that of *Xena: Warrior Princess*. While the writers found ingenious ways to highlight other performers, Lawless showed astonishing recuperative powers, helped by an intense regimen of therapy and a resolve to be "better than I was before the accident." As her father assured well-wishers in New Zealand, "Lucy is robust, fit, and keen and has a 'fix the damn thing and get on with it' attitude." On set in New Zealand barely a month later, Lawless herself viewed her ordeal with characteristic grit:

I believe that good and wisdom comes out of everything. And really this has been the toughest and most rewarding time of my life. I've been able to sort out many personal issues . . . and this metamorphosis could not have happened had I not been slowed down by this accident. I'm a much more peaceful person than I was. I'm happy in my life, I have a wonderful daughter, and I'm thrilled to be back at work.

Lawless believes Xena is "the best role for an actress on television in twenty years" and that, "personally, it has been a wonderful convergence of everything I'd ever done," from acting to riding ponies as a child. Musing on the fragile set of coincidences that led—just barely— to her winning the part, she admitted, "It almost makes me sick to think of it now." But perhaps, Lawless added playfully, other forces had also been at work:

While we were on our camping trip I read one of those New Year's features the country paper puts out—five days of horoscopes for everybody—and mine was this outrageous claim of "overseas travel predicted, fame and fortune are on their way." We were laughing *our heads off about it, and the next day that phone call came. . . . Yeah, I still have it, I photocopied and enlarged it, because it was such a hoot.*

• RENEE O'CONNOR—GABRIELLE •

Born on February 15, 1971, in Houston, Texas, Renee O'Connor grew up in the suburb of Katy. She recalled studying acting from age twelve at Houston's Alley Theatre:

Luckily for me they had a children's program, and so we would use these wonderful costumes and amazing clay sets. And it's funny because everything was make-believe, and here I am again, you know, at twenty-five years old and still doing it. I think that's where it all stems from—you know, that sense of play.

O'Connor's first, unconventional acting gig came at sixteen, prancing through a Six Flags amusement park as a succession of costumed cartoon characters:

It was the funniest thing you'd ever imagine! But it was wonderful because you are larger than life and can play comedy and it was very physical. So we would do shows where we would actually dance and have music and the voices would be over the top.

After a stint at the High School of the Performing and Visual Arts in Houston, O'Connor, then seventeen, moved to Los Angeles to hone her sense of play as a professional actress. In 1989 Disney cast her in the first of two serials on *The Mickey Mouse Club*, "Teen Angel," reviving an old series favorite, "Spin and Marty." Stretching from G-rated fare to HBO horror, O'Connor briefly appeared in an episode of *Tales from the Crypt*, directed by Arnold Schwarzenegger. In 1991 she played Cheryl Ladd's daughter in the miniseries *Changes*. "It was a Danielle Steel novel," she volunteered with an embarrassed smile. Two years later O'Connor starred as one of a group of students washed away by a river in the NBC movie *The Flood*. "It was based on a true story in Texas but filmed in Australia, which was so funny, especially since I'm from Texas. But it was pretty exciting."

Other feature films and TV roles followed. She appeared in another Disney production, *The Adventures of Huck Finn*, with Elijah Wood and Jason Robards. "It was a small part but it was wonderful, filled with humor, a nice period piece set in Natchez [Mississippi]." A guest appearance on *The Rockford Files* "was one of the highlights for me because I was—and am—such a fan of James Garner." Sandwiched between these and other performances, O'Connor appeared in two mythic action films for Renaissance Pictures: *Hercules and the Lost Kingdom* (1994) and the direct-to-video release of *Darkman II: The Return of Durant* (1995).

At her audition for the role of Deianeira in *Hercules and the Lost Kingdom*, O'Connor displayed considerably more humor than she had intended:

I just remember standing up on this chair in the middle of the room and playing this girl who

> Lucy Lawless on working with O'Connor: "I love acting with Renee . . . You must make the other character important, not yourself, so that you are listening to them and bringing them in."

> "Once again, Gabrielle's luck with men was harmed during the production of this motion picture."
> —Disclaimer from "Blind Faith"

wanted to be sacrificed to the gods, and then I ended up falling down and I hit some equipment in Rob Tapert's office! I kept apologizing, "Oh, no! I ruined all your things, I'm so sorry!

Tapert's good humor never faded, and he encouraged O'Connor to continue. Despite her misgivings, Tapert viewed the audition as a success: he had not lost equipment, he had gained an appealing lead actress.

When *Xena: Warrior Princess* was created in 1995, O'Connor won the key role of Gabrielle from a field of more than 400 aspirants. Willa O'Neill, who plays Gabrielle's sister Lila, called O'Connor "an incredibly giving actress" who made acting "a joy":

What I like about her is that she's actually interested in the skills of acting from just a playful point of view. She'll give good tips and she makes up little scenes and games off-camera to keep your acting fresh. She even gets the extras rocked up enough so that they're not static in the background. She'll say, "O.K., guys, now, we're just about to go to war and you're all gathering your stuff." I appreciate that she's making life a lot easier for everyone around her by being interested in what she's doing.

O'Connor summed up her approach to playing Gabrielle and her friendship with the Warrior Princess:

"Hooves & Harlots" Gabrielle (to Xena): "You know, I just thought of something! You're a Warrior Princess and I'm an Amazon Princess! That's going to make *such* a great story!"

They [Rob Tapert and R. J. Stewart] were looking for somebody spunky, spirited, who could hold her own with Xena eventually, and so that was the guideline I began with. And then I took the idea of her being a storyteller and really clicked with that. Everything that she hadn't seen before but had only heard through stories and from her readings, she now could see herself living through Xena. And I made her very romantic, sentimental, and sympathetic, full of the wonder and mystery of life. So she would be the opposite of Xena but wanted to be like her. And where Xena could be dysfunctional and Gabrielle would be her opposite, together *they make one person!*

The five-foot-three-inch, reddish-blond, green-eyed actress looks far more youthful than her twenty-six years. She has a gentle, kindly manner that recalls her character Gabrielle, though O'Connor said she envies Gabrielle's unwavering optimism. Off-camera she relaxes by rock climbing (her modest description for activities that have included ascending Mount Kilimanjaro!), kick boxing, jogging, Rollerblading, and—in sharp contrast to Gabrielle—horseback riding.

• TED RAIMI—JOXER •

Theodore "Ted" Raimi spent years playing "some of the most serious characters on earth" before bringing his superb comic talents to the cast of *Xena* as Joxer. Raimi grew up in a "loving and wonderfully supportive" Jewish family outside Detroit:

My father is quite an intellectual, who encouraged us to read, think, and ask questions all the time. And my mother is an incredibly unpredictable woman, who, when I was going to high school, for example, might come in one morning and say, "Let's skip school and go to the movies, what do you say?" And I'd say, "Great!"

It was also a family, Raimi said, where comedy was king:

I think my father and my mother both have this real offbeat, very biting sense of humor. We all took after it, and we always felt very comfortable being goofy around each other. We still do.

Raimi's decision at seventeen to try for a career in acting veered sharply from his family's business background. His paternal grandfather had immigrated from Holland and built a chain of eight appliance stores. His father ran a home-furnishings store, and his mother founded her own chain of lingerie stores (Raimi said he "could have

"Callisto"
Joxer: "Joxer the
Mighty at your
service . . . I'm fierce
and I have a lust for
blood . . . My
nickname is Bloody
Joxer." Xena: "If you
like the sight of
blood so much, keep
talking."

been the 'bra king' of Michigan"). But Raimi's father, swallowing any discomfort, suggested he go to New York City to audition for roles and, if acting did not work out, he could return and go to college.

Raimi's checkered career in fact led him through four colleges. "I spent the hardest, most horrible year of my life looking for acting jobs in New York," he said. "It was lonely and depressing, and all my buddies were having a great time in college." He "reluctantly returned" to Detroit to attend community college but when his older brother Sam began shooting *Evil Dead II* in North Carolina, Raimi dropped out to play Henrietta the monster "under a hundred pounds of makeup." He then enrolled in Michigan State University, where both his older brothers had studied. It was a move he quickly regretted:

It was like going to school in the Himalayas. You know, it's actually the first agricultural school ever in the United States. They are growing beans and raising cows, and I just wanted to act.

Raimi dropped out again and enrolled in New York University. But one day, while hammering boards for a play he could not act in because he was not a graduate student, Raimi decided, "This is ridiculous." He dropped the hammer and dropped out of school a third time, which did not ease his parents' concerns. "But I was so restless," he said, "because I couldn't figure out how to be the actor I wanted to be." The fourth time was the charm: Raimi studied theater at the University of Detroit, "which, as it turned out, was the best thing I've ever done in my life. I performed in nine plays in one year and learned an incredible amount about acting. But it took four schools to figure it out."

After moving to California in 1989, Raimi played everything from an author kissed by Pamela Anderson on *Baywatch* to a psychotic killer in the film *Skinner.* He starred as a sympathetic (though insane) fellow in *Lunatics: A Love Story,* and spent two years on the TV show *SeaQuest* (1993 to 1995) as the communications officer, Lieutenant Timothy O'Neill, who is "like [*Star Trek*'s] Lieutenant Uhura, but with lots of complexes!" Raimi also played a CIA computer programmer in the thrillers *Patriot Games* and *Clear and Present Danger*, which he relished for the chance to work with Harrison Ford. "It was educational, to say the least," he said, "watching a master at work, like a pianist sitting next to Vladimir Horowitz."

After *SeaQuest*, Raimi felt he had hit a career wall but the character of Joxer, in a rare act of heroism, came to his rescue:

> *I had just auditioned for a sitcom that seemed the stupidest thing I had ever read, I was disheartened, and thinking of going back to Detroit or New York. I bumped into Rob [Tapert], we had a nice conversation catching up on several years, and then he stopped and asked, "Would you like to go to New Zealand to play [Joxer]?" which he said might be a recurring part.*

Joxer, a self-proclaimed warrior who literally sings his own praises but cannot recruit anyone for a chorus, provides a light counterpoint to Xena's harsh world. The role was written originally for Wallace Shawn, a playwright and actor known for playing meek characters such as the high school teacher on *Clueless*. Raimi drew inspiration for playing Joxer from two of his favorite comic actors, Bob Hope and Woody Allen. Despite their different backgrounds—Hope from America's heartland and Allen a walking textbook of Jewish urban angst—they "are so similar," according to Raimi. "Both [their characters] are neurotic and tortured by a world they desperately want to be in but that will not let them in." Raimi could also draw on personal experience:

> *You know, there are two kinds of nerds in high school. The first kind knows he's a nerd and walks around holding his books desperately in front of him, hoping no one will smack them out. And I was the second kind, the guy who would go lomping down the hallways with thick glasses, having no idea*

"The producers wish to acknowledge the inspiration of Danny Kaye and pay tribute to the classic motion picture *The Court Jester.*"
—Disclaimer from "For Him the Bell Tolls"

"For Him the Bell Tolls"
Joxer (to Gabrielle): "I know nothing of this bumbling idiot of whom you speak. I'm the one and only Joxer."

he's a nerd. What did I know? I thought I was cool. And then I never understood it when kids would throw me up against lockers and beat the hell out of me.

Raimi told of meeting Robert Trebor, who plays the comical merchant Salmoneus on *Hercules,* and feeling a sudden bond:

> *We stopped and looked at each other. It was like negative universes meeting, it was really funny. Because what he is to Hercules, I am to Xena: you have two main characters and one funny, goofy guy. . . . The difference is that while Salmoneus is a pest like Joxer, he doesn't really need Hercules. He cares only about worldly things and is really the opposite of Hercules, and that's where the humor comes in. But Joxer wants to be just like Xena. He just never will be because he doesn't have any talent. And that's where the humor comes in, because she's the greatest warrior and he's the worst.*

The world of *Xena* at times follows Raimi off the set. Hudson Leick, who plays Callisto, recalls meeting him when she went "swing dancing," and although "it was really funny that Callisto was dancing with Joxer, we just burned up the rug." Raimi indeed cuts a striking contrast with his alter ego Joxer. Intelligent, witty, and sensitive, popular with cast and crew, he plays piano and trumpet, roots for the Detroit Tigers, reads voraciously, including science and science fiction, speaks half a dozen languages, and writes screenplays, among them an episode of *SeaQuest* called "Lost Land." Not least, said Hudson Leick, "He is one amazing dancer."

• HUDSON LEICK—CALLISTO •

Hudson Leick's dramatic roles have ranged from an angel on the CBS series *Touched by an Angel* to Callisto, who seems the devil's own creation, on *Xena: Warrior Princess.* Born Heidi Hudson Leick in Cincinnati, she took Hudson as her first name because it is her grandmother's maiden name, "and my roots are important." Leick modeled in France after high school but, she said, "I wasn't very good and wasn't getting a lot of work." On returning to the States she took an acting class at Nazareth College. For her "improv" she played a retarded person, and it taught her the power of acting:

> *Everyone started laughing at first because they thought it was really funny. But it wasn't funny to me, I had such a terrible time in high school and it was actually how I felt. And I portrayed this person as having a speech impediment and she was very slow. And she kept saying, "Don't, don't," because these people were throwing rocks at her. And as soon as the audience realized that she was being harmed, it changed everything. People who had made fun of someone because they're different suddenly saw another human being harmed by their laughter. And it was beautiful for me to be able to share that on that level.*

Heading for New York, Leick spent a year as a makeup artist and then two years with a renowned actor's workshop called the Neighborhood Playhouse, which she loved for its high standards but loathed for its "abusive" criticism of students. She went on to appear in an *ABC Afterschool Special* and *Law and Order*. In the TV movie *Hijacked,* she played a terrorist, and in the series *Melrose Place* she was a psychotic mischief maker—good training, it turned out, for her recurring role on *Xena*.

Casting director Beth Hymson-Ayer recalled why she went to the unusual step of courting Leick to try out for the part of Callisto:

> *I needed a nemesis for Xena who was a total opposite but with the same strengths and the same ferociousness that the old Xena had when she was in* Hercules. *And Hudson is just a real gutsy lady. She's very confident and you know she can stand up for herself.*

At her audition for Callisto, Leick was in a mood to rebel against the whole system of casting calls, which she felt were too impersonal:

It was a very small office, there were tons of other actresses [just outside]. And I felt no one understood what it was like to be me, to perform in front of all of them. I just didn't like it. And I thought, "You will respect me. I am a human being and I am here." I remember looking at every human being in the room and shaking all of their hands and saying, "Hello, and what's your name, who are you?" That kind of ruffled everyone's feathers. Not that they were upset, they were just, like, "Whoa! What is this? What is she about?"

Producer Liz Friedman recalled the session:

When Beth Hymson-Ayer said, "Any questions," Hudson said, "Yes, I have a question. Who is everybody?" And she went around to each person making incredibly close eye contact! It was spooky!

Later R. J. Stewart confided to Leick, "When you came in, everyone was so afraid of you! But I said, 'Well, if we're scared of her, she should get the part of Callisto!' "

Remarkably, Leick later won the part of Xena as well. In an episode called "Intimate Stranger," Callisto escapes from Tartarus by switching bodies with Xena. When Lucy Lawless suffered a riding accident, the ending was reedited to keep Xena in Callisto's body long enough to let Leick portray her in the next episode, "Ten Little Warlords." Leick delivered a fine, controlled performance as Xena, though she looks back uncomfortably on this unique interlude in the series and her own career:

It's something I just do not want to remember. I just showed up and tried to imitate something. I kept my voice at a lower octave, staying in more of a monotone, because I imagine Lucy as like John Wayne, you know? And Renee [O'Connor] would help me. I'd say, "What would she do, what would she do right now?" Because I had no clue what to do! And she'd put her arm on me and she'd show me. But I felt there was not a lot of spirit in my performance, and I kept thinking, "No one's going to like it. They're all going to say, 'Well, she's no Lucy Lawless.' " And I'm not.

Leick was less surprised by her casting call in 1997 for the series *Touched by an Angel,* despite her reputation for flamboyant villainy:

I'm really spiritual. I don't have a religion but I believe in something much greater than myself. I believe in soul-searching and finding kindness and love with another human being. And myself, for that matter. So when I went in for this role, I didn't just treat it as another role. . . . Because there's a part of me that is like Callisto and full of rage, but there's a part of me that is really angelic and . . . really soft. So I just connected to that part.

Leick considers one of the best aspects of working on *Xena* to be the strong presence of women in the cast and crew, which she said strongly influences the atmosphere on set:

The women on Xena *are amazingly kind, and we've bonded together. The testosterone level on* Hercules *is just so much stronger. You don't get the same feeling when you're working on* Xena. *You don't think, "O.K., I'm in this leather bikini"—but when I was doing* Herc, *I did feel that way.*

Off the set Leick relaxes with her dogs Griffin and Zu (short for Zulu), goes dancing, and enjoys yoga. Asked about her ambitions, she said:

I've had material things: money, men, beauty, some success. But there has to be more spiritually. More than people ever talk about on a group level, except maybe the Native Americans. Their idea of religion helps connect them to the earth. That's important to me.

Leick's charisma as Callisto led the editors in Los Angeles to dub the blond actress "Malibu Xena," much to Leick's amusement. Others on the production have called her "Xena Junior." Lucy Lawless went further still in praising Leick: "Well, I think we got something better than that. We got a much stronger foe because she was different and weirder and very strong." Asked whether Leick would continue to bedevil Xena as Callisto, Lawless said, "Well I certainly hope so. When you get a great foe, you don't want to lose them! She will always be welcome here with us."

• KEVIN SMITH—ARES •

Kevin Smith, who plays the god of war Ares, explained that the danger his character poses to *Xena* has as much to do with love as it does with war:

Every episode with these two, no matter what form it takes, is about a seduction. He's seducing her with the spoils of war. And there's always a certain sexual tension between them. He's the serpent, man.

Smith came to acting after spending several years as a musician and athlete. During his early twenties he was a guitarist and singer in a punk rock band that cut three albums and enjoyed a cult following on New Zealand's South Island. He also played rugby until, in 1987, he suffered his third concussion and feared he was becoming "punchy." While he was sidelined, Smith's wife alerted him to an ad for an actor to star in a touring production of *Are You Lonesome Tonight?: The Elvis Presley Story.* Armed with years of experience "doing Elvis impersonations at parties," Smith won the role. "I got a real charge out of it," he said, and although the musical closed in six weeks, it set him on a career in acting.

After spending several years with a theater company in Christchurch and playing villains on TV, he won the role of Hercules' jealous brother Iphicles in a second-season episode of *Hercules,* "What's in a

"The Reckoning"
Ares (to Xena):
"Your destiny is to rule the world—
with me."

Name?" Soon after, he was cast as Ares, a role that presented a very different challenge:

> I liked it straightaway, because I had just played Othello here, and there are similarities between Ares and [Shakespeare's character]. They're both regal. And although Othello did some monstrous things, people were drawn to him, he was charismatic. In the same way, Ares is charismatic despite his monstrous deeds. And on some level, even for a villain, you have to care about the character.

Smith found that Ares' villainy and his godhood both offered exciting dramatic possibilities:

> You can go to town. You can really explore the dark corridors. And, of course, as a god, there are no rules. There's no need to say, "Hey, gods don't do that." You're making up the rules as well. I think Ares does not see himself as a villain, but as absolutely necessary in the larger scheme of things. He thinks, "The world can't function without me being here." He's comfortable with who he is. And he's worldly, as gods go. In the first episode with Ares ["The Reckoning," on Xena], we see Ares' bachelor pad. Man, it has a Jacuzzi! A Jacuzzi! Here's a guy who likes wine, who likes to eat, who lives the good life.

While Iphicles is insecure, Ares projects supreme self-confidence. It's a part of TV convention, Smith explained:

> Bad guys are generally played with more smiles than good guys. It's something that's reasonably stylized, like wearing a black hat in a Western that signals, "I'm the bad guy." With Ares, at least it's black leather—it gives you a clue. Ares is like other successful villains in that he's sure of his place in the universe. And his smile shows his anticipation of ultimate victory: "O.K., it's not happening now, but it's going to come. Every defeat is just a bloody nose. You're going to come back strong."
> The villain's going to lose ultimately, of course. But in some ways villains have the emotional memory of a goldfish that swims

in a bowl with a rock, thinking, "Hey, nice rock. Hey, nice rock. Hey, nice rock." And I think with a villain, too, there's an enormous ego. So they're thinking, "This time!" Otherwise, you know, there would be scenes of Ares just holed up in his pad popping Prozac all day.

Smith briefly lived in North Hollywood and has worked in Australia, but he remains attached to his native New Zealand, saying, "This is my home, my spiritual base. I've got a couple of young sons, and in terms of quality of life, New Zealand may not be the perfect place, but after having a look around the world, we feel there's a lot of places worse to bring up kids than New Zealand."

• DANIELLE CORMACK—EPHINY •

Like Ephiny, her character on *Xena: Warrior Princess*, Danielle Cormack radiates a fierce independence. That quality did not help her, though, when she first tried out for roles on *Hercules* and *Xena*. Cormack described one ill-fated audition to play a female lawyer who defends Iolaus:

Here's a woman who stood against her own father. She's got integrity, she's standing on her own two feet. So I went into the audition with a sense of this character, the emotional price she's paid, her mannerisms, her determination to do good. And their response was "Could you be more vulnerable?"

The part went to another actress, who played the character as good-hearted but ditzy.

The refrain at the next few casting sessions grew familiar: "That was fine, Danielle, but could you play it more vulnerable?" Cormack was not amused: "I get sick of it because I'm quite passionate about playing what I believe is the heart of these characters. Let's give them some [conviction]." Encouraged by New Zealand casting director

Diana Rowan, Cormack trooped back to read for yet another part, thinking, "Hey, that's cool, as long as I don't have to be more vulnerable!" Cormack was not disappointed, nor were the producers: the character she read for was an Amazon warrior who was independent, strong, and fiery. Short of printing Cormack's name in the script, the writers had in effect custom-tailored for her the role of Ephiny.

Cormack was then twenty-four but already a veteran TV actress. She recalled how her career began simply as a childhood hobby:

> "To show sympathy for the Horde," Kaltaka was only served upon request during the production of this motion picture."
> —Disclaimer from "The Price"

> I used to do drama on Saturdays with a group of students from nine to fifteen years old. Lucy [Lawless] was there, she must have been about fourteen. And I went on to do youth theater. . . . We performed The Comedy of Errors, which made the news because we were the youngest Shakespearian troupe in New Zealand. Our production was put on television. And a casting agent saw me playing one of the lead roles, Adriana, and phoned to ask if I'd like to do television work.

At fifteen Cormack began a three-year stint in a stylish hour-long drama called Glos, at first working just six months a year while finishing school. She then moved to Paris and later to England, purposefully leaving her career behind for years. But on returning to New Zealand she landed a role in the TV series Shortland Street (after a street in Auckland) playing "a nice country girl":

> She was a nurse who had failed relationship after failed relationship. Miffed at the altar. The abortion scenario, the this, the that, the thus. You know, the typical sublime whore. The public loved her.

Shortland Street became a national phenomenon, and Cormack, as one of the fifteen original cast members, became a celebrity. "I'd walk down the street and hear, 'There's Allison!' " She responded by quitting after a year, a move that puzzled many but one she looked back on with satisfaction:

It was a good, solid paycheck every week, but I'm not here because of the money. And I think staying on a soap for several years is not healthy for an acting career in such a small community as New Zealand. The more they see you on that box, the more they're going to affiliate you with that one character. And after a year of working every single day, eight or nine scenes a day, five days a week, I pretty much got to do my emotional range within the character I was given.

Cormack has had a rich character to mine in Ephiny, who first appears in "Hooves & Harlots" as a quick-tempered warrior suspicious of Xena and contemptuous of Gabrielle. By episode's end, Ephiny has become Xena's staunch ally and Gabrielle's teacher and friend. Throughout the episode Cormack stands out even in background shots, her eyes flashing anger or intense resolve. Cormack recalled that the director encouraged her approach, though at times, she said, "I became so engrossed in everything on set that I forgot about the cameras and just kept looking around, taking it all in!"

Cormack is one of the few New Zealand guest stars on *Xena* who did not affect an American accent for her role. She described this as a conscious choice, though after seeing herself on TV it suddenly hit her, "Oh, the accent!":

I haven't had an opportunity to live in America or spend much time around America. And so therefore my ear for it isn't exactly perfect. So I figured I would much rather watch a performance in which I totally am [attuned to] that person, emotionally and in every other way, than watch someone who's just robotically speaking perfect American. . . . No, actually no one on set said anything to me about it.

Cormack has sought out and occasionally written unconventional acting projects. She starred in a movie shown at Cannes, *Topless Women Sit Around Talking About Their Lives,* which originated as a series of five-minute TV episodes. "They call it the micro-soap, for people with short attention spans," she said. "It's a whole new concept for New Zealand television." Despite the teasing title (the name of a film one of the characters is writing), *Topless Women* is a "slice of New Zealand life that reveals class differences and what young people are up to."

Though on *Xena* she projects the stature and bearing of an Amazon warrior, in person Cormack is diminutive and bubbles with energy, enthusiasm, and laughter. Her most serious insights are punctuated with quips and giggles that would startle Ephiny. But then the eyes flash that familiar intensity and resolve, and one sees why Ephiny looms as so large a presence on-screen.

• BRUCE CAMPBELL—AUTOLYCUS •

Bruce Campbell, who plays Autolycus, the self-styled "king of thieves," was born on June 22, 1958, in Royal Oak, Michigan. He grew up in Birmingham, a suburb of Detroit, and recalled taking an early interest in acting:

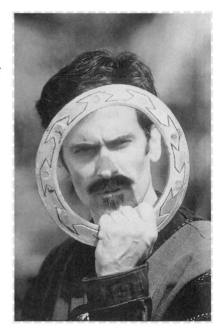

> *At age eight, I watched my father perform in a production of* The Pajama Game. *Realizing that adults could also participate in this form of make-believe left a lasting impression on young me.*

In a high school drama class in 1975, Campbell met Sam Raimi and assisted Raimi's magic act at bar mitzvahs and other off-Broadway productions. He described Raimi as a "kindred spirit" who shared his interests in acting and amateur filmmaking. "Throughout high school," he said, "we wrote, produced, directed, and acted in about fifty Super-8mm movies, developing the primitive skills that would help us in the future."

Disappointed by his film classes in college, which he said "failed to compare with my recent hands-on experience," Campbell dropped out and tried to break into TV and movies. During this period he met Rob Tapert, who was rooming with Sam Raimi's brother Ivan at Michigan State University. Tapert and Sam Raimi soon joined Campbell as ex-college students and in 1979 raised money for their own low-budget film, *The Evil Dead.* Like his two partners, Campbell shouldered many aspects of the production:

> *We all really had to "wear a lot of hats" on that film because our crew kept getting smaller and smaller. We wanted to finish the film and were willing to do anything in order to do it. I did my own "foley" footsteps for the film. I was the music editor, and Sam and I recorded a lot of the sound effects for the film.*

The Evil Dead was released in 1983, with Campbell as star and co-executive producer. Over the next decade, he appeared in two sequels, plus a string of genre films like *Maniac Cop* and *Sundown: A Vampire in Retreat* and the offbeat comedy *The Hudsucker Proxy.* Campbell added to his cult following by starring in *The Adventures of Brisco County, Jr.* (1993–94), a sly Western series on Fox television, and doing guest turns as the evil billionaire Bill Church on ABC's *Lois and Clark: The New Adventures of Superman.*

Married with one son and one daughter, Campbell works on a variety of film and television projects as an actor and director. He has continued his creative partnership with Raimi and Tapert, directing a first-season episode of *Hercules: The Legendary Journeys* ("The Vanishing Dead"), then appearing at the start of the second season as the thief and all-around mischief-maker, Autolycus. Campbell has since made several memorable appearances as Autolycus on *Xena,* and he even played the role of the Warrior Princess when Xena possessed his character's body in the episode "The Quest," during Lucy Lawless' hospitalization in October 1996.

Asked if the role of Autolycus was created with him in mind, Campbell first replied deadpan, "The truth is, all roles are created for me. I just don't have the time to do them all." Then, more seriously: "The role wasn't created for me. But Rob Tapert thought I would be right for it. Originally, I saw 'Auto' as an Errol Flynn type. The hammier the better."

As the broadly comic, grasping but ultimately good-hearted Autolycus, Campbell has won fans on *Hercules* and *Xena* alike, leaving

"Royal Couple of Thieves"
Autolycus: "Go on, Xena, I'll hold them off." Xena: "Are you kidding me?"
Autolycus: "I think I'm kidding myself. Go! Help those people!"

little doubt that the "king of thieves" will continue to create havoc on both shows in seasons to come.

• ERIK THOMSON—HADES •

Although the Greek myths portrayed Hades, the god of the dead, as a gloomy, somber presence, the writers on *Hercules* had in mind a more complex and spirited character. Diana Rowan, the New Zealand casting director, told the producers about Erik Thomson: "It is a case of whether you can grab him between his stints in the theater. But we ought to hook this guy ahead of time because you'll really like him." Thomson won the role, and he has become a staple player in the pantheon of Greek gods featured on both *Hercules* and *Xena*.

Thomson's journey to the Underworld began in the Scottish Highlands, where he was born in 1967. He immigrated to New Zealand at age seven and later gained admission to the country's sole national drama school, in Wellington. Graduating in 1990, he has worked widely on stage and on TV. New Zealanders also began to associate him with Lucy Lawless because of six commercials they filmed for the Auckland National Savings Bank, playing a married couple with a young child called Stanley. "Whenever I see her or read about her playing a role on Broadway," said Thomson, "I shake my head in disbelief. It's fantastic what she's accomplished!"

Thomson's career, too, was fast ascending, even though by way of the Underworld. After appearing in an early episode of *Hercules,* he won the role of Hades in 1995 during the series' second season. Hades was written as a spirited, wry, but overworked god, never having "enough staff" to classify all the dead, especially during rush periods like wars. Thomson credits George Mendeluk, who directed his first episode as Hades, "The Other Side," with setting the tone of

"No Fathers, Spiritual or Biological, were harmed during the production of this motion picture."
—Disclaimer from "Ties That Bind"

the character, along with the writers. "Mendeluk has a fairly Jewish sense of humor, for lack of a better way to explain it, and he evoked something of that quality from me."

At times Hades has appeared unable to cope despite his great powers, instead calling on Xena to set things right in the Underworld. In "Mortal Beloved," which Thomson shot after flying in from Australia for a long weekend, Hades sinks into depression after a mortal steals his Helmet of Invisibility. "I felt like Greta Garbo," Thomson said. "You know, 'I want to be alone.' And that was nice to play that side of it. A disempowered god. Just because it brought out an unusual side of the character."

Thomson's appearances as Hades became rarer after he went to Australia in 1996 for a featured role on another series, *Pacific Drive,* set on Australia's Gold Coast. "It's like *Melrose Place*," Thomson said, "not necessarily in quality but in the sense of being a popular show aimed at an adult audience for late-night viewing around the world." For Thomson the series was redeemed by the setting: "I'm a surfer and I was living for twenty months on the Gold Coast, which is a surfer's paradise. That was one of the reasons I took the job." Since then Thomson has returned to New Zealand and looks forward to supervising the Underworld more frequently.

Although Thomson has delighted in playing Hades, he recalled his astonishment on discovering the show's far-flung celebrity—and his own:

> *Bobby Hosea, who plays [Xena's lover] Marcus, told me he was in downtown L.A. to make a payment on his car, and the woman there said, "What are you doing on* Xena?*" And he told her, "I'm going down to the Underworld." She got excited at this and said, "Oh, if you see Hades, tell him I think he's gorgeous. Could you get a photograph with him?" And then I received a couple of fan letters from America. It's nice, but very strange!*

REPERTORY ACTORS

Like *Hercules, Xena* relies on New Zealand's superb but small acting community and frequently recycles actors in different guises. Here are just a few of the many talented members of the informal repertory company that populates these mythic landscapes.

• WILLA O'NEILL—LILA •

Twenty-four-year-old Willa O'Neill has recurring roles as Gabrielle's sheltered sister Lila on *Xena* and as the spitfire daughter of an Argonaut, Phoebe, on *Hercules*. According to O'Neill, the role of Lila was a natural fit:

> *I'm very good at playing young girls. For a long time I played girls with attitude. Which was O.K. And then I went through a phase of being a girl who has a lot of problems, like having a baby. But in the audition to play Lila, I really just had to stand there looking innocent and speaking in an American accent. That's fine, I like speaking that Californian American!*

Rob Tapert saw O'Neill playing Lila and had the role of Phoebe created for her. "I was really proud to receive that role," O'Neill said. "And it was perfect for me because I'm a bit of a guy's girl, and I'm in there fighting with the guys and still get to look pretty!"

An actress since age eight, O'Neill broke into theater by producing her own shows as a teenager. Several years ago she co-founded the Watershed Theatre, which stages offbeat plays in a basement in downtown Auckland. O'Neill found the first year an adventure in acting—and scavenging:

> *My partners and I got everybody's rubbish, basically. We said, "Hey, what are you throwing out? We're opening a theater. And so people threw all their rubbish our way and we managed to make a stage. In fact, a lot of the money that I've earned on Her-cules and* Xena *has gone into funding this theater space, which is O.K. by me because it's forwarding something I truly believe in. I just fell in love with the whole idea of the fringe arts in Auck-land surviving and having this home.*

O'Neill has performed dance and stand-up comedy, won the Kiwi equivalent of an Emmy (the Gofta) for best actress, and served for years on the executive board of New Zealand Actors Equity. "She's so energetic!" exclaimed Michael Hurst, the hyperkinetic actor who plays Hercules' friend Iolaus. What hasn't O'Neill done? "I still aspire to work internationally on feature films," she said. "Oh, and to sing in a jazz band."

• CHRIS GRAHAM—TOXEUS •

Chris Graham has made several villainous appearances on Xena. In the first season alone, as the vicious Toxeus he was killed (twice) in "Death in Chains" but made further mischief in the Underworld in "Mortal Beloved." A proud Maori, Graham lives at the top of a hill overlooking two hundred acres by a lake nearly three hours from Auckland. He is untroubled by the lack of modern conveniences like electricity, saying, "The land is beautiful and primitive. It's my little bit of paradise."

The attraction to *Xena,* he said, is the mythology. "I find that Greek history and myth are not unlike our Maori traditions. If you want me to play a role, I can think of people from my own people's history and stories." Could the flamboyant Toxeus ever return to *Xena* despite being decapitated in "Mortal Beloved"? "Well, since it's set in a mythical world," Graham said brightly, "nothing is certain. I could get my head back on. Look, I can do my own sewing, I'm a nineties kind of guy."

• EDDIE CAMPBELL—CRIAS •

Often in the background of *Hercules* (he urges Hercules to stop Xena in "The Warrior Princess"), Edward "Eddie" Campbell strides larger than life on *Xena* in "The Titans." Born in Edinburgh, Scotland, in 1949, Campbell discovered acting in the Marines when his outfit started an amateur dramatic society on Malta. For most of his career he has played "thugs, cops, generally people with a nasty edge." Even as a recurring "good" character on *Hercules,* the Argonaut Artemis, he spends much of his screen time seething about his old commander, Jason. Campbell had auditioned to play a murderous thief on *Xena* but was cast instead as the kindly Titan Crias, and delivered a poignant performance. "I was quite pleasantly surprised to be a nice guy," he said.

• GALYN GORG—HELEN •

When Galyn Gorg, an American actress who has also appeared on *Hercules,* auditioned to play "a sort of angel of death" on *Xena,* the casting director, Beth Hymson-Ayer, told her, "We're going to save you to play Helen of Troy," the world's most beautiful woman. Gorg's distinctive look matches her family background. "My mom's African-American, Choctaw, and Irish, and my dad's German," she said. During the eighties, Gorg danced on TV specials and in videos such as ZZ Top's smash hit, "Sharp Dressed Man." She later did comic turns on *Living Single* and *Fresh Prince of Bel-Air* and co-starred as a police lieutenant on *M.A.N.T.I.S.* (1994–95). But Gorg has found girl-next-door roles elusive, instead playing "a lot of prostitutes, a lot of bad girls." She has also appeared on *Star Trek: Deep Space Nine, Star Trek: Voyager,* and other "fantasy-oriented, sci-fi projects." Fortunately, Gorg said, "I love that sort of stuff!"

4

FROM SHEENA
TO XENA:

HEROINES OF THE SMALL SCREEN

In basing a weekly series on a female character who is deadly, volatile, and deeply flawed, Rob Tapert was pressing beyond the edge of American television programming. Compared with the vast men's club of TV sheriffs, detectives, and others who thrived on gunplay, fistfights, and similar pastimes, TV heroines before Xena formed a small sorority, whose weapons of choice were largely erotic, and barely concealed. Whether as jungle goddess, secret agent, or beautiful policewoman, the typical female action hero was no Mike Hammer in drag, but rather a blonde siren in uniform. She dispensed justice as surely as any man, but with greater delicacy and a keener fashion sense. The ratings successes of varied TV heroines made a show like *Xena* possible, yet few of these earlier women would have known quite what to make of Xena's toughness and independence, let alone her savage spirit.

The syndicated series *Sheena, Queen of the Jungle* provided television with its first memorable heroine, and, as befitted America in 1955, its most innocent. A gentle soul at one with nature, Sheena literally stood poised to swing into action on the nearest jungle vine. Originally a comic book icon, as portrayed by the Nebraska-born model Irish McCalla, Sheena commanded the jungle heights even on level ground, her five-foot-ten-inch frame projecting strength as well as beauty. Sheena's concerns were standard law-and-order fare, but transplanted to an exotic clime: saving simple villagers, simpler animals, and primeval lands from thieves, schemers, and the occasional witch doctor. Through 26 half-hour adventures, Sheena remained sweetly unaffected by brushes with menacing tribesmen, flights from

"Xena's body was not harmed during the production of this motion picture. However, it took weeks for Autolycus to get his swagger back." —Disclaimer from "The Quest"

elephant stampedes, and plunges into croc-infested rivers.

Although set in remotest Africa (portrayed, for budgetary reasons, by nearest Mexico), *Sheena* grounded its young heroine, in every sense, with the values of 1950s America. This dream woman was queen of her domain, but ruled no one. Though unmarried (also unkissed) and escorted only by the impeccably behaved and unaccountably pure-minded trader Bob, Sheena still lived a life of domestic bliss, cheerfully ministering to an only child, the playful chimpanzee Chim. A dutiful housekeeper on a grand scale, Sheena each week guarded her wholesome jungle abode against meddling outsiders.

While wrongdoers surfaced in every episode, no larger social issues troubled Sheena's world—a world wholly congenial to 1950s middle America. Black African tribesmen gladly deferred to the white jungle "queen" unless temporarily blinded by superstition or foolish traditions. By the end of every episode, even the most suspicious blacks had accepted Sheena as their wisest teacher and noblest friend.

Production values in *Sheena* were, if possible, even less in evidence than social realism. The Nassour brothers, who esteemed *Sheena* mainly as a tax write-off, spared no cost-cutting device in their search for television's smallest budget. All episodes but for a long-lost color pilot were filmed in black and white, Mexican extras were pressed into service as African tribesmen, and African animals appeared only by way of stock footage. Stunt doubling was rare, and McCalla, blessed with athletic ability and in any case too distinctive to double easily, did most of her own action scenes. This included hurtling through the air on vines until one day, weakened by a bout of dysentery, she lost her grip, crashed into a tree, and broke her arm. Thereafter a Mexican male circus acrobat in a blond wig and padded leotard passed as Sheena for airborne scenes.

Sheena scored well in viewer ratings, but the jungle queen could not overcome her greatest adversary, the Nassour brothers, who for reasons unknown ended production after the first year. McCalla went on to cinematic scorn for her portrayal of a spoiled young lady saved from an island of horrors in the cult film *She Demons* (1958). From there she moved directly to oblivion, unable to land more than a handful of roles before giving up acting altogether for her first love, painting. But by the 1970s McCalla surprised many by reemerging as an artist of Western vistas, then garnered new celebrity during the 1980s amid a wave of nostalgia for her role as Sheena.

Sheena would not likely impress modern audiences either as drama or as spectacle. Still, McCalla's fresh, earnest appeal, beauty, athleticism, and stature still seem just right for a role that combined innocence and assertion, purity and power. A fantasy figure for television's first generation of male (and many female) viewers, Sheena set the standard for a succession of superwomen, often garbed in modern attire but still kindred spirits to that pioneering jungle adventuress.

Over the next decades, American TV heroines kept pace with the sexual revolution but lagged well behind feminist dreams of an independent, assertive woman at least as skilled in self-defense as in seduction. Anne Francis stood out as a private eye on ABC's *Honey West* (1965–66), but the show failed after a season. NBC's *Police Woman* (1974–78) traded toughness for top ratings, as star Angie Dickinson spent much of her time dressed to kill. Though Dickinson's character, Sergeant Pepper Anderson, was courageous, she was also exceedingly vulnerable. As feminists everywhere gaped in dismay, Dickinson set a record for a series lead that may never be equaled, requiring rescue on more than forty separate occasions by a supporting character, her male partner and sometime lover, Sergeant Bill Crowley.

As Sergeant Dee Dee McCall, "the brass cupcake," Stepfanie Kramer played a tougher, though still alluring, breed of police officer for six years on NBC's *Hunter* (1984–92). Still, it was McCall's partner, the Dirty Harry clone Sergeant Rick Hunter, who handled the lion's share of action. Kramer finally quit the series after seeing her character's modest quota of heroics simply disappear behind Hunter's macho posturing.

"No Slippery Eels were harmed during the production of this motion picture despite their reputation as a fine delicacy in select cultures of the known world."
—Disclaimer from "A Day In The Life"

Beginning in the 1970s, female detectives flourished on TV, though none would ever have been mistaken for a character out of a Raymond Chandler novel. ABC led the way with the series *Charlie's Angels* (1976–81), displaying three glamorous private investigators. The portrayal of the Angels as intelligent and resourceful gave their adventures a feminist veneer. So, too, did the Angels' openness about sexuality.

Yet neither realism nor feminism was heavy on the minds of *Charlie's Angels* producers, Aaron Spelling and Leonard Goldberg. Rather, as Goldberg explained, "our motivation was the fact that action-adventure shows were dominated by inner-city realism starring such gruff types as Columbo and Baretta. We just thought, 'Why not inject some really stunning beauty into the genre and see what happens?' " The Angels obliged, using the power of flirtation to outmaneuver and put away scores of criminals. And, much as Superman kept his distance from Kryptonite, the Angels acted as if only loose-fitting garments could rob them of their powers, while bikinis, showers, and dazzling smiles would replenish their strength.

Goldberg knew to keep ratings high by pitching low. "We love to get them wet," he explained, "because they look so good in clinging clothes." For good measure, the Angels did the bidding of a male boss who lived for lechery and never met a crude double entendre he didn't like. The series worked hard to lure female viewers, lavishing the Angels with a wealth of new fashions to the point where episodes could have been shot on a catwalk as easily as a soundstage. And the Angels, for all their flirtation, somehow kept a fresh, innocent aura: men could melt but not touch.

Equally mild fantasies of powerful women occasionally made their way to series TV, after being trimmed of feminist edges that might be deemed too provocative. *The Bionic Woman* (1976–78), on ABC and then NBC, showed that a woman could have powers beyond those of almost any man—provided, of course, she first nearly died of injuries and was subsequently refitted with bionic legs, a bionic right arm, and a bionic right ear. Even so, the show's creator, Ken Johnson, said that

he modeled the bionic woman, Jaime Sommers, not after an action hero but rather his notion of an ideal date, someone "truthful, witty, and eminently attractive." And series star Lindsay Wagner took pride in conveying the softer, fragile side of Jaime Sommers, insisting, "I'm trying like hell not to be Wonder Woman."

Wagner's bionic swipe at Wonder Woman (1976–79) referred to a contemporary series on ABC and then CBS that marked the summit of heroic womanhood as portrayed by American TV. Wonder Woman, the daughter of an Amazon queen, was a comic book character of World War II vintage who left her idyllic life on Paradise Island to help battle the forces of evil. A patriotic fantasy figure in a time when women were serving on the home front as riveters, mechanics, and in other jobs long reserved for men, Wonder Woman could change instantly from her guise as a secretary into her red, white, and blue outfit, complete with wristbands to deflect bullets and a lariat to make even Nazi enemies tell the truth. Wonder Woman proved equally capable of quick changes on TV, in more ways than one.

Cathy Lee Crosby first played the Amazon princess in a two-hour pilot episode, in 1974. Though once a first-class athlete, the blond, beautiful Crosby was called on mainly to project poise in dangerous situations and allure toward dangerous masterminds. Even a climactic fight with staffs against a renegade sister was so delicate as to cast doubt on Wonder Woman's Amazon pedigree.

When ABC enlisted Wonder Woman two years later for weekly service against the Nazis, Lynda Carter took over the title role. Tall, dark-haired, with ballet training that helped her kick and otherwise punish assorted villains, Carter gave Wonder Woman a bit of brawn to go with her beauty. By 1977, when CBS picked up the series, Wonder Woman had become a modern-day crime fighter on a global scale, the hero of last resort against nuclear and other high-tech conspira-

cies. Both networks kept Wonder Woman safely in the realm of fantasy: no personal issues, let alone growth, diverted her (or viewers) from action-packed exploits. And chauvinists could take comfort in the fact that whenever Wonder Woman was not busy saving the world, she appeared content to work under cover as a sexy secretary to a male boss in her government agency.

Throughout the pre-Xena decades of American TV, the most thoroughly liberated and, when need be, lethal heroine was not American at all. The stylish cloak-and-dagger series *The Avengers* (1966–69), first produced for the British Broadcasting Corporation in 1961, paired Patrick Macnee, as the dapper secret agent John Steed, with Diana Rigg as Emma Peel, a talented amateur ready for any challenge. Peel's wry wit, unflappable manner, elegant dispatch of villains with judo flips and high kicks, and unapologetic independence all set her apart from her sister heroines on American TV. So too did her brand of sex appeal (the character's very name came from the equivalent British term "M-Appeal"): although she charmed mainly through intelligence rather than seduction, her boots and leather outfit hinted at a high-voltage libido lurking beneath her droll reserve.

It said much about the confines of American television programming that no network tried to build on the popularity of *The Avengers* with new action shows featuring characters like Emma Peel, but in-

stead let her remain a unique British curiosity. Nor did the networks ever air the adventures of Steed's first and toughest female partner, Cathy Gale. Before moving to big-screen stardom in the James Bond thriller *Goldfinger*, Honor Blackman played Gale with an edge that might have taken aback even Emma Peel. Blackman's Gale-force manner surely cowed American TV executives, who sensed that the public might not be ready for a heroine who bristled at hints of male condescension (especially by her partner) and who appeared just a little too sincere in thrashing the men who crossed her. Lucy Lawless herself was conscious of following in the bootprints of Emma Peel, though acknowledging that her own temperament inclined toward British comedy of manners rather than heroic spectacle.

> "Hooves & Harlots" Gabrielle: "I wanted to read philosophy and learn history and science ... But they didn't consider me a normal girl."

Despite traces of Emma Peel and Wonder Woman in Xena's makeup, the dearth of superheroines on American TV spurred Rob Tapert to seek role models for Xena farther east, in a rich Asian movie heritage. The Asian view of martial arts as aesthetic and even spiritual may have eased the way for Chinese actresses to gain acceptability as warriors. Unlike John Wayne and other Western heroes, who punched villains as a test of manly virtue, not as an art form, Asian action stars were in every sense martial "artists." It was scarcely coincidence that many leading ladies of Asian action cinema began their careers in opera and dance.

Hong Kong's first world-famous female star, the Taiwanese native Angela Mao Ying, grew up in a theatrical family and trained in Chinese opera from age eight. With her slight frame and wide-eyed look of vulnerability, she might have been typecast by Western filmmakers as a fragile beauty in need of a muscular male protector. But as Bruce Lee's sister in *Enter the Dragon* (1973), she fends off twenty thugs with crackling kicks, then takes her own life rather than submit to superior numbers. In that single scene Mao Ying distills the unbending will, ethereal grace, and lethal power of Asian action heroines.

The first Hong Kong actress promoted as a rival to Mao Ying in Kung Fu movies, Cheng Pei Pei, further highlighted the close connection between Asian cinema and gentler performing arts. Trained in ballet before going on to star in action films, Cheng eventually retired from acting and became a ballet teacher in Los Angeles, later reemerging in the film *Painted Faces* (1988) as a Peking Opera teacher. More recently Michelle Khan became a popular heroine in Kung Fu films after training in ballet.

"A lot of the female superheroines you see in Hong Kong fantasy and action films have the same kind of steely resolve we gave Xena," Rob Tapert said. He especially admired Brigitte Lin, whose heroines provided several of Xena's screen ancestors. In sharp contrast to action stars like Angela Mao Ying and Michelle Khan, Lin had meager martial arts skill, but the use of doubles and the surreal nature of her action scenes afforded sufficient cover. Lin's characters projected a fierce will, steeped in the tradition of Angela Mao Ying but with an explicitly erotic charge that amply compensated for her limits in action scenes. "In some respects," Tapert told Craig Reed of *Sci-Fi Entertainment*, "we Westernized her character from films like *The Bride with White Hair*. A volatile dark character, yet still very feminine, you never know what she's going to do next."

During her first season in syndication Xena battled or bonded with Amazons, Centaurs, kings, warlords, Ares the god of war, Hades in the Underworld, even Hercules, who crossed over from his own series to help the Warrior Princess rescue Prometheus. And viewers responded mightily: in 24 of its first 25 weeks, *Xena* became the most popular new syndicated series, finishing ahead of *Baywatch*, and just behind *Hercules* and *Star Trek: Deep Space Nine*." In its second season, *Xena* conquered a still larger share of the TV audience, outdrawing even its older brother, *Hercules*, and becoming the top-rated action hour in syndication.

Every group of TV viewers—men and women, adults, teenagers, and children—has contributed about equally to *Xena*'s fan base, though according to Rob Tapert the core followers are women and men ages eighteen to thirty-four. "*Hercules* has a much bigger audience among girls and boys ages four to six, the toy-buying demographic," Tapert told *Ms.* magazine. "*Xena*'s audience is older and probably a little hipper."

Critics agreed that Xena herself was a little hipper than other superheroes. Tributes appeared in such diverse pillars of Americana as *TV Guide, Entertainment Weekly* (which marveled at a spin-off series "so shrewdly done"), even the militantly hip *Village Voice* ("We don't need another hero, except for Xena"). Among many other dailies, the *Orange County Register*, in a feature by Kinney Littlefield on February 26, 1996, took respectful note that a pop culture phenomenon was picking up locomotive power:

> *As played by New Zealander Lucy Lawless, she's a strapping mythical she-ro with belligerent Shannen Doherty bangs, icy blue eyes and an icepick-sharp comedic sense. Her smarts are as big as her bulging biceps. . . . [Once a] good girl gone way bad, she bopped heads and slugged guts and did ninja moves and threw her chakram . . . and performed the "Xena touch" . . . like, well—like one of the guys. Yeah, you go, girl. . . . [Xena's] "archly off-the-cuff humor . . . makes her more witty, hip and humane than Lynda Carter's Wonder Woman" could ever claim to be.*

Even the staid *New York Times* warily circled *Xena* in a cover story for its Sunday TV magazine, acknowledging the show's clever mix of pop culture ingredients.

The favorable ratings and reviews only partly register *Xena's* impact. *Xena* and *Hercules* comics and novels sell briskly, and imposing Xena dolls (with removable sword and armor) have joined Hercules and Iolaus action figures in stores, where they prove irresistible to kids aged ten, fifteen, thirty, and up. Sarah Dyer, editor of "Action Girl" comic magazines and a collector of action figures, liked the way Xena, on TV and in toy stores, mixed femininity and fury. Getting down to the basics, Dyer explained: "She has cool-looking hair, but she kills people."

"Prometheus"
Gabrielle: "So do
you think Iolaus is
still in love with
you?" Xena: "His
love turned to hate
for a while. I'm not
sure how he feels
about me now."
Gabrielle: "What
about Hercules?"
Xena: "What about
him?" Gabrielle:
"You're not much for
girl talk, are you? Of
course, you're not
like most girls."

Xena rules in cyberspace, too, with scores of web sites springing up to explore every nuance of her adventures. Universal's official Internet forum for *Xena* early outstripped the bustling site for *Hercules* in total messages despite ceding the son of Zeus a year's head start. Early in the show's second season a web search revealed more than 7,200 entries for *Xena: Warrior Princess*. Among them are a number of wide-ranging and insightful forums where a sword is never just a sword, and impassioned articles leave no chakram unturned in the search for new layers of meaning.

Why *Xena* commands this extra measure of fan loyalty may have as many reasons as viewers, but it surely helps that no other series has ever fully served up this pungent formula of a dark heroine in a bright landscape, intense drama leavened by wild action and wry humor, and ancient settings for a modern-day friendship between two strong women. That distinctive brew has helped *Xena* join a parade of TV cult hits whose sole common trait was a uniquely memorable style: the Kennedyesque adventures of *Star Trek* in the sixties; the intricate plotting and technical wizardry of *Mission Impossible* through the seventies; the pulsing Caribbean rhythms and eye-catching flamingos, females, and other Floridian wonders of *Miami Vice* in the eighties. And, of course, the astoundingly successful intermarriage between ancient Greece and nineties California of *Hercules: The Legendary Journeys*.

Xena especially inspires women who had looked largely in vain for strong female role models on TV or elsewhere in American culture. "The fastest-growing audience who are now taking control of the remote are women," Lucy Lawless observed. "This show has caught a wave." In July 1996 *Ms.* magazine featured the sword-wielding, grinning Warrior Princess on its cover and lauded the series, in a profile by Donna Minkowitz ("Xena: She's Big, Tall, Strong and Popular"), for pioneering a new image of women:

Many feminists have been dreaming of mass-culture moments like this since feminism came into being. But we've almost never seen these fantasies realized. The Bionic Woman smiled too much. Even Cagney and Lacey worried about looking "overmasculine." No woman television character has exhibited the confidence and strength of the male heroes. . . . Until now.

The packed houses on the monthly "*Xena* night" at Meow Mix, a predominantly lesbian bar in New York City, attest to another source of fan fervor. Ever since Gabrielle's confession to Xena at the start of their travels together, "I'm not the little girl my parents wanted me to be," their friendship has generated speculation about a romantic "subtext." The producers have smiled at such perceptions, which at first greatly surprised them. But they have left the final word to each viewer, and certainly *Xena*'s portrayal of a deeply caring relationship between two women contributes greatly to the show's widespread appeal.

Xena's female fan club also counts many members who have yet to read their first issue of *Ms.* or even hear (or spell) the word "feminist." "I'm thrilled," Lucy Lawless told Donna Minkowitz of the hundreds of fan letters she has received from very young girls. "They write about how encouraging it is to see someone who's so strong. . . . I have all these photos of little girls with Xena costumes on." Rob Tapert added that Lawless had gotten a letter from a pair of five- and six-year-old sisters who refused to use their proper names. "They just wanted to be called Xena."

The outpouring of gratitude and affection from *Xena*'s female viewers was particularly satisfying to producer Liz Friedman. As a child Friedman had watched *Wonder Woman* on TV and winced at the daintiness that crept into the star's fight scenes, as if "she were afraid she might break a nail." Not so Xena, who "doesn't act in any ways associated with mass-cultural expectations of women." Friedman cited

a rule for the series: "Don't write Xena any differently than if she were a man." This extended to the friendship between Xena and Gabrielle, which is "based on love and compassion, unmodified by talk of boyfriends, lipstick, and other subjects that female conversations are supposed to feature."

Xena, of course, has her faults, and not simply the common foibles of typical TV heroes, for whom a failed relationship, a cigarette habit, or a weight problem might be enough to stamp them as vulnerable or quirky. Xena's flaws are on a whole other plane, from her past misdeeds as a plundering warlord to her ongoing struggle to rein in her rage. Perhaps this, above all, gives Xena her intensity and her equally intense fan loyalty.

Xena's very imperfections, setting her apart from the godlike, unshakably upright Hercules (and from the mass of TV heroes for over four decades), invite viewers to relate to her stumblings and her strivings. "I love playing Xena because she is not little Miss Perfect, not solely good," Lucy Lawless said. Indeed,

> "Ties That Bind"
> Xena: "Gabrielle, I want you to understand something. We both have families we were born into. But sometimes families change and we have to build our own. For me, friendship binds us closer than blood ever could."

goodness does not come easily to Xena, who in each episode must rise above her own savage nature before she can save others. Liz Friedman aptly summed up the difference between the two mythic adventurers, and the enduring appeal of each: "Hercules is the hero we hope is out there. Xena is the hero we hope is inside us."

5

XENA'S ADVENTURES:

EPISODE GUIDE

- -

THE FIRST SEASON

• 1. SINS OF THE PAST •

On a journey back to her native village of Amphipolis, Xena defeats soldiers and a Cyclops but cannot shake a spirited runaway named Gabrielle, who idolizes the Warrior Princess for her strength, courage, and independence. Xena's homecoming turns bitter when even her mother reviles her bloody past, echoing a warning by the warlord Draco, "There's no rest for the wicked!" But when Draco attacks Amphipolis, Xena risks her life to defeat him in single combat, regaining her mother's trust before riding on to make a fresh start with her new friend, Gabrielle.

> ### SINS OF THE PAST
>
> Writer: R. J. Stewart
> Story: Robert Tapert
> Director: Doug Lefler
> Original Air Date: Sept. 4, 1995
>
> #### • GUEST CAST •
>
> | | |
> |---|---|
> | Draco | Jay Laga'aia |
> | Cyrene | Darien Takle |
> | Hector | Stephen Hall |
> | Hecuba | Linda Jones |
> | Lila | Willa O'Neill |
> | Herodotus | Geoff Snell |
> | Perdicas | Anton Bentley |
> | Gar | David Perrett |
> | Cyclops | Patrick Wilson |
> | Old Man | Wally Green |
> | Kastor | Roydon Muir |
> | First Citizen | Huntly Eliott |
> | Boy | Winston Harris |

Highlights:

This is the ur-*Xena,* and it's a winner. Xena's hard-edged stoic manner, tinged with irony; her martial arts and acrobatic skills; her prowess with the chakram and use of pressure points; her struggle to atone for her past; and her budding friendship with Gabrielle are all effectively established. It is clear, too, that

Gabrielle will be more than a standard-issue humorous sidekick; she is instead a resourceful young woman whose love of stories, people, and life will inspire a Warrior Princess seeking to rediscover her humanity.

Casting Coup:

Jay Laga'aia as Draco creates a formidable antagonist.

Lucy's Take:

"We didn't really know what the show was and so we were all thinking on our feet. I had been a little overexcited and not quite centered enough heading into this episode. But the night before the first day of shooting I had terrible diarrhea, and it took everything out of me, which was exactly what was needed for going into the series. So I might have been a lot more hyped, a lot less natural had I not had that inauspicious beginning!

"Jay Laga'aia, who played Draco, is a really high-energy chap who never stops talking and doing acts and funny voices and dances. And if he weren't such an innately nice man, you would just hate this guy, but in fact he's such a good person that, astoundingly, you cannot dislike him. . . . Yeah, we all love him, we'd have him back in a heartbeat."

CHARIOTS OF WAR

Writers: Adam Armus & Nora Kay Foster
Story: Josh Becker & Jack Perez
Director: Harley Cokeliss
Original Air Date: Sept. 11, 1995

• GUEST CAST •

Darius	Nick Kokotakis
Cycnus	Jeff Thomas
Sphaerus	Stuart Turner
Argolis	Morgan Palmer
Hubbard	
Lykus	Patrick Morrison
Sarita	Ruth Morrison
Ugly Ruffian	Robert Harte
Tynus	Nigel Godfrey

• 2. CHARIOTS OF WAR •

Opposites attract when Xena, wounded while rescuing settlers from a marauding army, recovers at the home of a pacifist named Darius. Xena vainly urges Darius to fight for his homestead against the warlord Cycnus, but she is drawn to his quiet moral strength and to the warm life he has made with his three children. Darius implores her to stay and share that life, even after she kills Cycnus in battle. "I have never thought about having any of these things until now," she tells Darius but rides on, comforted by the knowledge that his family will be safe.

Highlights:

Fans still cringe at the memory of Xena directing Darius to push an arrow out through her back. Great acting by Lucy Lawless makes it easy to overlook that the gore is entirely off-screen. . . . The climactic chariot battle between Xena and Cycnus recalls the film classic *Ben-Hur.*

Lucy's Take:

"The cold! It wasn't actually the coldest day of the year, but it was the coldest *shoot,* because we were on water, we were getting water blown up into our faces, the wind as we charged through it on these real chariots was just horrendous. And I just remember huddling down in my coat—because we didn't have these big Michigan goose-downs at the time—and saying, 'This too shall pass, this too shall pass.' "

On the arrow-removal scene: "People may guess that I was remembering childbirth, and the *not* submitting to the pain because there's no other choice than to get through this. You know, these things have *got* to be done. So I just drew on that experience for that scene."

• 3. DREAMWORKER •

Xena must make her way through a maze of apparitions formed by the god of dreams, Morpheus, whose minions have kidnapped Gabrielle. At the end of this deadly dreamscape Xena finds her greatest foe: her intimidating and lethal evil half, created from her own thoughts, feelings, and nightmares. Xena finds that while she cannot kill her darker self—for that, too, is the "real" Xena—she can master it through sheer will.

DREAMWORKER

Writer: Steven L. Sears
Director: Bruce Seth Green
Original Air Date: Sept. 18, 1995

• GUEST CAST •

Manus	Nathaniel Lees
Elkton	Desmond Kelly
Storekeeper	Sydney Jackson
Swordsmith	Colin Francis
Baruch	John Palmer
Termin	Bruce Hopkins
Gothos	Mathew Jeffs
Mesmer	Michael Daly
1st Xena Warrior	Peter Phillips
2d Xena Warrior	Grant Boucher
Mystic Warrior	Lawrence Whareau
Dolas	Patrick Smith
Doppelganger	Polly Baigent

That insight, she exclaims, is "the key": not only to defeating Morpheus but also to accepting her past and trusting in her future.

Highlights:

A brilliant script by Steve Sears gives a fresh spin to Freudian as well as Greek myths, plunging Xena into the dark recesses of her psyche.

Mythic Connections:

The god Morpheus appeared to dreamers in human shapes. His name derives from *morphē*, Greek for "form," alluding to the dream god's ability to assume any guise.

Lucy's Take:

" 'Dreamworker' was wonderful fun. It came at the nadir of my marriage breakup. I think I put on an awful lot of weight in a great hurry. And when I see that one now, I go, 'Ooh, I remember what was going on then.' It was very thrilling to play my evil double. The large dark contacts that I wore completely change the shape of your face. Funnily enough, the size of your pupil makes a huge difference, not just darker, opaque, it was the fish eyes! The only difficulty [in playing a double role] is that you have to work the scene so you know exactly how long it takes which character to speak and what your reaction will be. I *enjoy* doing those things, they're a solo challenge, and I'm a solo challenge person, so I loved it."

CRADLE OF HOPE

Writer: Terence Winter
Director: Michael Levine
Original Air Date: Sept. 25, 1995

•GUEST CAST•

Pandora	Mary Elizabeth McGlynn
Gregor	Edward Newborn
Nemos	Simon Prast
Philana	Christine Bartlett
Weasel	Tony Bishop
Old Man	Alan De Malmanche
Kastor	Lathan Gains
Innkeeper	Paul Ninifie
Street Vendor	Paul Norell
Ophelia	Kirstie O'Sullivan
Young Man	Carl Straker
Cynara	Beryl Te Wiata

• 4. CRADLE OF HOPE •

Xena and Gabrielle walk into foster-parenthood when they find a baby by a riverbank, left to escape harm after a seer warns the local king that this child will one day take the throne. A woman named Pandora looks after the child, as well as a box she says must never be opened or else the gods' most precious gift, hope, would be lost. After recapturing Pandora's box from the king's ruthless minister, Nemos, Xena discovers that the king himself is a good man tormented by the death of his wife and young son. "Think, Gregor!" she tells the king. "This child *will* take your throne, but as your *heir*, not as your conqueror." The king asks Pandora to help care for his new son, and to share his new hope. Gabrielle later upends the box but finds it was empty all along. "What should we tell [Pandora]?" she asks Xena, who replies, "Hope has been and always will be safe. It's inside every one of us."

Mythic Connections:

Pandora, the first woman, created by order of Zeus, arrived on earth with a box containing all the world's evils and also hope. Despite warnings, Pandora gave in to her curiosity and opened the box, releasing all manner of plagues. By the time she closed the box, only hope remained. "Cradle of Hope" gives a new spin to the ancient tale, in which the granddaughter and namesake of Pandora devotes her life to keeping the box sealed.

In the series' first of many biblical allusions, "Cradle of Hope" adapts the tale of the infant Moses, floated down the Nile in a basket to save him from a Pharaoh's vengeance and then adopted by an Egyptian princess.

Highlights:

Masquerading as an exotic dancer, Xena convinces Nemos—and viewers—that she can please him beyond measure. Later she saves the child from Nemos' guards by hurling it skyward, slaying the attackers, and catching the child.

Lucy's Take:

"That was *wonderful* fun. That was the beginning of a slapstick thing that really set me on a roll for [later comical episodes like] 'Warrior . . . Princess' and 'Warrior . . . Princess . . . Tramp.' I like the gymnastics of playing multiple characters. . . . [The director] Michael Levine did a great job without being invasive."

• 5. THE PATH NOT TAKEN •

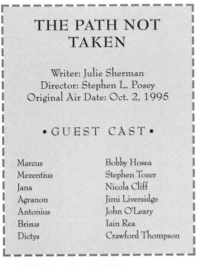

THE PATH NOT
TAKEN

Writer: Julie Sherman
Director: Stephen L. Posey
Original Air Date: Oct. 2, 1995

• GUEST CAST •

Marcus	Bobby Hosea
Mezentius	Stephen Tozer
Jana	Nicola Cliff
Agranon	Jimi Liversidge
Antonius	John O'Leary
Brisus	Iain Rea
Dictys	Crawford Thompson

The kidnapping of Princess Jana of Boeotia leads her fiancé, the prince of Colonus, to beg Xena's help in rescuing her. He suspects that the arms dealer Mezentius has arranged the kidnapping in order to spark a war between their kingdoms and supply both sides. Xena infiltrates Mezentius' band of mercenaries and reunites with her former lover, Marcus. When Marcus discovers Xena trying to free Jana, he alerts Mezentius. But when Mezentius aims an arrow at Princess Jana, Marcus rushes in front of her and is killed instead. A horrified Xena cuts down Mezentius with her chakram, then brings back Marcus' body to burn on a funeral pyre, mourning, "My friend. My friend."

Highlights:

In a deft parody of Western barroom brawls, Xena dispatches a succession of ruffians while Gabrielle, oblivious to the commotion, chats about their luck in finding a free table. . . . The torchlight funeral procession for Marcus is accompanied by a haunting dirge, sung off-camera by Lucy Lawless.

Casting Coups:

Bobby Hosea is affecting as Marcus. Stephen Tozer brings theatrical flair to the villainy of Mezentius.

Lucy's Take:

On the opening brawl: "That was the first action scene where I started to 'get it.' I guess I'd been training for a while at that stage. [Before this,] oh, I hated it, I hated it, I hated it, I used to *dread* another fight coming on. Now I quite enjoy it—it's sometimes all the exercise I get in a week [laughs], and my body is much more flexible. I move much faster from getting hit so much!"

• 6. THE RECKONING •

Ares, the god of war, frames Xena for murder in order to tempt her into using violence to save herself. He hopes to lure "his favorite disciple" to become once more the world's greatest conqueror. When prison guards whip her, Xena briefly succumbs to Ares' charm and her own rage, as she breaks her bonds and mercilessly beats her tormentors. But after striking Gabrielle in a frenzy, Xena pulls back in horror and returns to prison to await her execution. The next morning Xena finds a way to save herself without bloodshed by tricking Ares into revealing her innocence. Ares smiles at her cunning and bids her farewell, "Till next time."

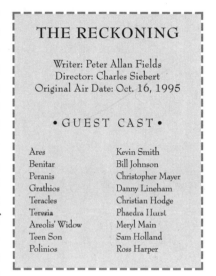

THE RECKONING

Writer: Peter Allan Fields
Director: Charles Siebert
Original Air Date: Oct. 16, 1995

• GUEST CAST •

Ares	Kevin Smith
Benitar	Bill Johnson
Peranis	Christopher Mayer
Grathios	Danny Lineham
Teracles	Christian Hodge
Teresia	Phaedra Hurst
Areolis' Widow	Meryl Main
Teen Son	Sam Holland
Polinios	Ross Harper

Mythic Connections:

Ares (called Mars by the Romans) was a blustery, headstrong braggart, but in "The Reckoning" he appears diabolical, charming, seductive—less like the Greek god of war than the Christian devil.

Highlights:

The relationship between Xena and Ares is fascinating in its complexity, revealing both antagonism and deep attraction.

Casting Coup:

Kevin Smith is menacing but also suave and charming as Ares.

Lucy's Take:

Laughing: "I was slightly afraid of what could be perceived as the S&M quotient in that episode [when Xena is bound in prison]. I have all *sorts* of nuts writing to me. Well, if you're wearing leather, you get a lot of notes, letters from lawyers and others who wanted me to—this is a quote—'walk all over me with boots,' they all think I'm some sort of dominatrix type [laughing again]. . . . But once I stopped being so jittery about that particular subject and just responded to the challenge [as an actor], I really enjoyed [that], and this show pushes the envelope in every direction."

• 7. THE TITANS •

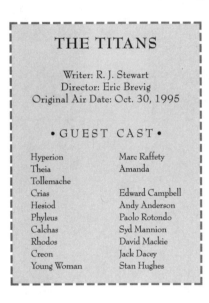

THE TITANS

Writer: R. J. Stewart
Director: Eric Brevig
Original Air Date: Oct. 30, 1995

• GUEST CAST •

Hyperion	Marc Raffety
Theia	Amanda
Tollemache	
Crias	Edward Campbell
Hesiod	Andy Anderson
Phyleus	Paolo Rotondo
Calchas	Syd Mannion
Rhodos	David Mackie
Creon	Jack Dacey
Young Woman	Stan Hughes

Be careful what you chant. Gabrielle unwittingly releases three Titans by reading from an ancient scroll. Xena cautions that the gods may have had good reason to encase these giants in stone, but Gabrielle dismisses this warning as "too cynical," until their leader, Hyperion, demands that she free hundreds of other Titans for a revolt against the gods. When Xena stands against Hyperion, he threatens to wipe out everyone in a village unless they surrender her. But after evading Hyperion's grasp, Xena traps him just long enough for Gabrielle to recite a second chant that turns the Titans back into stone.

Mythic Connections:

The Titans were a race of gods descended from Uranus (Sky) and Gaea (Earth), who ruled the world before the gods of Mount Olympus. When Zeus later overcame the oppressive Titans, he had them thrown into Tartarus, the lowest, most forbidding region of the Underworld.

Highlights:

The Titans are a towering triumph of clever camera work.

Lucy's Take:

"I met the director I liked most as a person of all of them, Eric Brevig. He had experience with special effects, so he came in to do the 'forced perspective,' [where] characters who are up close to the camera appear bigger. He was just a wonderful man, but had never directed before. And he produced an episode that didn't have enough heart in it. Also, it was the first episode *I* had ever done where it was not Xena's story [so much as Gabrielle's], and I didn't know what to do with it. I just kind of stumbled through it. It was more a *Hercules*-type structure [fighting the giants], and I was lost. So I felt crummy about that. Eric did a wonderful job with the effects. And we sort of sold it on that."

• 8. PROMETHEUS •

Xena sets out to save Prometheus, the Titan whose gifts to mankind of fire and healing are lost when he is chained to a mountain by Hera. She meets her cherished friend Hercules but refuses to turn over the Sword of Hephaestus that alone can break the chains, for she knows that whoever wields it to free Prometheus will be turned to ashes. The two heroes, accompanied by Gabrielle and Hercules' friend Iolaus, journey together until Iolaus is wounded fighting Hera's soldiers and Gabrielle stays behind to tend him. Rather than let Hercules die breaking the chains, Xena knocks him unconscious with her sword hilt. But when a giant bird carries her away, she hurls the sword down hundreds of feet to the son of Zeus in a last bid to save Prometheus. Hercules deflects it safely to break the chains and then catches Xena to complete their day's labors, as Prometheus gratefully

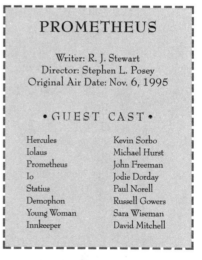

PROMETHEUS

Writer: R. J. Stewart
Director: Stephen L. Posey
Original Air Date: Nov. 6, 1995

• GUEST CAST •

Hercules	Kevin Sorbo
Iolaus	Michael Hurst
Prometheus	John Freeman
Io	Jodie Dorday
Statius	Paul Norell
Demophon	Russell Gowers
Young Woman	Sara Wiseman
Innkeeper	David Mitchell

waves, fire is restored to humans, and Iolaus regains his ability to heal himself.

Mythic Connections:

The Titan Prometheus created the human race and, in defiance of Zeus, gave it the gift of fire. Because of his disobedience he was chained to a mountain peak in the Caucasus, where every day an eagle gnawed at his liver. After many years Hercules slew the eagle with a poisoned arrow and broke the chains that bound Prometheus. In this retelling, Hercules' wicked stepmother Hera rather than his father Zeus is responsible for Prometheus' imprisonment.

Highlights:

Gabrielle recites to Iolaus a poignant fable of human yearning for love (adapted from Plato):

"Let me tell you another story. Once a long time ago all humans had four legs and two heads. Then the gods threw down thunderbolts and split everyone into two. Each half now had two legs and one head. But the separation left both halves with a desperate yearning to be reunited with each other because they still shared the same soul. And ever since then, all people spend their lives searching for the other half of their soul."

Casting Coups:

Kevin Sorbo as Hercules and Michael Hurst as Iolaus make for a star-studded episode. . . . Jodie Dorday is an oracle with talents in dance as well as prophecy.

Lucy's Take:

"Those 'egg men' [Hera's soldiers, emerging from eggshells]—oh, my God! The worst costuming ever, like something out of an Ed Wood movie. . . . Kevin [Sorbo] is great, he's always a pleasure to work with." On the challenge of playing Hercules: "If I were in his shoes I would always play the humanity rather than the god. That's intrinsically more interesting."

• 9. DEATH IN CHAINS •

The wily King Sisyphus does better than cheat death. When it arrives, in the person of the goddess Celesta, he chains his visitor and seizes her eternal flame. There are side effects: after Xena kills the bandit Toxeus, he later springs up none the worse for the sword wound through his body. Hades, god of the Underworld, explains to Xena that if the flame of his sister Celesta burns out, no one will be able to die, and eternal life—filled with suffering—will be the fate of all mankind. Xena agrees to rescue Celesta, aided by a young friend of Gabrielle named Talus, though he suffers from an incurable disease and knows that Xena's success will mean his own death. Toxeus and his band

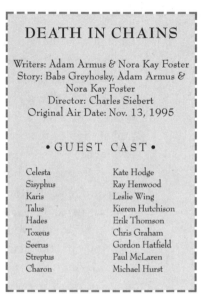

DEATH IN CHAINS

Writers: Adam Armus & Nora Kay Foster
Story: Babs Greyhosky, Adam Armus &
Nora Kay Foster
Director: Charles Siebert
Original Air Date: Nov. 13, 1995

• GUEST CAST •

Celesta	Kate Hodge
Sisyphus	Ray Henwood
Karis	Leslie Wing
Talus	Kieren Hutchison
Hades	Erik Thomson
Toxeus	Chris Graham
Seerus	Gordon Hatfield
Streptus	Paul McLaren
Charon	Michael Hurst

meanwhile celebrate their newfound immortality by hunting Xena in order to capture death for themselves. In the castle of Sisyphus, Toxeus seizes Gabrielle but Xena saves her by freeing Celesta with her chakram. As Celesta passes Toxeus with her flame, he falls dead at her feet. Then, to Gabrielle's horror, Talus follows Celesta toward a blinding light as he bids his friend farewell.

Mythic Connections:

Celesta is the writers' creation. Sisyphus, however, outwitted Thanatos (Death) when he came to take the king. Sisyphus bound him and threw him into a dungeon so that humans ceased to die. Ares, the god of war, freed Thanatos, who this time brought Sisyphus to account. But the king tricked Hades himself, escaping the Underworld and living to an old age. The gods were impressed but not pleased: after Sisyphus died, he was sent into Tartarus and compelled to roll a stone to the top of a hill for all eternity.

Highlights:

The likable Talus becomes the first in a long roll call of Gabrielle's male admirers to meet a sudden, tragic end.

Lucy's Take:

Laughing as she recounts a scene where rats fall on Xena while she crawls through a passage under the king's castle: "I thought they'd be lovely little lab rats, and I just let them dump these crates of *vermin* on me in the fiberglass sewer. I was supposed to dive hard to the bottom of the pipe, as soon as I felt them on me. But there was a long trail of slime at the bottom of the pile, so I really didn't want to, I left two inches between me and the pipe, just resting on my elbows and toes, I dropped my head, and they just kept dumping rats, and they yelled cut, cut, and these rats had all nestled on my body, nestled into my cleavage and legs, it was so disgusting! Oh, God, and they stunk, they stunk, and they just pooed everywhere. . . . It was really harrowing! Anyway, you 'dine out' on those [stories], and you laugh a lot afterward. But it was far more disturbing than I thought it would be. I don't know *what* I was thinking."

HOOVES & HARLOTS

Writer: Steven L. Sears
Director: Jace Alexander
Original Air Date: Nov. 20, 1995

• GUEST CAST •

Ephiny	Danielle Cormack
Tyldus	David Aston
Melosa	Alison Bruce
Krykus	Mark Ferguson
Terreis	Rebeka Mercer
Phantes	Colin Moy
Celano	Chris Bailey
Mesas	Antony Starr
Arben	John Watson
Magdelus	Aurora Philips
Eponin	Tanya Digan
Tor	Andrew Kovacevich

• 10. HOOVES & HARLOTS •

"To some of us you are a hero—a true Amazon," the Amazon Queen Melosa tells Xena, but it is Gabrielle who unwittingly becomes next in line to the throne after trying to save the queen's mortally wounded sister, Terreis. Gabrielle is inducted into the Amazon nation while Xena sets out to free a Centaur falsely accused of Terreis' murder. Aided by a quick-tempered but loyal Amazon named Ephiny, Xena discovers that the real murderer is the warlord Krykus, who hopes to spark a war between the Amazons and the Centaurs in order to steal both their lands. Xena saves the Centaur after defeating Melosa in a spectacular fight, earning the gratitude of an old en-

emy, the Centaur leader Tyldus. Then, at Xena's urging, Melosa and Tyldus join forces to defeat Krykus,
and replace their long hostility with the first steps toward a lasting peace.

Mythic Connections:

Both the Amazons, a nation of women warriors, and
the Centaurs, half horse and half man, appeared in Greek myth as exotic but unnatural creatures who caused havoc but were repeatedly
vanquished by heroes like Hercules. "Hooves & Harlots" gives a gentler, modern spin on the ancient legends by presenting both groups as
noble and peace-loving, once given the chance by Xena to overcome
their prejudices.

Highlights:

Another brilliant script by Steven Sears gives this episode both heart
and humor, centering on Gabrielle's immersion in Amazon rites, cus-
toms, and military training under the tutelage of Ephiny. The fight
between Xena and Melosa with "chobos," each holding two short
clubs, is a classic. So, too, is the scene of Amazons riding into battle
in chariots drawn by the Centaurs, in a triumph of special-effects
artistry. Gabrielle's use of the staff in that battle marks her emergence
as a warrior, though in her hands it is a tool for self-defense rather
than slaughter.

Casting Coup:

With her darting eyes and intense manner, Danielle Cormack makes
Ephiny a splendid foil for both Gabrielle and Xena.

Lucy's Take:

" 'Hooves & Harlots' was great fun because of Alison Bruce [who plays
Queen Melosa]. She's a good actress with a lot of charisma, and a nice
woman. . . . And we got wise to chariots in that episode, and rigged up
quite a machine. The [riding] scene is over in two minutes instead of
the eight hours we spent in the slimy old water! . . . Sometimes the

chariots were attached to trucks, but at other times you had to have the horses crossing, to give a sense of reality."

• 11. THE BLACK WOLF •

THE BLACK WOLF

Writer: Alan Jay Glueckman
Director: Mario Di Leo
Original Air Date: Jan. 8, 1996

• GUEST CAST •

Salmoneus	Robert Trebor
Xerxes	Kevin J. Wilson
Koulos	Nigel Harbrow
Flora	Emma Turner
Diomedes	Ian Hughes
Hermia	Maggie Tarver
Parnassus	Ross Duncan
Brigand	John Dybvig
Chief Guard	Jonathan Bell

Xena goes undercover to save a woman named Flora, who has fallen in love with one of a group of freedom fighters and been imprisoned with them. Assuring King Xerxes that she can discover who is the notorious rebel leader, the Black Wolf, Xena arranges to be jailed with them. Joining her soon afterward are Gabrielle (by design) and the peddler Salmoneus (by mischance), who assist Xena's plans to help the revolutionaries escape. But Xena must overcome the suspicions of Flora's lover, Diomedes, uncover a traitor in their band, and learn the identity of the Black Wolf, before she can spring her plan to free Flora and topple Xerxes.

Highlights:

When Salmoneus complains that Gabrielle is to blame for his being in prison (after she pelted a guard with fruit), she scolds him while Xena glares in disbelief, "This wouldn't have happened if you had kept your hands off my tomatoes!" Salmoneus also takes a stand for freedom, or at least free enterprise, by hawking "Black Wolf" logos and other merchandise.

Casting Coup:

Robert Trebor makes his first appearance as Salmoneus, a recurring character on *Hercules*.

Lucy's Take:

"It was a good-looking episode but hard to shoot. . . . I remember being in water [in a scene where Xerxes' minister of security, Koulos, tries to drown Xena], being in the tank, which was warm, no complaints about that. It's always such a good look, you know, being wet—plenty uncomfortable, but it looks great!"

Referring to actor Robert Trebor, known for his talent and his temperament: "Salmoneus was in this. He was really well behaved. I [had] thought, oh, crumb, here we go. But he perhaps sensed this and managed to pull his head in a bit. You know, he's got a good heart, but he can be a naughty boy."

• 12. BEWARE GREEKS BEARING GIFTS •

The Trojan War now centers on *two* women: the careworn but still beautiful Helen, struggling to break free of her husband, Paris, who cares only for glory; and her friend Xena, whom Helen urges to come to Troy. Gabrielle meanwhile finds herself drawn to a brave Trojan soldier named Perdicas, to whom she had been betrothed before leaving home for a life beyond her village. Not even Xena can save the walled city, which is fated to perish at the hands of the Greeks. But the Warrior Princess saves Helen from the traitor Deiphobus, and frees her to live with renewed purpose, as they leave the wreckage of Troy in the distance.

> ### BEWARE GREEKS BEARING GIFTS
>
> Writer: Adam Armus
> Story: Roy Thomas & Janis Hendler
> Director: T. J. Scott
> Original Air Date: Jan. 15, 1996
>
> #### • GUEST CAST •
>
> | | |
> |---|---|
> | Helen | Galyn Gorg |
> | Perdicas | Scott Garrison |
> | Deiphobus | Cameron Rhodes |
> | Paris | Warren Carl |
> | King Menelaus | Ken Blackburn |
> | Miltiades | Adrian Keeling |

Mythic Connections:

In this feminist retelling of Homer's epic tale, the drama relates not to Helen's beauty but to her soul. Will she dare leave the domineering Paris and a terrible war that haunts her dreams? Xena asks Helen, "What do you want to do?" Astonished, she says, "No one's ever asked me that before." Helen realizes with Xena's help that she must create her own destiny, independent of men, of wars, of capricious gods.

Highlights:

The battle into Troy by Xena and Gabrielle is harrowingly realistic. The Trojan Horse, the crowning glory of Ulysses' cunning, now attests to the ingenuity of Robert Gillies' prop crew.

Casting Coup:

Galyn Gorg gives the role of Helen surprising depth.

Lucy's Take:

"Scott Garrison played Perdicas. We had never before had a guest performer come up from the States and so completely fit in. What a charming, genuine individual, and really talented.

"That episode is when my back started to go downhill. I had really hurt it. And doing the fight on the last day was difficult, to say the least. I just kept quiet about it, I told them, my back's not great, my back's not great, but I didn't really deal with it. And in the next Couple of episodes, it really deteriorated. Because I was just overtraining. I'd be in the gym for an hour and a half, it would take me another half hour to get home, forty-five minutes to get cleaned, it was just a nightmarish existence. And I just thought I *had* to do it because I had never been gifted in, never practiced, the physical aspects of this job."

ATHENS CITY ACADEMY OF THE PERFORMING BARDS

Writers: R. J. Stewart & Steven L. Sears
Director: Jace Alexander
Original Air Date: Jan. 22, 1996

• GUEST CAST •

Orion	Dean O'Gorman
Polonius	Grahame Moore
Stallonus	Patrick Brunton
Kellos	Lori Dungey
Docenius	Alan De Malmanche
Euripides	Joseph Manning
Drunk	Bernard Moody
Twickenham	Andrew Thurtell
Gastacius	David Weatherley

• 13. ATHENS CITY ACADEMY OF THE PERFORMING BARDS •

Gabrielle enters a competition for bards, and wins handily by relating the exploits of her own greatest hero, Xena. She also bonds with the other contestants, including a youth named Orion, whose stars—and talent—augur greatness.

Highlights:

The highlights are flashbacks from earlier episodes, including Xena's appearances on

Hercules, and clips from the original *Hercules* with Steve Reeves and *Spartacus,* with Kirk Douglas and Jean Simmons. Robert Sidney Mellette, an aide on *Xena*'s writing staff, wryly explained:

> *A show like* Xena *is completely impossible to make. Think about it, every two weeks we present almost two hours of film. Most two-hour movies take as much as a year to make—more if you include writing and complete postproduction time. We average seven days of shooting per episode. Now, there are times when our producer in New Zealand says, "It can't be done! Not in this amount of time, and not for this amount of money." Most of the time we ignore him! . . . Well, in an effort to present the best show possible, we do what all great artists do, we steal! We'll steal time and money from future episodes. So shows like "The Titans" and "Hooves & Harlots" we shot in nine days. . . . Eventually, the bill comes due. . . . Clip shows like "Performing Bards" save a lot of production time. One of the unique things about that show was that it actually had a plot, which is more than can be said for most other TV series' clip shows. Also, it's kind of fun to have Kirk Douglas, Laurence Olivier, Tony Curtis, et al. as guest stars.*

Casting Coup:

Patrick Brunton, as the action-minded, street-wise bard Stallonus, offers a riotous send-up of Sylvester Stallone.

Lucy's Take:

"That was Renee's story, and I thought she did a great job. I really enjoyed the show. I thought the young guys were funny. And for a clip show, it was very entertaining."

• 14. A FISTFUL OF DINARS •

Shades of Indiana Jones, as Xena joins a quest for the Lost Treasure of the Sumerians, in order to keep an even greater prize from the wrong hands: ambrosia, the food

---

A FISTFUL OF DINARS

Writers: Steven L. Sears & R. J. Stewart
Director: Josh Becker
Original Air Date: Jan. 29, 1996

• GUEST CAST •

Thersites	Jeremy Roberts
Petracles	Peter Daube
Lycus	Richard Foulkes
Calicus	Huntly Eliott
Head Villager	Merv Smith
Klonig	Lawrence Whareau

that can turn a mortal into a god. Her traveling companions include an assassin, Thersites, and a warlord named Petracles, whom Gabrielle finds charming but Xena bitterly calls more dangerous than Thersites. She speaks from experience, for Petracles had seduced her as a youth with the promise of marriage, then left her. But when Thersites threatens to kill Gabrielle in a bid to seize the ambrosia and become a god, Petracles dies trying to save her. Xena kills Thersites and then rushes to Petracles, whom she finds holding a locket that Xena had given him for their engagement.

Highlights:

Xena's rescue of Gabrielle at the edge of a cliff is among the episode's rapid-fire thrills.

Casting Coup:

Jeremy Roberts as Thersites is an assassin who also steals scenes.

Lucy's Take:

"That was a good, fun one to shoot. Josh Becker [the director] has got a really good eye for the overall story, and knows how to see the world from each character's perspective. And Jeremy [Roberts, as Thersites] was a pleasure to work with. And the young boy who runs away and gets killed at the beginning of the episode was so intense. And we found out it was because to prepare himself for the role he had not eaten or slept for three days, so he could get into character for this brief role."

• 15. WARRIOR ... PRINCESS •

Mistaken identity produces both intrigue and farce when Xena poses as her exact look-alike, Diana, the daughter of King Lias, to protect her from killers trying to prevent her wedding to a foreign prince. Xena finds it is no easy matter to appear sweet, pampered, and helpless like the princess, and Diana has an even harder time trying to act convincingly like a superheroine—especially when she cries. Xena foils the murder plot just in time, for she is beginning to find the privileges of royalty surprisingly habit-forming.

Highlights:

In her first sustained comic turn, Lucy Lawless shines as Xena, Diana, Xena playing Diana, and Diana playing Xena. Best scene: Xena's rescue of Prince Mineus from a half dozen swordsmen while posing as the ineffectual Princess Diana. Diana later makes her own mark on her father, Lias, by splitting his crown with an overly eager toss of Xena's chakram. Best insult invoking a famous Greek philosopher: after an assassin is overpowered by Xena and exclaims, "You're not the princess!" she snaps, "You got that right, *Plato*."

WARRIOR...
PRINCESS

Writer: Brenda Lilly
Director: Michael Levine
Original Air Date: Feb. 5, 1996

• GUEST CAST •

Philemon	Iain Rea
Lias	Norman Forsey
Mineus	Latham Gains
Glauce	Patrick Smith
Tesa	Michelle Huirama
Timus	Jason Hoyte
Mirus	Jonathan Acorn
Lowlife	Ian Miller
Guard	Chris Bohm
Waif	Mia Koning

Lucy's Take:

"It was quite scary going into that, playing a new character when I'd been doing Xena so long. A wonderful challenge but hair-raising, to make yourself totally vulnerable again. It scares the living daylights out of you!

"Mike Levine directed it, and it was fun, fun, fun. So I was really disappointed when I heard that he couldn't make it back to do the triple[-character] episode [for the second season, 'Warrior... Princess...Tramp']. But, you know, all things turn out how they're supposed to, and the director we got for that one was superb. Those episodes were so exciting to shoot, because you never stop moving, you're in every scene at least twice, you've got to run out and change your clothes, and run back in, you've got to keep an idea of who you are and what your character knows at this stage: is it your character *pretending* to be Xena *pretending* to be the princess? It's that mental gymnastics that I love. By the end of the episode I am brain-dead."

• 16. MORTAL BELOVED •

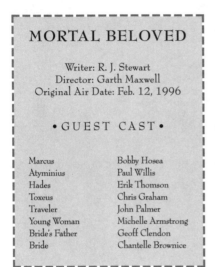

MORTAL BELOVED

Writer: R. J. Stewart
Director: Garth Maxwell
Original Air Date: Feb. 12, 1996

• GUEST CAST •

Marcus	Bobby Hosea
Atyminius	Paul Willis
Hades	Erik Thomson
Toxeus	Chris Graham
Traveler	John Palmer
Young Woman	Michelle Armstrong
Bride's Father	Geoff Clendon
Bride	Chantelle Brownice

Xena goes to the Underworld to help the soul of her slain lover Marcus. She finds all in turmoil: a maniac named Atyminius has stolen Hades' Helmet of Invisibility and usurped his power, making good souls suffer in Tartarus while letting the wicked loose in the Elysian Fields. Xena and Marcus, whom Hades grants a forty-eight-hour reprieve, track Atyminius back to the land of the living and stop him from renewing his murderous assault on young women. Marcus agrees to return Hades' helmet though it will mean his own return to Tartarus, where he had been confined because "you can't make up for a lifetime of evil with a single good deed at the end." But Xena moves Hades to overturn that judgment by pleading for her friend: "He learned to carry the Elysian Fields inside of him. Let him bring that love to paradise, where it belongs!"

Mythic Connections:

The Greeks considered the dead mere shadows of their living selves. Most souls dwelled forever in the dark, dreary expanse of the Underworld. But a handful were admitted to the Elysian Fields on the Isles of the Blessed at the western edge of the world; and the extremely wicked were sent to Tartarus, the lowest, most forbidding region of the Underworld.

Highlights:

A brilliantly written episode with a shattering climax. Xena's final act of violence shocks even Hades, and her tearful plea to the god of the Underworld reveals another dimension to this stoic heroine.

Casting Coup:

In an inspired cameo, Michael Hurst departs from his heroics as Iolaus on *Hercules: The Legendary Journeys,* and plays Charon the boatman like a New York City cabdriver picking up fares.

Lucy Lawless and Erik Thomson, who plays Hades, first worked together years ago as the parents of a boy named Stanley in a series of ads for the Auckland National Savings Bank.

Lucy's Take:

"Atyminius was played by a very nice gentleman called Paul Willis, who had this creepy manner when he was in character—sort of what you would expect of a pedophile, but in real life he was just the loveliest man. [The character Atyminius] was like a *horror* from my childhood. . . . I got to work with Bobby [Hosea] again. And I got to get out of my blasted corset [Xena enters the Underworld without her armor], so that was pleasant."

• 17. ROYAL COUPLE OF THIEVES •

Xena meets *The A-Team* meets *Raiders of the Lost Ark,* in a caper played for broad comedy. Her team consists of one irrepressible con artist, thief, adventurer, and narcissist by the name of Autolycus. Together they use guile and daring to steal a chest containing the most powerful weapon in the world, which is being auctioned at a gathering of ruthless warlords. Xena survives a fall overboard on the high seas, a battle with the deadly martial artist Lord Sinteres, attacks by soldiers, and, not least, her partnership

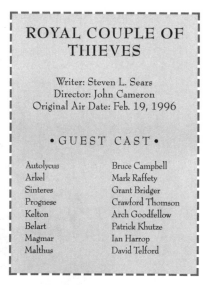

ROYAL COUPLE OF THIEVES

Writer: Steven L. Sears
Director: John Cameron
Original Air Date: Feb. 19, 1996

• GUEST CAST •

Autolycus	Bruce Campbell
Arkel	Mark Raffety
Sinteres	Grant Bridger
Prognese	Crawford Thomson
Kelton	Arch Goodfellow
Belart	Patrick Khutze
Magmar	Ian Harrop
Malthus	David Telford

with the resourceful but maddeningly roguish Autolycus. By adventure's end, though, Xena realizes that this self-proclaimed "King of Thieves" is kinder than he wants anyone to know.

Highlights:

Xena's sensuous "dance of the three veils" is accompanied by a musical score uncannily resembling the jazz-inflected theme song to the early sixties action show *Peter Gunn*. The writers call it the theme from *Peter Chakram*.

Casting Coup:

Bruce Campbell is charming and funny as Autolycus, the droll "King of Thieves" introduced on *Hercules: The Legendary Journeys*.

Lucy's Take:

"The redoubtable Bruce Campbell! Bruce is a great guy and just makes me laugh. He is ridiculously handsome for a start and when he puts that costume on with the beard and everything it just makes you giggle, it's awful. He's always doing great Sean Connery impressions, saying, 'Come on, Xena, sit on my lap,' and awful things like that, and it just makes me hoot. But the minute he takes that costume off, all that kind of flirtatiousness or anything extroverted like that just vanishes. He takes that costume off, he puts on his sandals and his socks that he wears under them, and he reverts to Mr.

Square. And yet when he's in that costume he is the slickest, most charming man.

"I realized on that episode that this series would contain elements that the audience couldn't predict. One time light, one time dark, one time a musical, for God's sakes!"

• 18. THE PRODIGAL •

Gabrielle freezes when bandits attack, and although Xena saves her life, she cannot save her friend's self-esteem. Seeing herself as a liability, a dispirited Gabrielle leaves Xena and returns to her home village of Potidaea. She finds it threatened by the bandit chief Damon and dependent on a hero for hire, Meleager the Mighty, who is now a drunkard living in fear. Using the skills Xena taught her, Gabrielle helps her sister Lila organize a defense against an army of brigands, and helps Meleager recover his confidence and defeat Damon in single combat. In rescuing her village, Gabrielle also overcomes her inner demons, and she rejoins Xena eager for fresh adventures.

THE PRODIGAL

Writer: Chris Manheim
Director: John T. Kretchmer
Original Air Date: Mar. 4, 1996

• GUEST CAST •

Meleager	Tim Thomerson
Lila	Willa O'Neill
Pharis	Alan Palmer
Damon	Steve Hall
Derq	Kelly Greene
Athol	Anton Bentley
Head Highwayman	Barry Te Hira
Elderly Driver	Wally Green

Highlights:

The scenes between Gabrielle and Lila reveal warm sibling bonds, mixed with the pain of long absence.

Casting Coup:

Tim Thomerson as Meleager the Mighty is the most hilariously dissolute hero since Lee Marvin's Oscar-winning role as the drunken gunfighter in *Cat Ballou*.

Lucy's Take:

"I went off to a convention in the States [while this was filmed]."

ALTARED STATES

Writer: Chris Manheim
Director: Michael Levine
Original Air Date: Apr. 22, 1996

• GUEST CAST •

Anteus	David Ackroyd
Icus	David de Lautour
Maell	Karl Urban
Zealot #1	Sean Ashton-Peach
Brawny Zealot	Jack Dacey
Zealot Guard	Peter Ford
Senior Zealot	Graham Smith
Zora	Teresa Woodham

• 19. ALTARED STATES •

"And I thought *our* gods were harsh!" Xena disdainfully tells the patriarch Anteus, who believes that the one true God has commanded that he sacrifice his beloved son Icus. But when Gabrielle goes into a hallucinogenic trance after eating bread prepared for Anteus by his eldest son Maell, Xena realizes that the command to kill Icus has come from his own brother. She defeats Maell but not before he shouts a "divine" command through a megaphone that Anteus kill Icus to prove his faith in God. Gabrielle lunges for the megaphone to issue a new command that Anteus spare his son's life, and Anteus obeys. Xena compliments Gabrielle on her quick thinking in imitating "the voice of God," only to hear Gabrielle deny ever getting hold of the megaphone.

Mythic Connections:

The biblical tale of Abraham and Isaac is given a daring secular spin by attributing the command to sacrifice Icus/Isaac to a jealous sibling rather than to God. Rob Tapert said, "I chickened out at the very last forty seconds of it," to avoid offending a great many religious people. "Even so, I watch that episode and say, 'I can't believe we did this.' "

Highlights:

Note Lucy Lawless' exuberant banter in the last scene, as she briefly steps out of character to joke with Renee O'Connor.

Lucy's Take:

"I have to admit it was one of those stories that I don't really enjoy filming that much because Xena is not emotionally invested in the story, it just goes from point A to point B. . . ." On the reverent ending to an irreverent story: "There had to be a nod to Greater America, I'm sure. . . . On the Internet they've written a lot about my walk and talk at the end. How all of a sudden they're allowed to see a new side to Xena, and she was lightening up at the end. Do you recall seeing that? . . . In fact, it was my first day back on set after I had hurt my back and I was having trouble walking, so if you watch it again you'll see I'm sort of walking away and I kept bumping into Renee. It was really funny. I kept forgetting my lines and we were running out of time, the sun was going down, and the only thing to do in that situation was to totally relax and let the words kind of flow out of you, and it just seemed to make things worse. But, yeah, I was just goofing around. It was a bit more Lucy, that's right, it wasn't a conscious effort to give a new insight into Xena!"

• 20. TIES THAT BIND •

Mourning becomes Elektra—with a vengeance, when Xena reconciles with a man claiming to be Atrius, the father who had abandoned her, only to lose him when villagers arrest him for treason. Bargaining for her father's life, Xena saves the village from an invading army by defeating its general, Kirilus, and seizing command of his troops. But on returning to find her father wounded and bound to a stake, she threatens a murderous revenge until Gabrielle stops her with an unfamiliar form of reasoning: a blow to the back of the head with a pitchfork handle. Xena recovers her senses and her good sense, forswearing vengeance even after her dying father urges her to strike down those who took him from her. Atrius then reveals his real form as Ares, the god of war, who had plotted to reawaken Xena's bloodlust but whom she now spurns along with her old ways.

TIES THAT BIND

Writers: Adam Armus & Nora Kay Foster
Director: Charles Siebert
Original Air Date: Apr. 29, 1996

• GUEST CAST •

Atrius	Tom Atkins
Ares	Kevin Smith
Kirilus	Stephen Lovatt
Rhea	Sonia Gray
Tarkus	Lutz Halbhubner
Andrus	Jonathon Whittaker
Areliesa	Nancy Broadbent
Slave Girl	Heidi Anderson

Highlights:

Seized by horror and rage as she spies her dying father in the distance, Xena screams at her soldiers, "Take the village!" It is a bloodcurdling moment that conveys why villagers once looked upon the Warrior Princess as a dread scourge.

Lucy's Take:

"I thought 'Ties That Bind' was really uneven, because I was out of commission for much of it. Some parts were really good and some parts were just . . . And I thought, poor Charlie Siebert, he's such a wonderful director and every time he directs, something happens to me. He was directing the first episode after I had the pelvic accident [in the second season]. That poor guy!"

On why she continues to do stunts despite a chronic bad back: "I don't know. Good workhorse body, generally. I'm sure this happens to everyone. Like Jackie Chan—I know he does these outrageous things but he's broken every bone in his body! And think of all the stunt people, too, who don't *ever* complain. I realize this is an occupational hazard and hopefully [my back] will never be this bad again."

• 21. THE GREATER GOOD •

THE GREATER GOOD

Writer: Steven L. Sears
Director: Gary Jones
Original Air Date: May 6, 1996

• GUEST CAST •

Salmoneus	Robert Trebor
Talmadeus	Peter McCauley
Ness	Jonathon Hendry
Photis	Natalya Humphrey
Kalus	Timothy James Adam
Nymis	Jason Tahau
Gorney	David Mitchell
Old Man	Kenneth Prebble

Gabrielle faces unimagined loss when a poisoned dart from an unknown source leaves Xena paralyzed and near death. Even from her bed, Xena directs the defense of a village against the warlord Talmadeus, aided by Gabrielle's masquerade as the Warrior Princess and by the carbonated water Salmoneus has been peddling as "Lord Seltzer," which the townspeople use to fire cork darts. But after killing two assassins in a last burst of will, Xena collapses and appears lifeless, leaving Gabrielle to mourn—and to stay in the village leading its desperate defenses, "for the greater good." Gabrielle holds off Talmadeus' soldiers with her staff to defend Xena's body, but is outmatched until Xena, her strength renewed, proves it will take more than one dart to kill a Warrior Princess.

Highlights:

Gabrielle weeps over Xena's body in a scene that underscores the power of their friendship. And Salmoneus displays unaccustomed depth in mourning the "proud warrioress."

Lucy's Take:

"Ah, that's the one with the silly old water fight. That was kind of a 'Renee episode' and I think I was very happy to let one go into her capable hands. . . . I just remember it was really dirty crawling around on the ground and the studio was filthy. And it was also the last episode we filmed before holidays. By that point you're completely [exhausted]. The penultimate one you're at your finest, your hardest-working, but the last one is difficult because everybody's brains slow down."

• 22. CALLISTO •

"You made me [who I am]!" exults Callisto, who was a child when Xena's army torched her village of Cirra, killing her mother and sister, and she is now a full-grown psychotic bent on vengeance. Xena remembers Cirra with terrible pain and guilt, for "that was one time when my army *was* responsible for the deaths of women and children." After Callisto and her cutthroats massacre villagers, Xena brings her in as a prisoner to stand trial while Callisto taunts, "Have you ever been tried for all of the things you have done?" But Xena's pity for Callisto fades after she escapes and abducts Gabrielle, leading the

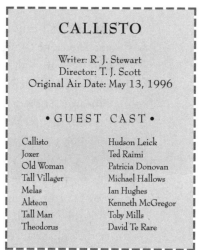

CALLISTO

Writer: R. J. Stewart
Director: T. J. Scott
Original Air Date: May 13, 1996

• GUEST CAST •

Callisto	Hudson Leick
Joxer	Ted Raimi
Old Woman	Patricia Donovan
Tall Villager	Michael Hallows
Melas	Ian Hughes
Akteon	Kenneth McGregor
Tall Man	Toby Mills
Theodorus	David Te Rare

Warrior Princess to track and defeat her nemesis in a fight on ladders

above a burning pyre. Spared by Xena, Callisto is led away in chains, still dreaming of revenge.

Highlights:

A classic episode that introduces Xena's greatest rival, "Callisto" also introduces the inept self-proclaimed warrior Joxer as a recurring comic foil; features Xena's anguished confession to Gabrielle about the torching of Cirra; pits Xena against Callisto in a chase on horseback across the dunes; and matches the two warriors in a brilliantly staged battle on ladders, inspired by the Hong Kong film *Once Upon a Time in China, Part 2*.

Casting Coups:

Hudson Leick as Callisto projects sensuality, psychotic glee, and a tantalizing hint of tenderness. Ted Raimi as Joxer recalls both Inspector Clouseau and Woody Allen, as he swaggers with neurotic bravado through one disaster after another.

Lucy's Take:

"It was the first time I met Hudson and she was very, very shy. I'm thrilled she came to us, but it was a difficult get-to-know-you period. . . . But even though I wasn't sure at first if I liked this person, I really respected her acting ability. And when that camera rolled or during rehearsal, she was there for me every time. . . . She has become a very valued member of the 'family' and I love her."

On her participation in the battle scene on the ladders: "I did quite a bit, really. . . . Yeah, we were [both on the ladders]. Of course they're rigged at the bottom so they're pretty safe and I fortunately did not have to go up in the dreaded harness, as every actor dreads because they hurt like crazy. We had a big long ladder on a teeter-totter, an industrial strength teeter-totter, and she and I did that, just using our balance. . . . Oh, there would have been nets underneath. . . . They take all precautions. I don't think we felt threatened. And

Hudson's really good, too. Not that she's athletic, but she's like a cat—she's got an amazing kick and she's very flexible and quick, she's really fast, so she keeps me on my mettle."

• 23. DEATH MASK •

Family reunions have not gone smoothly for Xena, whose mother greeted her with an outstretched sword in "Sins of the Past," and whose supposed father turned out to be Ares in "Ties That Bind." Now Xena's older brother Toris shows up and does little to bolster family values. Toris blames Xena for the death of their younger brother, who was killed while helping her repel the warlord Cortese from their home village. Despite his accusations, Toris himself feels guilt-ridden at having deserted Amphipolis while Xena stood her ground, and he now seeks to re-deem himself by murdering Cortese. Xena helps Toris bring Cortese to justice but dissuades him from killing the warlord, whose armies had devastated their family but whose defeat now helps reunite them.

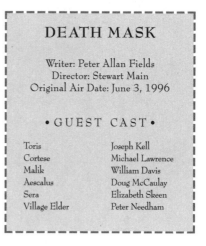

DEATH MASK

Writer: Peter Allan Fields
Director: Stewart Main
Original Air Date: June 3, 1996

• GUEST CAST •

Toris	Joseph Kell
Cortese	Michael Lawrence
Malik	William Davis
Aescalus	Doug McCaulay
Sera	Elizabeth Skeen
Village Elder	Peter Needham

Highlights:

The episode fleshes out Xena's past, revealing how the warlord Cortese robbed her of her younger brother, became an obsession that drove away her older brother, and set her on a path of plunder and destruction. As Xena confides to Gabrielle: "It was fighting him that twisted me into what I became."

Lucy's Take:

"Ah, yes! That chap that plays my brother, Joseph Kell, could take his tongue and shove it up the back of his nose through his throat and tickle his sinuses with his tongue. An extraordinary trick, and that's all I can say!"

IS THERE A DOCTOR
IN THE HOUSE?

Writer: Patricia Manney
Director: T. J. Scott
Original Air Date: July 29, 1996

• GUEST CAST •

Marmax	Ray Woolf
Ephiny	Danielle Cormack
Minoan Warrior	Tony Billy
Hippocrates	Andrew Binns
Hysterical Woman	Harriet Crampton
Runner	Edith
Democritus	Simon Farthing
Gangrene Man	Geoff Houtman
POW Leader	Paul McLauren
Blind Soldier	Adam Middleton
Thessalian Guard	Charles Pierard
Galen	Ron Smith
Head Wound Man	Deane Vipond

• 24. IS THERE A DOCTOR IN THE HOUSE? •

M*A*S*H and *E.R.* come to ancient Thessaly. Caught in the middle of a war, Xena and Gabrielle create a makeshift hospital in a temple despite vehement protests by the official healer, Galen. Xena sets up a system of triage, improvises a tracheotomy, amputates a limb to save a soldier with gangrene, and otherwise revolutionizes medicine while young Hippocrates records her techniques for a new generation of healers. Xena's greatest miracle of modern medicine—and faith—is her desperate discovery of CPR to revive Gabrielle after she goes into shock from a severe wound and dies. Xena also works a miracle of diplomacy by convincing a wounded general, Marmax, that there are no victors in war, only victims, and leads him to make peace with his longtime enemies.

Highlights:

An episode of exceptional power, featuring an extraordinary performance by Lucy Lawless. Verging on hysteria, Xena shouts at Gabrielle, "Don't you leave me!" and saves her friend in a scene of shattering intensity.

Lucy's Take:

"That was the singularly most rewarding episode—that and 'Warrior . . . Princess . . . Tramp' for me were the most rewarding ever. . . . This was a five-day episode [compared with the usual eight-day shoot], but it was amazingly intense, and so I had to be on every step of the way. God, I loved that! I loved to be under pressure. . . .

"In the scene where Xena loses her friend, you really see *raw Xena*. You see how great her need is. And then [as an actor] you've still got to keep a lid on it, or the audience is going to disengage at some point if you go into self-indulgence.

"Renee was just my savior in that episode because there came a time when we did the death scene and they asked if we could go for one more take and I said, 'Oh, I can't do it,' and I just about went mad, and Renee said, 'Yes you can, Yes-You-Can,' and I said, 'Oh, O.K., O.K., Renee, you're the boss.' And I did it and it was a fantastic take. So she was able to shore me up."

THE SECOND SEASON

• 25. ORPHAN OF WAR •

In an episode of *Hercules,* "The Gauntlet," Salmoneus chides Xena for her lack of "maternal instincts," then frantically explains, "Not that you *don't have* maternal instincts, but with all the *fighting* . . ." Indeed: Xena's maternal instincts led her secretly to give up her beloved infant son, Solan, to protect him from her enemies. Now, in yet another rocky family reunion, the nine-year-old boy tries to kill Xena, knowing only of her evil past and never suspecting she is his mother. But he soon finds her an inspiring guardian as she defends him and his foster father, the Centaur Kaleipus, against a warlord named Dagnine, who uses the fabled "Ixion Stone" to release the evil of the Centaur race and become a hideous giant. Xena kills Dagnine by triggering a huge crossbow, and leaves Solan in safety after forging a bond with her son deeper than she had dared hope for.

ORPHAN OF WAR

Writer: Steven L. Sears
Director: Charles Siebert
Original Air Date: Sept. 30, 1996

• GUEST CAST •

Kaleipus	Paul Gittins
Dagnine	Marc Ferguson
Solan	David Taylor
Meklan	Alexander Campbell
Seer	Stephen Papps
Daylon	Peter Tait

Mythic Connections:

Not many mortals in the ancient world were so evil as to spend eternity in Tartarus, but Ixion doubly qualified: he became the world's first murderer, a Thessalian version of the biblical figure Cain; and then, for good measure, tried to seduce Zeus' wife, Hera. Zeus fooled Ixion by forming a cloud to resemble Hera, and the result of this mating was Centaurus, who fathered the dissolute race of Centaurs. "Orphan of War" brightens this tale by portraying Ixion as a good person who made the Centaurs a noble race by capturing their evil qualities in a single stone.

Highlights:

A flashback in which Xena, garbed in a black cape and hood, bids Kaleipus to raise her son, is visually and emotionally jolting.

Lucy's Take:

"I loved the first little fight sequence—all credit to the editor and stuntees and everybody else who was in it. I loved the first time I gave the baby up, but I thought the last, parting scene [where Xena refrains from revealing she is Solan's mother] played way too long. . . . I was disappointed in the way I performed it. I would have kept the lid down harder, held it down tighter, so that the pain was greater. I kick myself about that one. . . ."

On Xena's horror at giving away her child: "I got the idea she should go off to throw up. I had the idea she was going to go there and just vomit, she's so sick at what she just did. So if you ever see it again you know that's what she's going to do!"

• 26. REMEMBER NOTHING •

Frank Capra's classic movie *It's a Wonderful Life* is given an unlikely but effective retelling, as Xena learns what life would have been like had the Warrior Princess never existed. The three Fates, grateful to Xena for repelling an attack on their temple, let her live in a world where she had remained a peaceful villager. But grim sur-

REMEMBER NOTHING

Writer: Chris Manheim
Story: Steven L. Sears & Chris Manheim
Original Air Date: Oct. 7, 1996

• GUEST CAST •

Lyceus — Aaron Devitt
Maphias — Robert Harte
Mezentius — Stephen Tozer
Krykus — Mark Ferguson
Clotho — Rebecca Kpacka
Lachesis — Micaela Daniel
Atropos — Elizabeth Pendergrast
Slave boss — Chris Graham
Caputius — Slade Leef

prises await her: without a Warrior Princess to slay predatory warlords like Mezentius, Krykus, and Caputius, they have joined forces to conquer new lands; and without a Warrior Princess to save Potidaea from raiders, Gabrielle has grown up an embittered slave girl. Even Xena's joy at finding her younger brother Lyceus still alive is tempered by his insistence that he would rather die fighting for freedom than surrender to tyrants. At last, battling with Lyceus against the three warlords, Xena sheds blood and is returned to her original world, more at peace with her choices in life and, as she tells Gabrielle, "more myself than I've ever been."

Mythic Connections:

The three Fates were daughters of Nyx (Night): Clotho spun the thread of a person's life, Lachesis determined the length, and Atropos cut it at the appointed time.

Highlights:

An excellent script abounds in clever twists and offers a warm look at the ties between Xena and her brother Lyceus.

Lucy's Take:

"I thought Renee was brilliant. I thought she was really great. [Laughing about Renee's hardened character in this episode:] Such an awful little tramp! And I thought I looked stupid. Too much blubbering in the bloody cages [where Xena and Lyceus are imprisoned]. 'Potsie Webber' [referring to the character Anson Williams made famous on the sitcom *Happy Days*] directed that episode, and I remember him yelling like crazy at the boy who played my brother, Aaron Devitt, trying to wring a good performance out of him. It happens with young men, usually, that you can only yell at them so long and they come to a little crisis point where they start to laugh. They say, 'This is ridiculous, this cannot be happening to me.' And he just started to laugh. Anson was just ragging on him, trying to get some Methody-type performance out of him, which was ridiculous because this boy was untrained. He had all the raw material and no sort of craft. And so I went out the back with Aaron and we talked about acting and I tried to get him to loosen up and have some fun with me and just listen [to my character] and 'bring me in.' And I think he did have more fun but it gave him a terrible shock about acting. He said he'd never do another part without going away to drama school. . . . Yes, Aaron was very much like my [real] brother Daniel. And I really like [Aaron]. He's such a nice young man."

• 27. GIANT KILLER •

GIANT KILLER

Writer: Terence Winter
Director: Gary Jones
Original Air Date: Oct. 14, 1996

• GUEST CAST •

Goliath	Todd Rippon
David	Anthony Starr
Dagon	Calvin Tuteao
Jonathan	Dale Corlett
King Saul	Dennis Hally
Sarah	Emma Brunette

Goliath never looked so appealing as in this retelling of the biblical story of David's battle with the towering Philistine champion. Here Goliath is a giant with a heart, who once saved Xena's life in battle and has since been tracking the brutish, and still larger, Gareth, who murdered his family. Xena finds that Goliath has been used by the Philistines as a mercenary to persecute the Israelites, and tries to convince her old friend to quit. But when Goliath refuses, she first battles him herself, then devises a strategy to let the pious young Israelite, David, defeat his far more powerful foe.

Highlights:

The remarkable action scenes are highlighted by clever camera work to create a thirty-foot giant and weave him convincingly into the battles. . . . Gabrielle shares a tender moment with David, who recites his most famous Psalm, "The Lord Is My Shepherd."

Lucy's Take:

"I remember the lovely big skeletons lying about [the remnants of a battle of giants]. It was like being in an elephants' graveyard. I also liked doing the forced perspective [camera work]. . . . Poor old Goliath was miscast, just physically miscast. He had skinny legs . . . and they deepened his voice to try to make him more majestic, more of a threat. . . ."

On cutting the last act from the episode: "That's right. We had Xena battle a bigger giant, and he's supposed to be a thicker and more scary one. But we cut that whole thing out because who cares, once Goliath is gone? Why should we care about the other giant even though he is bigger?"

• 28. GIRLS JUST WANNA HAVE FUN •

A Halloween episode that is weird, startling, and riveting. Xena and Gabrielle set out to stop Bacchus, a god who commands a cult of young maidens whom he has turned into vampire-like predators called Bacchae. The two heroines are joined by the boastful, bumbling Joxer, and by the head—just the head—of the minstrel Orpheus, whose music can calm the Bacchae but whose body has been stolen by Bacchus. Along the way Xena battles Bacchae; flying skeletons known as Dryads; and Gabrielle, who is bitten by one of the Bacchae and transformed into one herself. On realizing that no human can kill Bacchus, Xena allows Gabrielle to bite her, too, and then flies at Bacchus with the sharpened bone of a Dryad, destroying him and lifting his curse from Gabrielle, Orpheus, and the Bacchae maidens.

> ### GIRLS JUST WANNA HAVE FUN
>
> Writers: Adam Armus & Nora Kay Foster
> Director: T. J. Scott
> Original Air Date: Oct. 21, 1996
>
> • GUEST CAST •
>
> | | |
> |---|---|
> | Joxer | Ted Raimi |
> | Orpheus | Matthew Chamberlain |
> | Bacchus | Anthony Ray Parker |

Mythic Connections:

Dionysus, also known as Bacchus, was the god of wine and the center of a cult of women known as Maenads, who engaged in frenzied dancing on hillsides while carrying torches. Their outbursts of violent madness were the subject of several tales, one of them centering on Orpheus, a musician who charmed all of nature when he sang and played the lyre. When he stopped sacrificing to Dionysus, the Maenads tore him apart. Only his head was saved, and it floated down the river Hebrus calling out for his lamented wife, Eurydice.

Highlights:

A sensual episode with striking visuals and Joseph Lo Duca's hypnotic music, including an ancient precursor of hip-hop and an Arabic chant as the Bacchae dance beneath the gaze of their master.

Lucy's Take:

"Xena didn't have a lot to do emotionally, so those episodes are not always my favorite. But there was an awful lot going on, it was very colorful. I've got some strong images from that like Matt Chamberlain [as Orpheus]. . . . Poor Matt! The whole episode, because his body was blue-screened out, he always had to wear sort of a blue robe and blue pajamas. The whole week we treated him like a head! The funny thing with monsters and heads is that nobody wants to eat with them, or at least they're not seen as people, you know. The last hours of filming, when he became whole again, I went, 'Oh, Matt!' I was so ashamed because I had kind of ignored him all week.

"The poor chap who played Bacchus [Anthony Ray Parker] left home at two in the morning, and at four in the morning he was sitting in makeup. It took six or eight hours and he wasn't used until four that afternoon. So the poor guy had been in that claustrophobic head all that time.

"And I was working with Ted Raimi again, whom I just love. . . . He's just bloody funny. We adore him."

On the wild episode: "I don't mind making those leaps. And we don't mind unsettling our audience a bit. You know, 'you'll laugh, you'll cry, you'll love us, you'll hate us, but you'll keep watching' is the name of our game. Just never bore them! The reaction to this episode was very polarized on the Internet, but you know you'll get that because we like to push boundaries. And T.J. more than most!"

• 29. RETURN OF CALLISTO •

Callisto tests Gabrielle's goodness, idealism, and pacifism when she murders Perdicas just a day after he and Gabrielle had married. When Gabrielle appears bent on revenge, Xena reluctantly teaches her to use a sword but counsels, "You need to mourn," hoping to keep her friend from an act of violence that could harm her body and soul. Gabrielle slips alone into Callisto's lair but cannot bring herself to kill even this most hateful creature, and she is instead taken prisoner. So, too, is Xena, but a diversion by Joxer helps her break free, and she catches Callisto after a chariot race along the shore. The two tumble into quicksand, leading Callisto to sparkle at the thought of their spending eternity in Tartarus together, but Xena uses her chakram and whip to pull herself out while Callisto sinks to her death.

RETURN OF CALLISTO

Writer: R. J. Stewart
Director: T. J. Scott
Original Air Date: Oct. 28, 1996

• GUEST CAST •

Callisto	Hudson Leick
Joxer	Ted Raimi
Perdicas	Scott Garrison
Theodorus	David Te Rare

Highlights:

For the first time, Gabrielle feels the rage that had long possessed Xena, but, at the moment of truth, her humanity proves stronger than Callisto's cruelty. . . . The chariot race between Xena and Callisto is among the most spectacular action scenes in this or any other series.

Lucy's Take:

"I loved the episode. We originally shot it differently. We shot it where I do try to save her and she dies anyway. I get the whip and try to throw it to her. I hesitate but I do it, so that I could have a little bit of moral high ground in the next episode: you see, when she comes back and accuses me of murdering her, I say, 'No, I did try to save you, you hag,' that sort of thing. But when I had my accident they just quickly reedited everything."

• 30. WARRIOR . . . PRINCESS . . . TRAMP •

WARRIOR . . .
PRINCESS . . . TRAMP

Writer: R. J. Stewart
Director: Josh Becker
Original Air Date: Nov. 4, 1996

• GUEST CAST •

Joxer	Ted Raimi
King Lias	Norman Forsey
Philemon	Iain Rea
Agis	Chris Bailey
Alcibiades	Simon Fa' Amoe
Nurse	Collette Pennington

Greek tragedy meets French farce when Xena encounters two look-alikes: the sweetly naive Princess Diana and the scheming, lustful, but not overly bright Meg. The three take turns impersonating each other, with riotous results. Lucy Lawless has a comic field day playing a dizzying succession of characters (Xena playing Diana, Diana playing Meg, Meg playing Diana, Diana playing Xena, etc.). Oh, yes: Xena foils two kidnappings (Diana and her new baby), and Meg gets an unexpected second chance in life as a cook in the royal kitchen.

Highlights:

Poor Joxer is lost without a scorecard to keep track of the different characters: he backs away from Meg's advances, convinced she is Xena; then tries to seduce Xena in the dangerously mistaken belief that she is the ever hospitable Meg.

Lucy's Take:

"Josh Becker, who directed, set up the perfect creative environment. It was really stimulating and we ad-libbed some of those scenes fiercely. One of my favorite jokes is when Meg comes out holding the chakram and calls it 'my trusty . . . *shamrock!*' That was Josh's joke, but it did work beautifully. . . .

"My ad-libs? Well, I had ad-libs for other people. And some of the more physical things—for example, on [Meg masquerading as Xena] 'torturing' Gabrielle in the prison [casually pulling her hair to get her back inside]. We all did a bit of ad-libbing. Once of my add-ins [as Meg] was putting the hickey on Joxer. And he ad-libbed, 'And that ain't all' [when Joxer is boasting to Gabrielle about Xena's supposed advances toward him], and he was about to show Gabrielle his . . . who knows what! . . ."

• 31. INTIMATE STRANGER •

Having written the first-season episode "Dreamworker" on the power of nightmares to invade our lives, Steve Sears plays diabolical variations on the theme in "Intimate Stranger." Callisto enters Xena's guilt-ridden dreams over her failure to save her foe, beckons her to the Underworld, steals her body, and returns to Earth. Xena, now trapped in the Underworld in Callisto's body, persuades Hades to release her for one day so she can send Callisto back to Tartarus. Xena intercepts Callisto as she is about to burn alive everyone in Amphipolis, and, with her last reserves of strength, hurls a dart into Callisto's neck. The two warriors meet again in the dream world, where Xena forces Callisto to face the many people she has slaughtered, and leaves her foe in Tartarus while she returns—still in Callisto's body—to the land of the living.

INTIMATE STRANGER

Writer: Steven L. Sears
Director: Gary Jones
Original Air Date: Nov. 11, 1996

• GUEST CAST •

Callisto	Hudson Leick
Joxer	Ted Raimi
Ares	Kevin Smith
Theodorus	David Te Rare
Cyrene	Darien Takle
Arleia	Lee-Jane Foreman
Gressius	Michael Cooper

Highlights:

Watching two superb actresses, Lucy Lawless and Hudson Leick, play each other's roles is a unique treat.

Lucy's Take:

"They quickly reedited the whole ending so that we do not get our own bodies back [as originally written], so that Hudson can play Xena in the next episode. Everyone was scrambling to rewrite, reedit, 'rerationalize' everything. . . . No, I did not reshoot the last scene, because I was flat on my back in the Burbank Hospital [after the fall from the horse].

"It was so incredibly hard to play someone else's character. I knew that Hudson could play Xena as well as anybody possibly could given the time frame. And it took *me* five days of agony to find out how to make the connection between me and Hudson and [then figure out how to play] Callisto. . . . The director was pushing for physical gimmicks [to signal Callisto's character], but that's not the way to get the essence of a character. That's just masking. . . . Well, Hudson moves in sort of a spidery or feline way and so I can do that, which looks ridiculous on my physique but it's all I had to hang on to. And certain stupid things like mimicry of her voice, which I didn't do very well. And then only on the last two days did I begin to understand where the heart of Callisto was, and how to [find a connection with Hudson].

"Then I realized the very thing: Hudson would tell me about her childhood, her adolescence, and on the face of it, it seems diametrically opposed to my own, but when I think about it she was everything that I [might have been]. Her life was everything that I would simply not *allow* myself to be at the same age, which is not to say [those qualities] were not there. My conditioning just squelched it out of me."

• 32. TEN LITTLE WARLORDS •

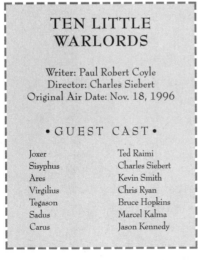

TEN LITTLE WARLORDS

Writer: Paul Robert Coyle
Director: Charles Siebert
Original Air Date: Nov. 18, 1996

• GUEST CAST •

Joxer	Ted Raimi
Sisyphus	Charles Siebert
Ares	Kevin Smith
Virgilius	Chris Ryan
Tegason	Bruce Hopkins
Sadus	Marcel Kalma
Carus	Jason Kennedy

It's just one of those days on Earth and Mount Olympus, when Ares becomes a drunkard, Xena's spirit remains in Callisto's body, and Gabrielle begins picking fights for trivial reasons. Someone has stolen Ares' sword, and with it his godly powers, and invited ten warriors to compete for the sword and immortality. Meanwhile, without a god of war, peaceful people like Gabrielle have lost the self-discipline to control their anger, and only warriors like Xena and Ares himself can now control their passions. Xena and Ares slip into the competition and expose it as a hoax planned by Sisyphus, whom Hades has promised to make the new god of war if he delivers "the world's

ten best warriors" to the Underworld.
Xena retrieves the sword for Ares, who
confines Sisyphus to the Underworld, re-
stores Gabrielle's peaceful ways, and reunites Xena's body and spirit on earth
while sending Callisto's body back to lan-
guish in Tartarus.

Highlights:

Ares appears more thoroughly likable as a mortal than he had ever
been as a god, and his partnership with Xena against a pack of murderous warlords is appealing.

Casting Coup:

Hudson Leick plays Xena during Lucy Lawless' recuperation from her
fall; and while Lawless' Xena remains definitive, Leick credibly shifts
from psychotic archvillain to savvy superheroine.

• 33. A SOLSTICE CAROL •

The ghosts of Christmas past and future visit
Charles Dickens' *A Christmas Carol,* relo-
cating his tale in pre-Christian Greece while
slyly updating it. A king embittered by the
loss of his wife Analia thirty years ago bans
celebration of the Solstice and orders his
clerk Senticles, a former toy maker, to close
an orphanage for failure to pay the heavy
royal taxes. Hoping to shock the king into
changing his ways, Xena visits him in the
guise of Clotho, the Fate of the past, and
shows him a floating vision of Queen Analia,

A SOLSTICE CAROL

Writer: Chris Manheim
Director: John T. Kretchmer
Original Air Date: Dec. 9, 1996

• GUEST CAST •

Senticles	Joe Berryman
King Silvas	Peter Vere Jones
Lynal	Daniel James
Melana	Sher Booth

in reality Gabrielle veiled and suspended by a rope. Later, disguised as
Lachesis, the Fate of the present, Xena brings the king to see the effects of his cruelty on the orphanage. Mistaking the woman who
heads the orphanage for Atropos, the Fate of the future, the king

pleads for a second chance and has his wish granted beyond measure when she reveals herself as Analia and reconciles with her husband.

Highlights:

Xena and Gabrielle defeat the king's guards using toys fashioned by Senticles; to Xena's amazement, one is an action figure of Hercules bearing a startling resemblance to Kevin Sorbo. . . . Lucy Lawless offers a broad comic take on the Fates (Dickens' ghosts) of the past and present.

Lucy's Take:

"I don't read scripts until generally four days before the first day of shooting, and I think I read that one about two days before. All of a sudden I had to pull out these two extra characters. And I only ever do that once I get into a costume. You know, it's just a total surprise for me what's going to come out! I have all these options and maybe the director doesn't like one, so I've got to go in a completely new direction. But [with so little time] I had to fake it, just as Xena would have, in order to pull out those two new characters, which worked out fine. For one [of the Fates] I drew on [the character of] Julia Child, because she struck me as having just the most outrageous voice."

• 34. THE XENA SCROLLS •

THE XENA SCROLLS

Writers: Adam Armus & Nora Kay Foster
Story by: Robert Sidney Mellette
Director: Charlie Haskell
Original Air Date: Jan. 13, 1997

• GUEST CAST •

Jacques S'er   Ted Raimi
Ares   Kevin Smith
John Smythe   Mark Ferguson
Nikos   Ajay Vasisht
Executive   Rob Tapert

Double roles for Lucy Lawless and Renee O'Connor move Xena's adventures forward to 1940s Macedonia, where the archaeologist Janice Covington (O'Connor) and her ditzy companion Melinda Pappas (Lawless) come upon the historical find of the century: the Xena Scrolls. Pappas, daughter of a renowned scholar who spent his life searching for the scrolls, proves surprisingly adept at translating fragments relating epic deeds of the Warrior Princess and her friend from Poteidaia. The scrolls have other admirers: Jacques S'er claims to be an officer in the

Free French Army who must guard the secrets of long-lost mystical powers from the Nazis, while a fortune hunter named John Smythe would happily kill all three for this treasure. Instead Smythe is killed by Ares, who emerges from long repose in a tomb and demands that a descendant of Xena—Pappas—set him free to wreak new havoc in a world at war. Ares menaces Covington and Jacques S'er (who is really a timid brush salesman from New Jersey), but the spirit of Xena takes control of Pappas' body, battles Ares, and entombs him once more.

Mythic Connections:

The splendid conceit of this episode is that Xena was a historical figure whose actual deeds—preserved by the recently discovered Xena Scrolls—inspired the series *Xena: Warrior Princess*.

Highlights:

The clever final scene flashes forward to the 1990s, where Ted Kleinman (Ted Raimi) pitches ideas for a series to an unnamed mogul, played by executive producer Rob Tapert. Kleinman's suggestions echo themes from *The Evil Dead* and other films produced by Tapert and Sam Raimi, and are dismissed with "Done that," until he suddenly piques his superior's interest with a copy of the Xena Scrolls.

Casting Coup:

Ted Raimi is hilarious as Jacques S'er (a descendant of Joxer), whose accent abruptly crosses the ocean from Paris to New Jersey.

Lucy's Take:

" 'The Xena Scrolls' was a bit of a landmark for me personally, because I flew into a huge rage with the director, Charlie Haskell. Charlie had been the second-unit director on *Hercules* for a very long time. And I've known him for many years, since my very first gig ever, [the New Zealand TV show] *Funny Business,* way back when. I even quite fancied him then, I think! Anyway, Charlie Haskell is a great guy and he wouldn't mind me telling this story in terms of just honesty about life.

"I got very angry and I didn't know why. It's just the rotten feeling I had about the way I was being covered [by the camera], and it took me days to put my finger on what was wrong. Charlie had come from *Hercules,* and for him I was just Lucy from seven years ago. And he had covered the show as if I was fifth-string. I couldn't put my finger on what was wrong, but there was no presentation of a 'star.' And I, as an animal, didn't like it, and I, as a business person, sensed there was something wrong with that. He was just reading the script as if it was totally isolated from the show *Xena: Warrior Princess.* And so he gave no credence to the fact that Xena, the main character, in whatever guise, is still the star. I don't think I got one close-up. You know, if you're counting close-ups, a close-up tells the story. And it doesn't matter where she is, you have to present the star. You see, stars are not born, they are *crafted* and they are *presented.* I don't mind playing second-string to Renee, but I will not play second-string to Ares, or whomever. It's all in a matter of presentation, how you frame the shot, where you stick an actor in a scene. And Charlie was not mindful of that. And it took me until two days left on the shoot to work out what the hell was wrong.

"That was a huge turning point for me, where I started to go, no, that ain't going to happen again. And I started to 'take my power,' if you will, to understand what the business is about and take some measure of control. Because I realize that directors very often have come off of a million other shows. They don't know the show as well as I do. And I will still bow to their input—they are the final arbiters, generally, unless I really feel something is wrong. And with me it's a gut feeling, and I'm learning how to put forth that in a constructive manner."

• 35. HERE SHE COMES . . . MISS AMPHIPOLIS •

Lucy Lawless, a former Mrs. New Zealand ("in the days when New Zealand cared about such differences!"), enters the fictional realm of beauty pageants when Xena competes for the crown of "Miss Known World" to thwart a saboteur. This is the first episode to be directed (as well as written) by a woman, and it carries a strong feminist line on the exploitative nature of beauty contests. But humor is king, or queen, here, as Xena, posing as Miss Amphipolis, must submit to a talent competition, survive the clawing of desperate contestants, and affect a dainty femininity to please the judges. And the winner is: Miss Artiphys, a secret transvestite, who accepts the award after the leading contestants withdraw rather than compromise their self-esteem.

Highlights:

Salmoneus makes a worthy precursor to Bob Barker and other Miss America MCs, never more so than in rehearsing his "girls" in a notably chaotic musical routine. . . . When Gabrielle, posing as an agent for Miss Amphipolis, recoils on seeing her client's ornate dress, Xena obligingly hacks off the offending ribbons with her sword.

Casting Coup:

Geoff Gann, a female impersonator, is outrageously funny as Miss Artiphys.

Lucy's Take:

Comparing her experience in the Mrs. Zealand contest with the pageant on *Xena:* "There was a lot of camaraderie between the women in real life and there were a couple of girls who were pretty anxious to win and didn't like to fraternize with us. But otherwise, no, [the two worlds] didn't really cross over."

HERE SHE COMES . . . MISS AMPHIPOLIS

Writer: Chris Manheim
Director: Marina Sargenti
Original Air Date: Jan. 20, 1997

• GUEST CAST •

Miss Artiphys	Geoff Gann
Salmoneus	Robert Trebor
Lord Clairon	John Sumner
Palatine of Parnassus	Stan Wolfgramm
Doge of Messini	Calvin Tuteao
Regent of Skiros	Tim Lee
Miss Skiros	Katherine Kennard
Miss Messini	Simone Kessell
Miss Parnassus	Jennifer Rucker
Pageant Matron	Brenda Kendall

DESTINY

Writers: R. J. Stewart & Steven L. Sears
Story by: Robert Tapert
Director: Robert Tapert
Original Air Date: Jan. 27, 1997

• GUEST CAST •

M'Lila	Ebonie Smith
Julius Caesar	Karl Urban
Niklio	Nathaniel Lees
Brutus	Grant Triplow
Sitacles	Slade Leef
Telos	Grant Boucher
Vicerius	Mark Perry

• 36. DESTINY •

Originally entitled "Why and Where," the episode reveals in flashbacks the origins of Xena's fighting skills, her rise as a military leader seeking only to guard her native Amphipolis, and her turn to the dark side after being betrayed by another conqueror, Julius Caesar. While commanding a pirate ship, Xena has an affair with Caesar, a Roman captive, but releases him and later greets him as a friend, only to be caught and crucified on Caesar's orders, Xena is saved by a slave girl named M'Lila whom she had once protected. But when M'Lila is killed by Roman troops while defending Xena, Xena flies into a murderous rage, declaring, "A new Xena is born today, with a new purpose in life . . . death!" These memories flood back as Xena lies dying from a wound, and as her spirit leaves, a vision of M'Lila reminds her that she has a destiny to fight evil, and urges her to find a way, some way, to return to the land of the living.

Mythic Connections:

Rob Tapert's story was inspired by reading Colleen McCullough's novel on Julius Caesar, *First Woman*.

Highlights:

These are, as Caesar would say, legion: the slave girl M'Lila's fight on the ship and use of a knife embedded in a sail to slide thirty feet down to the deck; M'Lila's tutoring Xena about pressure points; Xena's seduction of Caesar; the harrowing crucifixion; Xena's violent frenzy after M'Lila's death; and her vision of M'Lila on the cross, intercut with a montage of scenes with Gabrielle. Composer Joseph Lo Duca scored M'Lila's scenes with distinctive Gaelic melodies and songs, underscoring her origins "in western Gaul."

Lucy's Take:

"I was working with Rob [Tapert], which I'm still not sure I like, because when Rob's working as director, he's not *my* Rob. I have to work out a new relationship with him. . . . Working together was slightly uncomfortable for me until I realized, ah, it's simply that I have to [adjust] in the way I deal with Rob during the day. And then it was fine.

"I would have liked this to be a two-hour script. It just got pared down and pared down, and it would have been great in an hour and a half, if that's possible. But it was not to be. But it also left open a lot of doors for us to go back to if we do revisit Julius Caesar. I just started [reading] a script and there is mention of him. So he will turn up again."

• 37. THE QUEST •

Perhaps sensing that only Autolycus, "the King of Thieves," could steal the role of Xena while Lucy Lawless recovered from her injuries, the writers had Xena's spirit inhabit his body, in order to find the ambrosia that could reunite her body and spirit. As he prepares to steal Xena's casket before it can be ceremonially burned, Autolycus stumbles into a brewing civil war among the Amazons, with Ephiny urging Gabrielle to assume the throne after Queen Melosa is slain by the power-hungry warrior Velasca. Although Velasca has Autolycus jailed, he escapes with his fellow prisoners Gabrielle and Ephiny, and races to find the ambrosia, aided by the fabled dagger of Helios that can unlock a gateway to the food of the gods. Velasca tracks him, breaks his hand, and climbs toward the ambrosia in hopes

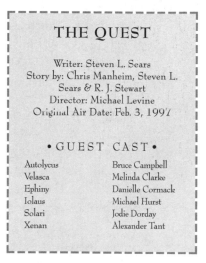

THE QUEST

Writer: Steven L. Sears
Story by: Chris Manheim, Steven L. Sears & R. J. Stewart
Director: Michael Levine
Original Air Date: Feb. 3, 1997

• GUEST CAST •

Autolycus	Bruce Campbell
Velasca	Melinda Clarke
Ephiny	Danielle Cormack
Iolaus	Michael Hurst
Solari	Jodie Dorday
Xenan	Alexander Tant

of becoming a god. But Xena's spirit enters Gabrielle, who sends Velasca hurtling into a fiery pit while saving just enough ambrosia to revive her friend.

Mythic Connections:

Ambrosia (meaning "immortal") was the food of the gods. Nectar was their drink. Together the two substances conferred immortality.

Highlights:

Overjoyed at seeing Xena suddenly manifested, Gabrielle kisses her—or thinks she does, until finding herself face to face with Autolycus, the repository of Xena's spirit. . . . Gabrielle, her powers enhanced by Xena's spirit, engages Velasca in a short but stirring fight on ropes to gain the ambrosia.

Casting Coups:

Who *isn't* in this episode? In a bid to offset the near absence of Lucy Lawless, the episode features several actors in recurring roles, including Bruce Campbell as the roguish Autolycus, Danielle Cormack as Ephiny, and Michael Hurst as Hercules' friend Iolaus. Melinda Clarke, sounded out about playing Xena when the role was originally cast, does not get to devour the ambrosia but effectively chews the scenery as the villainous Velasca.

Lucy's Take:

"This episode was a cover-up for my accident, of course. I mean, I was stuck in other people's bodies for weeks! I didn't have anything to do with any of those episodes until afterward, and I went into the ADR [automated dialogue replacement] booth and voiced those scenes [well after the filming]." On the footage of her in the casket: "That would have been my first days back, yes. We could have just done the Bobby Ewing thing [from the series *Dallas*], you know: had me wake up [later] in the show in the middle of a bad dream!"

• 38. A NECESSARY EVIL •

"To fight an immortal I *need* an immortal," Xena tells Gabrielle after the renegade Amazon Velasca, defeated by Xena, not only revives but becomes a god after eating ambrosia. Xena's choice for this mission is her deadly rival Callisto, whom Hera had rescued from Tartarus and granted immortality in exchange for her attempting to kill Hercules. Xena tempts Callisto with the chance to take Velasca's remaining ambrosia and become a god herself. Despite Gabrielle's revulsion at teaming with the woman who slew her husband, she realizes it is necessary to keep Velasca from destroying the entire Amazon nation under its new queen, Ephiny. Pitting Velasca and Callisto against each other on a bridge, Xena upends both immortals, who fall into an ocean of lava where they can battle harmlessly for eternity.

A NECESSARY EVIL
Writer: Paul Robert Coyle
Director: Mark Beesley
Original Air Date: Feb. 10, 1997

• GUEST CAST •

Velasca	Melinda Clarke
Callisto	Hudson Leick
Ephiny	Danielle Cormack
Solari	Jodie Dorday

Highlights:

Velasca gives an impassioned speech renouncing Artemis, goddess of the Amazons, before destroying her temple with lightning bolts. She then commands a terrified villager to tell everyone what she has done but kills him as he flees, remarking, "He wouldn't have told it right, anyway."

Casting Coup:

Jodie Dorday plays Ephiny's second-in-command, Solari, as a shrewdly calculating but loyal enforcer.

Lucy's Take:

"[Melinda Clarke] was nice—I didn't even remember that she was one of the [prospective] Xenas [two years earlier]. But, you know, I'm sure she's happy with the way life's worked out. She also was getting married at the time."

• 39. A DAY IN THE LIFE •

A DAY IN THE LIFE

Writer: R. J. Stewart
Director: Michael Hurst
Original Air Date: Feb. 17, 1997

• GUEST CAST •

Hower	Murray Keane
Minya	Alison Wall
Zagreus	Willy De Wit
Gareth	Jim Ngaata
Largo	Tony Billy

R. J. Stewart's clever script recounts in humorous fashion a typical day for Xena and Gabrielle, showing how these adventurers give new meaning to seemingly mundane events. "Waking up" involves a fight with attacking bandits; lunch features a wrestling match with the spirited entree, a giant eel. Along the way, Xena casually engineers the destruction of a warlord's entire army by a giant, whom she then defeats with a last-minute strategy involving the world's first kite.

Highlights:

Xena's battle with the giant Gareth is a marvel of special effects, originally filmed for the episode "Giant Killer" by director Gary Jones, but moved to "A Day in the Life" for reasons of time.

"A Day in the Life" fueled speculation about the possibility of a romantic relationship between Xena and Gabrielle. Among the alleged signposts: Gabrielle cautions Hower, a man smitten by Xena, that Xena wouldn't marry because "she likes what I do" too much, before "correcting" herself and saying, "She likes what *she's* doing"; Xena and Gabrielle share a bath and giddily splash water at each other; Gabrielle and Xena stretch out side by side to sleep under the stars, and Gabrielle expresses her gratitude to Xena by kissing her on the cheek.

Lucy's Take:

" 'A Day in the Life' was a landmark. Michael Hurst directed, and that was charming. And we really got to expand our characters, because there was no paradigm for this episode. We had not done anything like it before, so we all just kind of went crazy and it was good, cheeky fun. Because [Renee and I] got to fill in the gaps [in our characters and relationship] in our own silly way. I think we brought a lot more of ourselves. I know I did anyway. You get to see a lot more of Lucy in there.

"You know what was pure Lucy: when the eels were thrashing, and you get to see the slow motion of me pulling silly faces. Well, that was kind of outtakes. Because the water stank so bad, it was so smelly and slimy. The eels are so primal and disgusting to touch that I wanted to howl. I was just trying not to laugh, because I'm in such a disgusting situation. . . . Yeah, these were real eels, and they move in all directions—and their skin moves in the opposite direction. They are the foulest creatures I've ever touched. We've done rats and eels now, but I don't know what's next!"

On Gabrielle's much analyzed line to Hower: "Oh, that was just Renee having a gag. Yeah, she said, 'Oh, why don't I say this?' and everybody said, 'Yeah, yeah, say that.' So we did, and then we moved on. That's how this whole fuss was created. It's just us goofing!"

• 40. FOR HIM THE BELL TOLLS •

Joxer finds his inner hero in a comedy inspired by the film *The Court Jester*, about a troubadour (Danny Kaye) who becomes a daredevil swordsman whenever he hears the snap of fingers—and reverts to his bumbling ways on hearing a second snap. In "For Him the Bell Tolls," Aphrodite bets her son Cupid that she can make any man into an irresistible lover, and takes Joxer as the ultimate test of her powers. She turns Joxer into a suave and dashing hero by ringing a bell, a

FOR HIM THE BELL TOLLS

Writers: Adam Armus & Nora Kay Foster
Director: Josh Becker
Original Air Date: Feb. 24, 1997

• GUEST CAST •

Joxer	Ted Raimi
Aphrodite	Alexandra Tydings
Cupid	Karl Urban
Ileandra	Mandie Gillette
Sarpedon	Craig Parker
Barus	Ross Jolly
Lynaeus	Craig Walsh-Wrightson
Aria	Rachale Davies

spell that lasts until another ring leaves him as comically ineffectual as ever. Unfortunately Joxer's charm overwhelms a princess engaged to be married to a foreign prince, and threatens to trigger a war between the two kingdoms. With Lucy Lawless still recovering from her accident, Renee O'Connor as Gabrielle handles the troubleshooting heroics, facing down Aphrodite and undoing the harm wrought by Joxer's dazzling but misguided adventures.

Mythic Connections:

Aphrodite (the Romans called her Venus) was the goddess of love, at once irresistible and irresponsible.

Highlights:

Viewers will gape in disbelief—and delight—at Joxer's convincing gallantry as he romances Princess Ileandra and engages in several duels, including the final battle in Aphrodite's temple. Adding to the surreal quality of the episode, Joxer sings his own theme song, appropriately entitled "Joxer the Mighty."

Casting Coups:

Ted Raimi is doubly brilliant (in a role made famous by his idol Danny Kaye), handling low comedy and high adventure with equal flair. Alexandra Tydings is superb as the ever mischievous, dazzling, petulant, and humorous Aphrodite, a recurring character introduced on *Hercules*. And seventeen-year-old Mandie Gillette, beautiful and innocent as Princess Ileandra, is a perfect comic foil for Ted Raimi's Joxer.

Lucy's Take:

"Well, I was probably sitting in a wheelchair in L.A. at the time." On Xena's appearance in two scenes: "I acted that with somebody dressed as Joxer."

• 41. THE EXECUTION •

Pride comes before a falling-out, as Xena's suggestion that Gabrielle's faith in a convicted defendant may be misguided provokes a bitter, wounded response. The defendant is Meleager the Mighty, a warrior who once saved Gabrielle's town of Potidaea but now awaits execution for murder. Persuaded by his claims of innocence, Gabrielle helps him escape from prison but is shocked when Meleager later confesses that he might have been guilty, for he was too drunk to remember what happened on the day of the murder.

Xena investigates further, though, clears Meleager, and finds that the venerable judge Arbus is so intent on an execution that he has conspired to kill everyone who knows Meleager is innocent. Realizing that where Arbus is concerned, justice is blind to the truth, Xena exposes the judge as a power-mad hypocrite and rescues both Meleager and a chastened Gabrielle.

THE EXECUTION

Writer: Paul Robert Coyle
Director: Garth Maxwell
Original Air Date: Apr. 7, 1997

• GUEST CAST •

Meleager	Tim Thomerson
Arbus	Tony Blackett
Sullus	Douglas Kamo
Elysha	Ranald Hendriks
Old Woman	Ann Baxter

Highlights:

Gabrielle stands up to Xena, challenging her with her staff rather than let her overtake Meleager and send him back to prison.

Casting Coup:

Tim Thomerson is once more funny and engaging as the heroic but somewhat befuddled Meleager.

Lucy's Take:

"I've talked to Rob [Tapert] about it and we decided that they made a mistake in having Tim Thomerson play a cleaned-up drunk, because a character that's a drunk is funny. A *reformed* drunk is not. But Tim was great fun to work with."

• 42. BLIND FAITH •

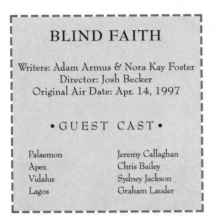

BLIND FAITH

Writers: Adam Armus & Nora Kay Foster
Director: Josh Becker
Original Air Date: Apr. 14, 1997

• GUEST CAST •

Palaemon	Jeremy Callaghan
Apex	Chris Bailey
Vidalus	Sydney Jackson
Lagos	Graham Lauder

The Western movie theme of the young gunslinger looking to make his mark by killing the reluctant "fastest gun" is transplanted from Montana to Mycenae, as Palaemon kidnaps Gabrielle in order to provoke Xena into a duel to the death. Xena sees at once that Palaemon is redeemable: a decent person who has yet to discover what honor and glory are really about. Blinded by a splash of the poison sumac, Xena rushes to save her friend rather than her eyesight. She drags Palaemon with her to find the men who are holding Gabrielle and preparing her to become their king's new bride. Gabrielle's alarm over her impending royal nuptials is not eased by her discovery that the king is already dead, and that she is to be a pawn in a sham ceremony that will allow the minister Apex to assume power—as soon as she is cremated. Xena retrieves Gabrielle's casket just before it is consumed by flames and defeats Apex with the help of Palaemon, who realizes that absorbing Xena's values will be more precious than any trophy of battle.

Highlights:

Gabrielle sends up her own character's history by pleading that she should not be forced to marry the king, because "All the men I get serious about seem to wind up dead."

Casting Coup:

Sydney Jackson is effete but sensitive as the eunuch Vidalus, who helps Gabrielle and later saves Xena's eyesight with oil from a rare Egyptian plant in his garden.

Lucy's Take:

"I spent a week trying ways to set my eye focus at, say, twenty meters [to appear blind]. Jeremy Callaghan [as Palaemon] was a really neat guy. And fascinating, with all of these interesting stories from his past, though he looks so young. He grew up in New Guinea and told about having school for just two hours in the morning—and all they owned was one exercise book, one pencil, and a hunting knife. And then the kids would go out in gangs for "bushcraft" the rest of the day, and kill pigs and so forth. And then, because he was very good at tennis, he went away to a tennis camp in Japan for a year when he was fifteen, and experienced Japanese regimentation and what we would consider brutality. Most, most interesting! And such a funny guy. [As an actor] he'll just get better and better, because he's very intelligent and he has a lot of history to feed on. And he's just a super guy."

• 43. ULYSSES •

The adventurer Ulysses gains unexpected help from the Warrior Princess on returning from Troy to his kingdom of Ithaca. Despite warnings from the sea god Poseidon that he will destroy Ulysses, Xena fights side by side with Ulysses to recapture his ship from pirates, then weathers the turbulent journey to his island. Convinced by Poseidon that his wife, Penelope, is dead, Ulysses confesses that he scarcely knew her on leaving to fight ten years at Troy, and that he realizes that Xena is his true soul mate. Xena, too, is strongly attracted to the handsome and courageous Ulysses, but on reaching Ithaca

ULYSSES

Writer: R. J. Stewart
Director: Michael Levine
Original Air Date: Apr. 21, 1997

• GUEST CAST •

Ulysses	John D'Aquino
Penelope	Rachel Blakely
Meticles	Tim Raby
Layos	Carl Bland

they find Penelope much alive and loyally keeping a band of plundering suitors at bay. Ulysses strikes them down with a hail of arrows and wistfully reunites with Penelope after Xena rejects him, refusing to take him away from his wife and kingdom.

Mythic Connections:

On his ten-year journey home from Troy, Ulysses passed the island of the Sirens, whose ethereal singing lured men to their deaths. Ulysses had his sailors place wax in their ears, but he himself listened to the Sirens after ordering his men to lash him to the mast and refuse to release him till they were safely past. Another band of heroes, the Argonauts, also survived the Sirens' call by having Orpheus, the greatest of minstrels, play a song of his own. "Ulysses" adapts both myths. Xena first lashes Ulysses to a post (Xena: "I'm going to tie you up." Ulysses: "I'm game. What do you have in mind?" Xena: "Saving your life."); but when he breaks free, she keeps him from jumping overboard by singing until they are safe.

Highlights:

Xena has fought many duels, but never before using her voice, as she does against the Sirens. The stringing of the mighty bow by Ulysses takes a fresh twist, for Xena secretly helps, suggesting that behind every great male myth there stands a Warrior Princess.

Casting Coup:

Rachel Blakely is winning as the hard-pressed but resourceful Penelope.

Lucy's Take:

"The actor who played Ulysses was somewhat miscast. I just did the best I could to make it believable that Xena could fall in love head over heels with Ulysses, without letting down my character."

• 44. THE PRICE •

Xena has run a gauntlet, fought countless battles, suffered near-fatal (and even fatal) wounds, been crucified, entered the dread realm of Hades, and never shown fear. Until now. The advance of "the Horde," an alien, implacable force of primitives who give and expect no mercy, who once flayed her soldiers alive, sends her and Gabrielle on a desperate escape through the woods and into a river. They take shelter in a fortress whose demoralized Athenian defenders turn to the Warrior Princess, with her towering military reputation and iron will, as their only hope. But as Xena takes command she begins to lose her humanity, vowing a war of total destruction that appalls Gabrielle, who wants to explore paths to peace and healing. Xena spurns Gabrielle's way ("There is nothing about these people that we can or should understand!") until she finds that her friend's humanity holds the key to their survival.

> ### THE PRICE
>
> Writer: Steven L. Sears
> Director: Oley Sassone
> Original Air Date: Apr. 28, 1997
>
> • GUEST CAST •
>
> | | |
> |---|---|
> | Menticles | Paul Glover |
> | Mercer | Charles Mesure |
> | Garel | Tamati Rice |
> | Galipan | Mark Perry |
> | G'Kug | Justin Curry |

Highlights:

An episode of sustained intensity that reveals Xena at her darkest and suggests the terror she must have inspired as a ruthless warlord, a breaker of nations. Among many powerful scenes, Xena's speech to motivate "her" Athenian troops carries extraordinary power. When they clamor around her imploring, "Tell us what to do, Xena!" she strides toward them along the ramparts and mockingly repeats, "Do?" Then, suddenly raising her sword, she yells, "We are going to kill 'em all!"

Lucy's Take:

"That was great fun. We had a new director, Oley Sassone, who was really good. I had a wee tantrum with the writers, which I was only partly right about. Because there was a paragraph where Xena says, 'Listen to the Horde out there screaming, they are so evil, they are so stupid.' And that was one of two moments where I [strongly objected]. I said, I'm not saying that, because that makes my character complicit in the stupidity. And Xena's allowed to be wrong and she's allowed to be afraid, but she's not allowed to be stupid. And that just makes her part of the evil instead of simply wrong.

"But I liked the fact that Xena, and I think the audience also liked the fact that Xena is still dangerous. It just woke them up to the fact that this is not the girl in the white hat. And also I played it like she was right. You know, it surprises me that people have had such a negative reaction because there is a particular scene where I ad-libbed just one word, but it made all the difference, I thought, to my character. It showed where my character was coming from. It was 'This is war, Gabrielle, what did you expect?' And I ad-libbed, 'Glamour?!' Because Xena had the view, when you go to war, this is what it's really like. And you bleeding-heart liberals! You know, you tree-huggers, if you went to Bosnia, what did you think it would be like? I wanted people to discover their own hypocrisy [about war]."

• 45. LOST MARINER •

LOST MARINER

Writer: Steven L. Sears
Director: Garth Maxwell
Original Air Date: May 5, 1997

• GUEST CAST •

Cecrops   Tony Todd
Hidsim   George Henare
Basculis   Nigel Harbrow

Cecrops the sailor hasn't slept soundly in three hundred years. Cursed by Poseidon to wander the seas until love redeems him, he appears almost equally bitter toward Athena, who granted him immortality. Cecrops laments the loss of his one true love, Tarae, from whom he was separated by Poseidon's whirlpool Charybdis but who watched him from the shore every evening until she died—the only woman whose love could truly save him. Xena, who has boarded this cursed vessel with Gabrielle, is convinced that Athena must have kept Cecrops alive for good reason, and persuades him to sail once more to Tarae's village. As they approach Charybdis, Poseidon offers to help Cecrops if he will kill Xena, but Cecrops refuses—an act of pure love that sets him free at last, to enjoy both land and life.

Mythic Connections:

Cecrops, the son of Gaea, or Mother Earth, had the upper body of a man, the lower body of a serpent. He was the first king of Attica, a region including the city of Athens, to which he helped give its name. The sea god, Poseidon, and the goddess of wisdom, Athena, each claimed Athens, and named Cecrops to judge their claims. Cecrops awarded the city to Athena, who became the city's patron deity. As Cecrops declares in "Lost Mariner," the bards never bothered to relate what happened to him after that fateful judgment against Poseidon.

Highlights:

Cecrops' pained recounting of his love for Tarae is mesmerizing. . . . Poseidon and Charybdis are among the computer-generated wonders of Kevin O'Neill's special-effects team.

Casting Coup:

Tony Todd as Cecrops projects an intensity that gives his encounters with Xena and Gabrielle great power.

Lucy's Take:

"The director, Garth Maxwell, is a New Zealander and he's such a delight for us to work with. And it's the episode we filmed with a cyclone. . . . No, not Charybdis, an actual cyclone. That day where you see us being washed up on the shore, there was a tropical cyclone at the time. And the normally placid little beach was washing up over the edge of the bank and there were gale-force winds out. . . ."

On Cecrops' vessel: "Yeah, it's a real ship. Rob [Tapert] had a thing built on it, and it's called 'Rob's Folly.' He's always wanted a boat. He cares so much about fishing, really. It's where his heart is. And so they built this big boat. It's on a barge and they can just change the uppermost construction to make it a Phoenician sailing yacht, a pirate ship, or whatever it has to be. . . . Well, it doesn't sail, it's under motor. And we go out in the harbor [to film] and have to battle sun position and wind, and just about every single line in that episode had to be looped! . . . Oh, that was great fun. That was the one where Renee ate [raw] squid. . . . Yeah, actual squid. It absolutely was.

"Tony [Todd] is terrific. Yeah, he's a good, strong actor and he had an awful lot of dialogue to carry. He has a lot of charisma, a lot of presence on the screen."

• 46. COMEDY OF EROS •

COMEDY OF EROS

Writer: Chris Manheim
Director: Charles Siebert
Original Air Date: May 12, 1997

• GUEST CAST •

Joxer	Ted Raimi
Draco	Jay Laga'aia
Cupid	Karl Urban
Pinullus	Anthony Ray Parker
Bliss	Cameron Russel
Craigan	Barry Te Hira

Xena's life is an ongoing struggle to rein in her rage—except in "Comedy of Eros," where she must instead contain a sudden attraction to her foe, the warlord Draco. The Warrior Princess is not the only one suffering the arrows of outrageous romantic fortune: Cupid's baby, Bliss, has flown off with his father's quiver of love-tipped arrows and is happily shooting at random passersby. Other targets include Gabrielle, who now craves the affections of Joxer; and Draco, who is smitten with desire for Gabrielle. The sudden flowering of unlikely love is especially inconvenient for Xena, who is trying to save a temple of Hestial virgins from Draco's slave-raiding soldiers. Piecing together the mystery, Xena has Cupid break the spell for everyone, but Draco, who vows to reform in order to win Gabrielle's favor—and Joxer, who has fallen for Gabrielle in a way no mere Olympian could alter.

Mythic Connections:

Eros, or Cupid, the son of Aphrodite, was portrayed in the later Greek world as a child or baby whose arrows were tipped with gold, to create love, or with lead, to cause revulsion.

Highlights:

Gabrielle proudly sings "Joxer the Mighty," a tribute to and by her new hero ("With Gabby as his sidekick, Fighting with her little stick . . .").

Lucy's Take:

"That episode [featured] a whole lot of silliness and running around. It was a delight to shoot. Charlie Siebert is a marvelous director and I will do anything for him, because on two separate occasions I have gotten horribly ill on his episodes: one was the time when I hurt my back and another time when I broke my pelvis. . . . So I will never say no to Charlie Siebert. Anything he wants me to say or do, I will do."

THE AMERICAN WAY
OF ENGLISH

M any New Zealand actors, having grown up watching Hollywood TV shows and movies, can speak with an American accent. But some find it difficult to shift their way of speaking from Kiwi to Californian. To smooth the transition, the producers hired a dialogue coach, Warren Carl, to help actors over rough spots in pronunciation. The following memo from Carl is on prominent display in the New Zealand casting office. It is a wondrous guide to linguistic adjustment, offering pointers on how to slur words and fail to pronounce consonants in order to speak like a real American:

As you are aware, this series is shot with an American accent. Having worked for several months on this series, I've found some consistent questions from actors. Please realise that working with an accent adds to a list of distracting technical elements (i.e., hitting marks, correct eye lines, line memorization, character motivation, fast-paced filming) that can fluster even the more experienced actor. Point being, the more prepared you are, the less you will be thrown on the day of filming. Unfortunately, I've noticed that the accent is the first thing to go out the window during those whirlwind times.

I hope this list of tips and ideas will assist in your preparation.

This series is shot in what we call a non-regional American accent; *not Southern, Jewish New York, Bostonian, or Texan. Please do* not *take examples from any New York cop shows,* Gone With the Wind, *or reruns of* Dallas. *The accent we're seeking is actually closest to a "Californian" variety. A good example of such an accent can be heard on such shows as* Melrose Place *or* Baywatch. *Seen in small doses, these shows can be learned from before the brain-numbing effect of the programme sets in.*

Things to note:

Lazy Consonants

It is what might be considered a "lazy" accent—in that we [Americans] don't often articulate our consonants. For example, the word "matter" would be pronounced "madder"—with the "d" sound replacing the articulated "t" sound. Similarly the word "later" becomes "lay-der." I recommend going through your spoken lines and write "d"s over any words where this might apply. Obviously this rule does not apply to words like "commitment" and "important." I highly recommend making accent changes on your script to give yourself a visual reminder when learning your lines—e.g., "I'll see you later, Hercules.*"*

Slurring Words

Also, in the lazy accent department, we have the habit of slurring our words together—e.g., "All I had to do was ask" looks/sounds like "Alleyehadtadoowuzask." We don't overarticulate; the words are clear but the jaw is fairly still, almost frozen. I've come across countless actors speaking with their jaw flapping away, articulating every consonant, trying to "do" an American accent. Too much work; you should actually be doing less (relaxed jaw, lazy tongue), to produce the correct sound. Again, have a listen to those prescribed shows to hear the relaxed Californian sound.

The "R"

The single most repeated problem is the dropping of the "r" sound. The British and Kiwi accents do not use this "r" sound at all, but an American accent does. For example, the word "matter" might be pronounced "mattuh" by a Kiwi. Nothing will give you away as a non-American more than a dropped "r." Please go through your script and underline *all "r"s in your spoken dialogue. You* must *sound them; the lazy rule does not apply in this instance. If there are two "r"s in a word, they must be sounded—e.g., "forward." Again, underlining your script will give you a visual reminder when learning and practising your lines.*

At some point before filming commences we'll have the chance to run through your dialogue to correct and fine-tune your accent.

Memorising Lines

I must ask you to have your dialogue permanently emblazoned on your memory so that any alterations to pronunciation won't throw off your concentration. Remember, television is a technical medium and can be very confusing—the last thing you want to worry about is remembering your lines.

Further Research

If you wish to delve further into the study of an American accent, I highly recommend the booklet and tape called Non-regional American Accent for British Actors, *by Dr. David Alan Stern.*

How to Pronounce

For example:
Iolaus = Ee oh lus
Hera = Hair a
Salmoneus = Sal moan e us

I hope none of this information frightens you but instead assists you so that you may more fully enjoy your filming with us. I look forward to meeting you and will happily answer any further accent queries at that time.

Dialogue Coach

A XENAVERSE TIMELINE

- -

X *ena* is set in ancient Greece, but the Warrior Princess is far too fast and agile to be confined by mere place names and dates. During the first two seasons alone, Xena traveled a mythic landscape spanning thousands of miles and several millennia. Here are a few landmarks on her legendary journeys through time and space.

• Xena saves Icus from human sacrifice in a tale based on the biblical story of Abraham and Isaac ("Altared States"). Abraham lived earlier than 2000 B.C.

• Xena helps free Cecrops from a 300-year curse ("Lost Mariner"). Cecrops was known to legend as the first king of Attica, a region that included Athens. He would have reigned before 1500 B.C.

• Xena fights for Troy against the Greeks ("Beware Greeks Bearing Gifts"). The city of Troy, on the western shore of what is now Turkey, was destroyed shortly after 1200 B.C.

• Xena helps Ulysses take back his kingdom on the isle of Ithaca ("Ulysses"). Ulysses returned home ten years after the Trojan War.

• Xena helps young David defeat Goliath ("Giant Killer"). David ruled the united kingdom of Judah and Israel from 1000 to 960 B.C.

• Young Homer relates a story about the freedom fighter Spartacus ("The Athens Academy of the Performing Bards"). This was no small feat, since Homer lived between 900 and 800 B.C., while Spartacus led a revolt of slaves and gladiators from 73 to 71 B.C. Euripides, also featured in "Performing Bards," lived from 484 to 406 B.C., a few centuries after Homer but before Spartacus.

• Xena returns to her native village Amphipolis, joined by Gabrielle from the village of Potidaea ("Sins of the Past"). Amphipolis in northern Greece was founded by Athens in 437 B.C. on the east bank of the Strymon River. It later became the Roman capital of Macedonia. Potidaea was a coastal city founded by Corinth around 600 B.C., less than 100 miles southwest of Amphipolis.

• Xena inspires the young physician Hippocrates with her modern medical practices despite the protests of the tradition-bound healer Galen ("Is There a Doctor?"). Hippocrates (460–377 B.C.) lived centuries before Galen (A.D. 127–199), who was known for his scientific method.

• Xena crosses paths with Julius Caesar ("Destiny"). Gaius Julius Caesar lived from 100 B.C. until his assassination in 44 B.C.

• Xena stops Ares from breaking free and causing more bloodshed ("The Xena Scrolls"). As the scholars who subtitled this episode attest, the historical record places this event in 1942.

PRODUCTION CREDITS

STARRING:

Lucy Lawless as Xena

Renee O'Connor as Gabrielle

Produced by: Renaissance Pictures in association with Universal

Television Enterprises

Executive Producers: Rob Tapert

Sam Raimi

Co-Executive Producer: R. J. Stewart

Supervising Producer: Steven L. Sears

Produced by Eric Gruendemann

Producer: Liz Friedman

Coordinating Producer: Bernadette Joyce

New Zealand Producer: Chloe Smith

Music by Joseph Lo Duca

Directors: Various

Robert Weisbrot claims to have been a more or less productive citizen before discovering *Xena: Warrior Princess*. He is the author of several books, including *Freedom Bound: A History of America's Civil Rights Movement*. A professor of American history at Colby College, he lives in Waterville, Maine.